Crime and Criminal Justice

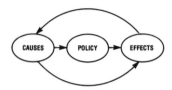

Policy Studies
Organization Series

Crime and Criminal Justice

Issues in Public Policy Analysis

edited by

John A. Gardiner
University of Illinois
at Chicago Circle

Michael A. Mulkey
National Institute of Law Enforcement and Criminal Justice

Lexington Books
D. C. Heath and Company
Lexington, Massachusetts
Toronto   London

31191

Library of Congress Cataloging in Publication Data

Main entry under title:

Crime and criminal justice.

    1. Criminal justice, Administration of—United States—Ad-
dresses, essays, lectures. 2. Corrections—United States—Ad-
dresses, essays, lectures. I. Gardiner, John A., 1937-
II. Mulkey, Michael A.
HV8138.C68   364'.973   75-749
ISBN 0-669-99507-x

Published simultaneously in Canada

Printed in the United States of America

International Standard Book Number: 0-669-99507-x

Library of Congress Catalog Card Number: 75-749

Contents

31191

              Charging and Plea Bargaining: The Roles of Prose-
              cution and Defense, *Michael A. Mulkey*   121

Chapter 12   Courts Policy: The Recommendations of the Na-
              tional Advisory Commission, *George F. Cole* and
              David W. Neubauer   131

Chapter 13   "For the Salvation of Children": The Search for
              Juvenile Justice in the United States, *Jameson W.
              Doig*   139

Chapter 14   What Works? Questions and Answers about Prison
              Reform, *Robert Martinson*   155

Chapter 15   New Perspectives on Corrections Policy, *Erika S.
              Fairchild*   189

              Notes   198

              Index of Names   201

              Index of Subjects   205

              About the Editors and Contributors   213

Acknowledgments

Chapter 2, "Crime and the Criminologists," originally appeared in the July 1974 issue of *Commentary* magazine. Reprinted by permission of the author.

The preparation of Chapter 4, "Sources and Limitations of Data in Criminal Justice Research," was supported by a National Science Foundation (RANN Division) grant, GI-43949.

The preparation of Chapter 9, "Public Participation in the Criminal Justice System," was supported in part by a National Science Foundation (RANN Division) grant, GI-39277.

Chapter 14, "What Works? Questions and Answers about Prison Reform," originally appeared in *The Public Interest,* No. 35 (Spring 1974). Copyright © 1974 by National Affairs, Inc. Reprinted by permission of the author and publisher.

1

Crime and Criminal Justice: Issues in Public Policy Analysis

John A. Gardiner and Michael A. Mulkey

Over the last ten years, crime and criminal justice have been among the most hotly debated issues in American politics. "Conservative" candidates for public office routinely decry "crime in the streets," call for "more police protection," protest delay in the courts, and ask why correctional institutions don't "do something" about repeat offenders. "Liberal" candidates just as vehemently condemn police "repression" and illegal searches and seizures, and call for gun control legislation, social programs to reduce "the root causes" of crime, and court sentences which invoke community-based programs rather than institutionalization. The pages of the criminal code are a battleground for the contending forces as opponents and proponents of various forms of behavior seek to criminalize or decriminalize them; and the procedures utilized by criminal justice agencies are debated as Constitutional imperatives or handcuffs on the police.

Despite the salience of crime and criminal justice as focal points for public concern and debate, very little is known about the validity of the prescriptions so vociferously advocated by all sides. While social scientists have become quite interested in the etiology of crime, factors associated with various categories of offenses and offenders, and the organizational dynamics of police, court, and correctional agencies, we know relatively little about crime and criminal justice programs. Certainly the failings and excesses—the arrests and convictions of the innocent, the violations of civil liberties, and the frequent recidivism by convicted offenders—have been well documented by official crime commissions, investigative journalists, and the advocates of various reforms. What is strangely lacking from these debates, however, is substantive evidence that current programs are or are not achieving their objectives or that proposed Alternative A is more likely than Alternative B to achieve a given set of goals.

The articles presented in this volume have been prepared to partially remedy this gap, both by bringing together current knowledge about the major issues in the field and by identifying major areas where future research is needed. Our goal is to provide a survey of the fundamental issues that must be addressed in any analysis of the policies which—consciously or unconsciously—govern crime and criminal justice policy in America. To limit the scope of this volume to a workable size, we have

1

been obliged to exclude certain topics. First, we have restricted the symposium to the United States and to the state and local settings which are the center of American criminal justice. Second, we have perhaps arbitrarily limited our analysis to programs *directly* dealing with crime problems, although it is frequently argued that the level of crime in a society is as much influenced by the success or failure of educational, health, welfare, and housing programs as it is of agencies and programs specifically related to crime and criminal justice. While these omissions necessarily limit the comprehensiveness of the volume, we hope that the methods of analysis presented will be applicable to other areas.

The first part of this volume addresses basic issues involved in undertaking policy analysis and assessing crime policy. In Chapter 2, James Q. Wilson argues that most of the criminological literature of the twentieth century has been of little prescriptive value—analyses of the *causes* of crime have produced few suggestions for policy-makers who are expected to "do something" about crime. In Chapter 3, Robert P. Rhodes articulates the problems confronting policy analysts because of the essentially contradictory value premises underlying crime and criminal justice programs. To avoid some of these conflicts, Rhodes suggests a focus on the impact of programs on crime victims.

The next two chapters introduce the very serious problems involved in gathering and analyzing data concerning crime and criminal justice policies. In Chapter 4, Roger B. Parks reviews current data resources and points out serious questions of data validity and dangers inherent in using for policy analysis purposes data collected for other reasons. Finally, Parks suggests strategies which policy analysts can use to cope with these problems. In Chapter 5, Wesley G. Skogan reviews data derived from surveys of citizen attitudes toward and evaluations of criminal justice agencies, noting their limited value thus far in either assessing program impact or advising administrators on promising changes.

The following chapters illustrate the ambiguities and conflicting values present in American crime and criminal justice policy. In Chapter 6, Carl Akins reviews the issues involved in labeling behavior as criminal and in removing that label, taking examples from the field of "victimless" crimes. In Chapter 7, Michael D. Maltz reviews the amorphous concepts of "organized crime" and "white-collar crime," noting the frequent similarities between the behaviors condemned by these concepts and other values highly esteemed in American life. Maltz further documents the perils of policy analysis in an area in which the available indicators are almost as undecipherable as the phenomena they are supposed to measure. Finally, in Chapter 8, Lief H. Carter analyzes the value conflicts which arise between the twin policy goals of flexibility and uniformity, reviewing the evidence on how they are applied by criminal justice agencies and suggesting that the conflicts are likely to continue.

Part II of the symposium shifts the focus to the participants in policymaking and the major policy issues currently confronting them. Chapter 9 surveys a relatively new phenomenon in criminal justice, the widespread use of volunteers to supplement, and at times to challenge, official criminal justice agencies and their programs; while the number of volunteer programs is growing rapidly, Thomas J. Cook and Frank P. Scioli, Jr., find almost no systematic comparative evidence of their successes or failures. In Chapter 10, Leonard Ruchelman analyzes the multiple (and frequently conflicting) objectives assigned to police agencies and the evidence available concerning attainment of these objectives. Looking at current disputes regarding police patrol, departmental organization, and community relations, Ruchelman stresses the critical importance of developing better performance measures to identify the most effective policy alternatives.

Chapters 11 and 12 focus on issues relating to the adjudication phase of the criminal justice process. In Chapter 11, Michael A. Mulkey explains the critical roles played by prosecutors and defense counsel in establishing the charges to be levied against defendants and negotiating guilty pleas; the low visibility and lack of standards and goals surrounding these issues raise major questions for analysts of both the substantive and procedural aspects of court systems. In Chapter 12, George F. Cole and David W. Neubauer review the disparities between our historic ideals concerning criminal adjudication and the realities of "assembly-line justice." They then analyze the implications of the 1973 National Advisory Commission on Criminal Justice Standards and Goals Report, noting that while these standards may increase efficiency and fairness in the courts, they are unlikely to affect crime rates.

Chapter 13 analyzes the unusual system which has developed in the United States to deal with juvenile offenders. James W. Doig articulates the high aspirations and apparently low success rates of juvenile institutions; the evidence is very sparse that they have significantly contributed to any reduction of juvenile delinquency or rehabilitation of convicted offenders. Indeed, there is more evidence that the wide discretion vested in juvenile agencies has generated both a lack of procedural fairness and widespread racial, sex, and class discrimination. To counteract these abuses, many groups are advocating community-based juvenile programs and even reduced emphasis on coercive intervention of any form in the lives of juveniles.

The final chapters of this volume deal with American correctional institutions and programs. In Chapter 14, Robert Martinson summarizes thirty years of research attempting to evaluate the effectiveness of a wide variety of correctional programs; in general, he finds little persuasive evidence that any of them have had an appreciable impact on recidivism. Erika S. Fairchild concludes in Chapter 15 that, these findings notwithstanding, many correctional systems are moving toward modifications in the currently popular "medical treatment" model of corrections, establishing community programs to replace massive maximum-security institutions, and involving the offenders themselves in program decision-making. As was the case in the chapters dealing with police and court policy issues, Chapters 14 and 15 reinforce the arguments made at the beginning of this book: prescriptions for change in criminal justice must recognize the importance of identifying and weighing often conflicting societal goals, must develop more powerful indicators of program impact, and must focus for decision-makers' consideration the implications of each policy alternative. Unless these steps are taken, as James Q. Wilson noted in Chapter 2, the policy analyst will serve only as a spokesman for his personal prejudices and preferences.

**Part I
Definitional Problems: Policy Analysis
and the Goals of Crime Policy**

2

Crime and the Criminologists
James Q. Wilson

The "social-science view" of crime is thought by many, especially its critics, to assert that crime is the result of poverty, racial discrimination, and other privations, and that the only morally defensible and substantively efficacious strategy for reducing crime is to attack its "root causes" with programs that end poverty, reduce discrimination, and meliorate privation. In fact, however, at the time when their views on crime were first sought by policy-makers (roughly, the mid-1960's), social scientists had not set forth in writing a systematic theory of this sort. I recently asked three distinguished criminologists to nominate the two or three scholarly books on crime which were in print by mid-1960 and which were then regarded as the most significant works on the subject. There was remarkable agreement as to the titles: *Principles of Criminology,* by Edwin H. Sutherland and Donald R. Cressey, and *Delinquency and Opportunity,* by Richard A. Cloward and Lloyd E. Ohlin. Agreement was not complete on the validity of the views expressed in these books. Quite the contrary; criminologists then and now debate hotly and at length over such issues as the cause of crime. But these two books, and others like them, are alike in the way questions are posed, answers are sought, and policies are derived—alike, in short, not in their specific theories of delinquency, but in the general perspective from which those theories flow. And this perspective, contrary to popular impression, has rather little to do with poverty, race, education, housing, or the other objective conditions that supposedly cause crime. If anything, it directs attention away from factors that government can control, even if only marginally, to move beyond the reach of social policy altogether. Thus when social scientists were asked for advice by national policymaking bodies on how to reduce crime, they could not respond with suggestions derived from and supported by their scholarly work. In consequence, such advice as they did supply tended to derive from their general political views rather than from the expert knowledge they were presumed to have.

I

In the 1960's the prevalent social-science perspective on crime found its most authoritative development in the treatise by Sutherland and Cressey whose seventh edition appeared in 1966, just after President Johnson appointed his crime commission. In this work Sutherland and Cressey reviewed various "schools of criminology" and faulted all but the "sociological" approach, according to which criminal behavior is learned by a person in intimate interaction with others whose good opinion he values and who define crime as desirable. The "classical" theories of Bentham and Beccaria were rejected because their underlying psychological assumptions —that individuals calculate the pains and pleasures of crime and pursue it if the latter outweigh the former—"assume freedom of the will in a manner which gives little or no possibility of further investigation of the causes of crime or of efforts to prevent crime." The hedonistic psychology of Bentham, in short, suffered from being "individualistic, intellectualistic, and voluntaristic." Theories based on body type, mental abnormality, or mental illness were also rejected because the available data were inconsistent with them. Criminals were no more likely than law-abiding persons to have a certain stature, to be feeble-minded, or to suffer from a psychosis.

As for poverty—defined as having little money—Sutherland and Cressey's references to its impact were few and skeptical. Sutherland was quoted from his earlier writings as observing that while crime was strongly correlated with geographic concentrations of poor persons, it was weakly correlated (if at all) with the economic cycle. That is, crime might be observed to increase as one entered a poor neighborhood, but it was not observed to decrease as neighborhoods generally experienced prosperity. Furthermore, Albert K. Cohen (to whom Sutherland and Cressy refer approvingly) had shown that much of the delinquency found among working-class boys was "non-utilitarian"—that is, consisted of expressive but financially unrewarding acts of vandalism and hell-raising—and that these acts were more common among this group than among middle-class boys. If economic want were the cause of crime, one would predict that delinquency for gain would be more common among those less well-off and delinquency for "fun" more common among the better-off. Yet the opposite seemed to be the case. "Poverty as such," Sutherland concluded, "is not an important cause of crime."

Nor could being a member of a minority group and experiencing the frustrations produced by discrimination explain crime for Sutherland and Cressey: while the experience of Negroes, whose crime rate was high, might support such a theory, that of the American Japanese, whose crime rate was low, refuted it. Poverty and racial segregation might serve to perpetuate crime, however, to the extent that these factors prevented persons from leaving areas where crime was already high and thus from escaping those personal contacts and peer groups from which criminal habits were learned.

There were in 1966 other theories of crime in addition to Sutherland and Cressey's. Most of these were reviewed in their treatise and though criticisms were sometimes made, the governing assumptions of each were quite compatible with what the authors described as the sociological approach. Sheldon and Eleanor Glueck, for example, produced in the 1950's a major effort to predict delinquency, and while the idea of predicting delinquency became controversial on grounds of both fairness and feasibility, their empirical data on factors that helped cause delinquency were not seriously challenged. They argued and supplied data to show that among the key variables distinguishing delinquents from non-delinquents were those related to family conditions—chiefly stability, parental affection, and the discipline of children. Walter B. Miller also argued that delinquency was in large part an expression of the focal concerns of lower-class youth. Toughness, masculinity, "smartness," the love of excitement, and a desire for personal autonomy were valued by lower-class persons to a greater degree than by middle-class ones, and acting on the basis of these values, which were maintained by street-corner gangs, inevitably placed many lower-class boys (and some girls) in conflict with the laws of the middle class. Albert K. Cohen further suggested that delinquency was in part the result of lower-class youth striving, not simply to assert their focal values, but to repudiate those middle-class values which they secretly prized.

These and other sociological theories of crime, widely known and intensely discussed in the 1960's, had certain features in common. All sought to explain the causes of delinquency, or at least its persistence. All made attitude formation a key variable. All stressed that these attitudes were shaped and supported by intimate groups—the family and close friends. All were serious, intelligent efforts at constructing social theories, and while no theory was proved empirically, all were consistent with at least some important observations about crime. *But none could supply a plausible basis for the advocacy of public policy.*

This was true for several reasons. By directing attention toward the subjective states that preceded or accompanied criminal behavior, the sociological (or more accurately, social-psychological) theories directed attention toward conditions that cannot be easily and deliberately altered. Society, of course, shapes attitudes and values by its examples, its institutions, and its practices, but only with great difficulty, slowly, and imprecisely. If families inculcate habits of virtue, law-abidingness, and decorum, it is rarely because the family is acting as the agent of society or its government, but rather because it is a good family. If schools teach children to value learning and to study well, it is not simply because the schools are well-designed or generously supplied, but because attitudes consistent with learning and study already exist in the pupils. One can imagine what government might do if it wished to make good families even better or successful pupils even more successful: more resources might be offered to reduce burdens imposed by want, but the gains, if any, would likely be at the margin.

If it is difficult by plan to make the good better, it may be impossible to make the bad tolerable so long as one seeks to influence attitudes and values directly. If a child is delinquent because his family made him so or his friends encourage him to be so, it is hard to conceive what society might do about this. No one knows how a government might restore affection, stability, and fair discipline to a family that rejects these characteristics; still less can one imagine how even a family once restored could affect a child who by now has left the formative years and in any event has developed an aversion to one or both of his parents. Government could supply the lower class with more money, of course, but if a class exists because of its values rather than its income, it is hard to see how, in terms of prevailing theory, increasing the latter would improve the former.

If, similarly, the lower class has focal concerns that make crime attractive or even inevitable, it is not clear how government could supply it with a new set of values consistent with law-abidingness. Indeed, the very effort to inculcate new values would, if the sociological theory is true, lead the members of that class to resist such alien intrusions all the more vigorously and to cling to their own world-view all the more strongly. Peer groups exist, especially for young people, as a way of defending their members from an alien, hostile, or indifferent larger society and for supplying them with a mutually satisfactory basis for self-respect. A deviant peer group—one that encourages crime or hell-raising—would regard any effort by society to "reform" it as confirmation of the hostile intent of society and of the importance of the group.

II

The problem lies in confusing causal analysis with policy analysis. Causal analysis attempts to find the source of human activity in those factors which themselves are not caused—which are, in the language of sociologists, "independent variables." Obviously nothing can be a cause if it is in turn caused by something else; it would then only be an "intervening variable." But ultimate causes cannot be the object of policy efforts precisely because, being ultimate, they cannot be changed. For example, criminologists have shown beyond doubt that men commit more crimes than women and younger men more (of certain kinds) than older ones. It is a theoretically important and scientifically correct observation. Yet it means little for policymakers concerned with crime prevention since men cannot be changed into women nor made to skip over the adolescent years. Not every primary cause is itself unchangeable: the cause of air pollution is (in part) certain gases in automobile exhausts, and thus reducing those gases by redesigning the engine will reduce pollution. But social problems—that is to say, problems occasioned by human behavior rather than mechanical processes—are almost invariably caused by factors that cannot be changed easily or at all, because human behavior ultimately derives from human volition—tastes, attitudes, values, or whatever—and these aspects of volition are in turn formed either entirely by choice or are the product of biological or social processes that we cannot or will not change.

It is the failure to understand this point that leads statesman and citizen alike to commit the causal fallacy—to assume that no problem is adequately addressed unless its causes are eliminated. The preamble to the UNESCO charter illustrates the causal fallacy: "Since wars begin in the minds of men it is in the minds of men that the defenses of peace must be constructed." Yet the one thing we cannot easily do, if at all, is change, by plan and systematically, the minds of men. If peace can only be assured by doing what we cannot do, then we can never have peace. If we regard any crime-prevention or crime-reduction program as defective because it does not address the "root causes" of crime, then we shall commit ourselves to futile acts that frustrate the citizen while they ignore the criminal.

Sutherland and Cressey commit the fallacy; yet, being honest scholars, they provide evidence in their own book that it *is* a fallacy. "At present," they write, "the greatest need in crime prevention is irrefutable facts about crime causation and sound means for transforming that knowledge into a program of action." Suppose it could be shown that their own theory of crime causation is irrefutably correct (it may well be). That theory is that individuals commit crime when they are members of groups—families, peers, neighborhoods—which define criminal behavior as desirable. The policy implication of this, which the authors draw explicitly, is that the local community must use the school, the church, the police, and other agencies to "modify" the personal groups in which crime is made to appear desirable. No indication is given as to how these agencies might do this and, considering what the authors and other sociologists have said about the strength and persistence of family and friendship ties, it is hard to see what plan might be developed.

But we need not merely raise the theoretical difficulties. A series of delinquency-prevention programs have been mounted over the decades, many if not most of which were explicitly formed on the strategy of altering primary-group influences on delinquents. Almost none can be said on the basis of careful, external evaluation to have succeeded in reducing delinquency. Sutherland and Cressey describe one of the most ambitious of these, the Cambridge-Somerville Youth Study in the late

1930's. The differences in crime between those youths who were given special services (counseling, special educational programs, guidance, health assistance, camping trips) and a matched control group were insignificant: " 'the treatment' had little effect." Perhaps a better program would have had better results, though it is striking that for some a "better" youth project is one that moves beyond merely providing concentrated social-welfare services to delinquents because these services do not address the "real" cause of crime. William and Joan McCord, in *Origins of Crime,* for example, draw the lesson from the Cambridge-Somerville study that the true causes of delinquency are found in the "absence of parental affection" coupled with family conflict, inconsistent discipline, and rebellious parents. They are quite possibly correct; indeed, if I may speak on the basis of my own wholly unscientific observation, I am quite confident they are correct. But what of it? What agency do we create, what budget do we allocate, that will supply the missing "parental affection" and will restore to the child consistent discipline supported by a stable and loving family? When it comes to the details of their own proposals, they speak of "milieu therapy" in which the child is removed from his family and placed in a secure and permissive therapeutic environment of the sort developed by Dr. Bruno Bettelheim for autistic children. Conceding that such a program is frightfully expensive, they urge that we attempt to reach fewer children than under conventional programs, and presumably keep each child for a relatively long period. That parents, children, taxpayers, or courts might object to all this is not considered.

Attempts to explain the causes of crime not only lead inevitably into the realm of the subjective and the familial, where both the efficacy and propriety of policy are most in doubt; they also lead one to a preference for the rehabilitative (or reformation) theory of corrections over the deterrence or incapacitation theories. Sutherland and Cressey recognize this: "On a formal level it may be observed that attempts to explain criminal behavior have greatly abetted at least the official use of the treatment reaction." One may deter a criminal by increasing the costs or reducing the benefits of crime, but that strategy does not deal with the "causes" of criminality, and hence does not go to the "root" of the problem. Stated another way, if causal theories explain why a criminal acts as he does, they also explain why he *must* act as he does and therefore they make any reliance on deterrence seem futile or irrelevant. Yet when Sutherland and Cressey come to consider the consequences of treating criminals in order to reform them, as opposed to punishing in order to deter them, they forthrightly admit that "there is no available proof" that treatment increased or decreased crime, and that "the methods of reformation . . . have not been notably successfully in reducing crime rates." Careful reviews of the major efforts to rehabilitate criminals amply support this judgment.[1]

Policy analysis, as opposed to causal analysis, begins with a very different perspective. It asks, not what is the cause of a problem, but what is the condition one wants to bring into being, what measure do we have that will tell us when that condiion exists, and finally what policy tools does a government (in our case, a democratic and libertarian government) possess that might, when applied, produce at reasonable cost a desired alteration in the present condition or progress toward the desired condition? In this instance, the desired condition is a reduction in specified forms of crime. The government has at its disposal certain policy instruments—rather few, in fact—that it can use: it can redistribute money, create (or stimulate the creation of) jobs, hire persons who offer advice, hire persons who practice surveillance and detection, build detention facilities, illuminate public streets, alter (within a range) the price of drugs and alcohol, require citizens to install alarm systems, and so forth. It can, in short, manage to a degree money, prices, and technology, and it can hire people who can provide within limits either simple (e.g., custodial) or complex (e.g., counseling) services. These tools, if employed, can affect the risks of crime, the benefits of noncriminal occupations, the accessibility of things worth stealing, and the mental state of criminals or would-be criminals. A policy analyst would ask what feasible changes in which of these areas would, at what cost (monetary and nonmonetary), produce how much of a change in the rate of a given crime. He would suspect, from his experience in education and social services, that changing the mental state of citizens is very difficult, quite costly, hard to manage organizationally, and may produce many unanticipated side-effects. He would then entertain as a working hypothesis that, given what he has to work with, he may gain more by altering risks, benefits, alternatives, and accessibility. He would not be sure of this, however, and would want to analyze carefully how these factors are related to existing differences in crime by state or city, and then would want to try some experimental alterations in these factors before committing himself to them wholesale.

In sum, the criminologist, concerned with causal explanations and part of a discipline—sociology—which assumes that social processes determine behavior, has operated by and large within an intellectual framework that makes it difficult or impossible to develop reasonable policy alternatives and has cast doubt, by assumption more than by argument or evidence, on the efficacy of those policy tools, necessarily dealing with objective rather than subjective conditions, which society might use to alter crime rates. A serious policy-oriented analysis of crime, by contrast, would place heavy emphasis on the manipulation of objective conditions, not necessarily because of a belief that the causes of crime are thereby being eradicated, but because behavior is easier to change than attitudes, and because the only instruments society has for altering behavior in the short run require it to assume that people act in response to the costs and benefits of alternative courses of action. The criminologist assumes, probably rightly, that the causes of crime are determined by attitudes which in turn are socially derived, if not determined; the policy analyst is led to assume that the criminal acts *as if* crime were the product of a free choice among competing opportunities and constraints. The radical individualism of Bentham and Beccaria may be scientifically questionable, but it is prudentially necessary.

The other most important work of the 1960's in the field of criminology, *Delinquency and Opportunity* by Richard A. Cloward and Lloyd E. Ohlin, would appear to be an exception to the general criminological perspective of the day. Writing in 1960, Cloward and Ohlin developed an influential theory of delinquency in big cities. A delinquent gang (or "subculture"— the terms are used, for reasons not made clear, interchangeably) arises in response to the conflict that exists between socially-approved goals (primarily monetary success) and socially-approved means to realize those goals. Certain youths, notably of the lower class, desire conventional ends but discover that there are no legitimate means to attain them; being unable (unwilling?) to revise these expectations downward, they experience frustration and this may lead them to explore illegitimate ("nonconforming") alternatives. Some lower-class youth may aspire to middle-class values ("money and morality," as the authors put it) while others may aspire only to success in lower-class terms (money alone). The barriers to realizing those aspirations are found in part in cultural constraints derived from the immigrant experience (Southern Italians and Sicilians, for example, allegedly do not value schooling highly), but in larger part in structural difficulties, chiefly the fact that education is costly in money outlays and foregone earnings.

In its brief form, the theory of Cloward and Ohlin would seem to be in sharp contrast to the general sociological perspective. Delinquency may in their view be learned from peers, but it is learned because of the gap between aspirations and opportunities, and opportunities in turn are objective conditions determined by government and the social system. Education, they claim, is the chief source of opportunity. One therefore expects them to end their book with a call for cheaper, more readily available educational programs. But they do not. Indeed, less than one page is devoted to policy proposals, amounting essentially to one suggestion: "The major effort of those who wish to eliminate delinquency should be directed to the reorganization of slum communities." No explanation is offered of what "slum reorganization" might be, except for several pages that decry "slum disorganization." Their analysis leads the reader toward the material desires of life as the key factor (indeed, that is all the lower classes are supposed to value), but stops short of telling us how those material desires are to be realized. Their theory states that "each individual occupies a position in both legitimate and illegitimate opportunity structures" (they rightly note that this is a "new way" of viewing the problem), but they do not speak of the costs and benefits of illegitimate as opposed to legitimate opportunities. Instead, the individual who is confronted with a choice among kinds of opportunities does not *choose,* he "learns deviant values" from the "social structure of the slum."

Thus, when the authors come to speak of policy, they have little to say about what determines the choice of illegitimate opportunities (nobody has chosen anything, he has only 'learned" or "assimilated"), and thus they have no theoretical grounds for suggesting that the value of legitimate "opportunities" should be increased (e.g., better-paying jobs for slum youth), or that the benefits of illegitimate ones should be decreased (e.g., more certain penalties for crime), or that "opportunities" for goal gratification be replaced by direct goal gratification (e.g., redistributing income).

III

Explaining human behavior is a worthwhile endeavor; indeed, for intellectuals it is among the most worthwhile. Those who search for such explanations need not justify their activity by its social utility or its policy implications. Unfortunately, neither intellectuals nor policymakers always understand this. If the government becomes alarmed about crime, it assumes that those who have studied crime most deeply can contribute most fully to its solution. Criminologists have rarely sought to show statesmen the error of this assumption. Much of their writing is "practical," much of their time is "applied." To a degree, of course, criminological knowledge may assist criminologists' actions: careful study and conscientious learning can help one avoid obvious errors, attack popular myths, and devise inventive proposals. But it is also likely that the most profound understanding may impede or even distort, rather than facilitate, choice, because much of this knowledge is of what is immutable and necessary, not of what is variable or contingent.

In the mid-1960's, when the federal government turned toward social scientists for help in understanding and dealing with crime, there was not then in being a body of tested or even well-accepted theories as to how crime might be prevented or criminals reformed, nor was there much agreement on the causes of crime except that they were *social,* not psychological, biological, or individualistic. In fact, there was not even much agreement that crime was a major and growing problem—scholars noted the apparent increase in crime rates, but (properly) criticized the statistical and empirical weaknesses in these published rates. While these weaknesses did not always lead the critics to conclude that crime was in fact not increasing, some scholars did draw that conclusion tentatively and their criticisms encouraged others to draw it conclusively.

Nor were scholars very farsighted. Having established beyond doubt that crime rates were strongly related to age differences, few scholars (*none* that I can recall) noted the ominous consequences for crime of the coming-of-age in the 1960's of the products of the postwar "baby boom." Similarly, while some scholars had shown by cross-sectional studies that the proportion of a city's population that was nonwhite was powerfully correlated with assaultive crimes, few to my knowledge drew the obvious implication that, unless this correlation was spurious, the continued in-migration of blacks to large cities would inflate crime rates. Once the various national commissions were underway, however, scholars associated with them (notably the group associated with the Task Force on the Assessment of Crime, under the direction of Lloyd Ohlin) began to work vigorously on these issues and produced a number of reports that showed vividly the impact of demographic changes on crime rates.

The major intellectual difficulty governing the relationship of social scientists to policymakers with respect to crime was not the presence or absence of foresight, however, but rather the problem of how to arrive at policy proposals in the absence of scientific knowledge that would support them. The crime commission did not develop new knowledge as to crime prevention or control; as Professor Ohlin later described it, existing "social-science concepts, theories, and general perspectives were probably of greater utility to the staff and the commission in forming the final recommendations than the inputs from new knowledge development efforts." What were these "concepts, theories, and general perspectives"? One, cited by Ohlin, consisted of "grave doubts" about the effectiveness of the criminal-justice system and of rehabilitation and treatment programs. From this, Ohlin and his colleagues drew the conclusion that "the criminal-justice system should be used only as a last resort in the control of undesirable conduct." From that inference, in turn, the commission adopted the view that offenders should be "diverted" from the system and recommended a broad policy of "deprisonization."

There are no doubt ample grounds in humane sentiment for finding fault with prisons, but at the time of the commission's work there were scarcely any well-established *scientific* grounds. That "treatment" had failed seemed clear, but "non-treatment" had failed just as clearly: persons on probation might be no more likely to "recidivate" than those in prison, but neither were they much less likely. As for deterrence, there was, when the commission deliberated and Professor Ohlin advised, virtually *no* scientific material on whether prison did or did not deter. It was not until 1966, fifty years after criminology began as a discipline in this country and after seven editions of the leading text on crime had appeared, that there began to be a serious and sustained inquiry into the consequences for crime rates of differences in the certainty and severity of penalties. In any case, the commission scarcely dealt with the deterrence or incapacitation functions of prison.

In short, criminology could not form the basis for much policy advice to the commission. Yet that did not prevent criminologists from advising. Professor Ohlin is entirely honest about this: "The relevant social-science literature was descriptive and analytical. There were relatively few experimental or controlled studies of the effectiveness of particular programs or policies. . . . Sociologists serving as consultants to the commission proved reluctant to draw out . . . action recommendations. . . . When they did try to do this, the recommendations were often *more influenced by personal ideological convictions than by appropriately organized facts and theories* . . .*" [emphasis added].

Social scientists did not carry the day on the commission (they could not, for example, get their view on marijuana accepted), but the effect of their advice, based on personal belief rather than scholarly knowledge, was clear. Working with sympathetic commission members in small task forces, the advisers stimulated and participated in a process that—as Professor Ohlin later put it—"led to far more liberal recommendations by the commission than one would have thought possible at the outset given the conservative cast of its membership."

There is nothing whatsoever wrong with social scientists trying to persuade others of their policy beliefs, just as there is nothing wrong with lay commission members trying to persuade sociologists of their beliefs. There *is* something wrong with a process of persuasion colored by the mistaken notion that one party is an "expert" whose views are entitled to special consideration because of their evidentiary quality. There is no way of knowing to what extent commission members believed what the sociologists were saying was true, as opposed to merely plausible or interesting. But based on my own experience in advising national commissions, including the crime commission, I am confident that few social scientists made careful distinctions, when the chips were down, between what they knew as scholars and what they believed as citizens, or even spent much time discussing the complex relationships between knowledge and belief. I certainly did not, and I do not recall others doing so.

IV

Having alluded to my own role as a policy adviser, let me amplify on that experience to reinforce, by self-criticism, the point I am making. I was not in 1966 a criminologist, nor am I now. I came to crime, if I may put it that way, as a consequence of my study of police administration and its political context, and found myself labeled an "expert" on crime because of that interest and perhaps also because of the desire of governmental consumers of "expertise" to inflate, by wishful thinking, the supply of such persons to equal the demand for their services.

Once I found myself, willy-nilly, in the crime business, I found that my ideas on the subject—apart from those formed by my own empirical research on policing—were inevitably influenced by the currents of academic opinion about me. The effect of these currents is not to persuade one of what is true, but to persuade one of what is important. In my case, I did not absorb from criminological writings a set of policy conclusions about whether criminals can be deterred or rehabilitated, but I did absorb a set of interesting facts about crime: for example, that crimes are age-specific, that victims contribute to their victimization in most assaultive crimes, and that published crime rates are unreliable. All of these things were (and are) true, but of course they are not directly related to the policy question of what is to be done about crime.

In short, I did not, any more than Professor Ohlin, have in 1966-68 empirically supported policy advice to offer statesmen dealing with crime. What I then realized, as did Professor Ohlin, was that many of those seated about me, urging in the strongest tones various "solutions" to crime, were speaking out of ideology, not scholarship. Nor was this only true of my colleagues on the crime commission. Walter Reckless, for example, in the 1967 edition of his text, *The Crime Problem,* states flatly that punishment "does not . . . prevent crime," though he adduces no systematic evidence to warrant such a conclusion. Charles R. Tittle and Charles H. Logan provide other examples of this unsupported assertion in their review of the more recent literature on deterrence, a review that nevertheless concludes by observing that "almost all research since 1960 supports the view that negative sanctions are significant variables in the explanation of conformity and deviance. . . . Sanctions apparently have some deterrent effect under some circumstances." [2]

What I only later realized was that criminologists, and perhaps sociologists in general, are part of an intellectual tradition whose focal concerns are with those aspects of society that are, to a great extent, beyond the reach of policy and even beyond the reach of science. Those matters that are within the reach of policy have been, at least for many criminologists, defined away as uninteresting because they were superficial, "symptomatic," or not of "causal" significance. Sociology, for all its claims to understand structure, is at heart a profoundly subjectivist discipline. When those who practice it are brought forward and asked for advice, they will say either (if conservative) that nothing is possible, or (if liberal) that everything is possible. That most sociologists are liberals explains why the latter reaction is more common even though the presuppositions of their own discipline would more naturally lead to the former.

Notes

1. See, for example, Leslie T. Wilkins, *Evaluations of Penal Measures* (New York: Random House, 1969); and Chapter 14 of this volume.

2. Charles R. Tittle and Charles H. Logan, "Sanctions and Deviance: Evidence and Remaining Questions," *Law and Society Review* 7 (Spring, 1973), p. 385.

3

Political Theory, Policy Analysis, and the Insoluble Problems of Crime
Robert P. Rhodes

It is currently fashionable and accurate to characterize criminal justice planning and evaluation efforts as fragmented, eclectic, uncomprehensive, and without a theoretical foundation for public policy. However deplorable to some people, this state of affairs is largely inevitable, for disjointed planning and evaluation efforts in criminal justice today reflect not merely uncertainty as to solutions, but strong disagreement as to the nature of our criminal justice problems.[1] If political theory is, in some sense, concerned with means and ends; and if current policy problem definitions in criminal justice imply the value of multiple outputs or ends for the criminal justice system; and if such ends are competing, as we think they are—then the problems of criminal justice will remain insoluble, subject to incremental, approximate solutions at best. Policy analysis models which emerge from contending problem definitions will, for the most part, reflect the lack of consensus.

Political Theory and Problem Definition

Competing problem definitions exist at present throughout the political community, among interest groups, actors in the subgroups and organizations in the criminal justice system, and among academic groups as well, not excluding policy analysts. Disparate problem definitions emerge from mind-sets as evaluation models which are, themselves, the functions of contending organizational roles [2] and interest-group perspectives of police, prosecutors, defense counsels, trial and appellate judges, civil libertarians, criminal justice planners, and the general public. Political interests formed by organizational roles and group behavior establish the parameters of policy, objectives, standards, and even indicators as measures of success for goal fulfillment. Examples of such evaluation models that emerge from mind-sets are due-process models, administrative-efficiency models, class-conflict models, law-enforcement models, and social-control models. Of course, the most vigorous efforts of policy analysts to remain detached and objective will not prevent value conflicts in policy analysis. Some conflicts of value in criminal justice are formally institutionalized, as in the adversary system; others reflect social tensions that stretch far beyond the criminal justice system.

31191

Political science can make a major contribution to criminal justice evaluation in three areas. First, it can measure the impact and consequences of government programs on securing formal objectives.[3] Second, policy analysis can measure, although with great difficulty, the impact of programs on informal objectives, the unwritten agenda of policy, such as income and budget redistribution.[4] Third, it can bare the competitive mind-sets now in use for evaluation by both practitioners in criminal justice and social scientists. The third of these contributions, the focus of this chapter, is crucial in a subject area as value-laden as criminal justice, for the clarification of problem definitions, value assumptions, and goal inconsistency in various perspectives is preliminary to identifying conflicting mind-sets in dialogue concerning criminal justice reform. We believe this will be, for the most part, a thankless task, for the basic value structures within competing theoretical perspectives command tenacious loyalties in all of us. Yet theoretical consciousness [5] of inevitable value bias in policy analysis is necessary to reveal the difficulty of problem definition in criminal justice.

Those who are explicitly interested in a general political theory of criminal justice have largely ignored the area of policy analysis. Some of the general-theory literature, often sociological, calls for major reordering of the social structure, an alternative as vague in its program and consequences as it is unlikely to occur.[6] There is also an exploding literature involving the politics of crime at a descriptive level.[7] The theoretical point of departure for this literature is either David Easton's much quoted definition of government as "the authoritative allocator of values in society" [8] or Harold Lasswell's equally well-known definition of political study as inquiry into who gets what, when, and how.[9] What does seem in short supply are critical assessments of outputs and the values attached to their measurement as they apply to manageable policy goals.

Data and Values

The problem is not lack of data alone, although anyone who has engaged in criminal justice evaluation knows the data problems to be anything but minor. Criminal justice agencies and departments are swimming with data, but many of the data are useful only for internal administration, official reporting, and public relations. There is no question that systematic data collection needs to be undertaken for evaluation purposes, but the determination of what data to collect, what they are to measure, and for what objectives requires a value judgment and reflection on the nature of the problem.

For example, traditional uniform crime reporting is a useful indicator of police activity, but misleading as an indicator of actual criminal behavior, which often goes unreported. The use of data generated by current efforts of the Law Enforcement Assistance Administration to measure criminal behavior through victimization surveying generally avoids the problems of unreported crime. However, although victimization surveying is a valid and reliable measure of legally defined criminal acts,[10] it is not necessarily an accurate measure of the seriousness of crime from the aggregate perspectives of the victims who suffer. Nor do any of these indicators reflect the more generalized perspectives of the public, which is more apt to respond to a publicized incident in the newspaper than to a statistical formulation. Obviously, the public perspective is immeasurably more important to the local police chief and mayor.[11] Finally, systematic data collection of legal decisions at crucial stages in the courts is essential to evaluate systemic management problems such as crowded dockets, delay, or excessive workloads. But if it is not offender-based (i.e., if it does not identify offenders by name or code), no control can be applied to past offenses to compare the effectiveness of defense counsel or to analyze discriminatory practices. If data are offender-based, their use may interfere with juvenile justice, with its emphasis on sealed records, or with the rights of privacy. As a practical matter, data processing and retrieval systems may be quietly opposed by local law enforcement because they will interfere with efforts by the police to clear the streets of prostitutes and pickpockets by extra-legal sweep arrests, or hinder attorneys who rely on low-visibility decision-making to minimize adversary conflict and maximize efficiency.

Different types of data assume that certain policy objectives are to be measured, and cannot easily be applied to other problems. The problem is not simply technical, but involves the fact-value dichotomy with which policy research must persistently struggle. Different facts often presuppose particular values and social objectives within an explanatory paradigm.

Political Paradigms in Criminal Justice

At present, there is a wide variety of political paradigms which measure the allocation of values in criminal justice. Some are conscious, scholarly attempts to model behavior. With others, theoretical awareness about implicit concepts, goals, and indicators of value vary in sophistication. Nevertheless, a wide variety of models, weltanschauungs, or mind-settings are used by criminal justice scholars and practitioners to evaluate what is going on. By a paradigm or model, in this context, we simply mean a conceptual framework of goals and indicators to measure goal attainment with regard to the operations of the criminal justice system in its broadest dimensions. No suggestion is made here of the necessity of internal symmetry, carefully defined components, or well-defined parameters and boundaries, for we are concerned with perceptual limitations about the meaning of facts due to a value bias built into a commonly used frame of reference.

Obviously, the policy evaluator will attempt to be rigorous in developing, within a carefully constructed framework of behavioral theory, quantified objectives related to policy goals and operationalized indicators of goal fulfillment. But the conception of goals and objectives usually begs a problem definition.

As an illustration, a goal to reduce recidivism may be pursued by community-based treatment centers and work-release and furlough programs. The evaluation of the program goal might, in simplified terms, compare recidivism rates among a stratified sample of offenders in such centers with a similar sample of offenders from traditional incarcerating institutions. Assuming that the primary problem is the reduction of recidivism through modern correctional treatment, some "risk" of law-breaking by the experimental sample of released prisoners must be tolerated. But the police problem definition is more apt to emerge from a day-to-day concern with increases in criminal behavior. Incarceration is 100 percent effective during the time of sentence, and the mind-set of the officer is not usually consonant with the short-term risk.[12] Moreover, the police perspective may have merit if the recidivism rate is only marginally reduced by community-based treatment and serious offenses increase. There is evidence that the impact of community-based treatment on recidivism is marginal.[13] On the other hand, the program budget analyst may point to the fact that community-based treatment is cheaper than traditional incarceration, whatever its impact on recidivism.[14]

Similar conflicts in value occur in drug program evaluation. Drug squads measure their success by arrests and hard evidence against users and sellers, not necessarily by the offender's social recovery. Methadone clinics and Synanon-type centers consider the abandonment of illegal drug use and social adjustment their goal. But Alcoholics Anonymous might react with mixed emotions to indications of success from both police blotters and methadone clinics if a rapidly increasing pattern of alcoholism filled the social vacuum left by former illegal drug users.

The group which commissions an evaluation, be it police department, court, department of correction, foundation, or government agency, will largely define the normative policy objectives and, consequently, the nature of the problem. Each group will inevitably "tunnel" perceptual reference for evaluation and explanation, as will actors in various subgroups in the criminal justice system, in the academic community, and in the general public, each revealing its unique interests, values, and social roles.

Space does not permit a full catalog of models which have emerged from distinct mind-sets to evaluate criminal justice policy. Many civil libertarians and defense attorneys prefer due-process models, which evaluate by drawing comparisons between court rules, as ideal conditions, and actual practice, although procedural barriers to fact-finding may result in less protection for potential victims through lower and slower conviction rates. The recent debate in New York State over corroborating testimony in rape cases is instructive here.[15] The same might be said for liberalizing bail [16] and Miranda warnings.[17]

Closed-system production-flow models and utility curves tend to be favored by court administrators and trial judges with heavy dockets, and by cost-benefit-oriented planners, because they emphasize administrative or economic efficiency as a value.[18] Of course, what is administrative utility from one point of view may be assembly-line justice from another. Professionally oriented police planners and administrators opt for models that measure police output in terms of clearance rates, response time, and criminalistic skills. Street-wise officers, while responding to administrative measures for promotion, informally evaluate performance in terms of social control, keeping the peace, preventing riot and disorder, maintaining morale, or simply keeping themselves out of trouble.[19] Finally, conflict-oriented social theorists frequently prefer the class-conflict model, which emphasizes and measures inequities in the social structure, reflected in criminal justice, often with little concern for detection, apprehension, and deterrence.

The Insoluble Problems of Crime

We are not discounting the utility of any of the above perspectives for evaluating subgoal attainment. We are suggesting that such perspectives are at times insufficient for comprehensive planning and evaluation, for subgoal problem definitions are sometimes too insular or inconsistent with other valued objectives of the system. That is, maximizing goal attainment in one problem area may be dysfunctional for goal attainment in another.

For example, the adversary system, prized by civil libertarians, contradicts administrative efficiency at many junctures; and vigorous law enforcement in high-crime areas—using tactical squads and police dogs—may reduce burglary and armed robbery downtown, but at the cost of community relations and urban harmony. Utilizing "professional" standards for recruiting and training police officers, civil-service testing, lateral entry, specialization, educational attainment, all may be in the short run contradictory with the goal of minority representation on the force.[20] In other areas, mention has been previously made of subgoals such as the continuance of low-visibility decision-making by prosecutors or police in the administration of justice versus high-visibility administrative control permitted by rapid-retrieval information systems, and of improvements in rehabilitation techniques which may require higher social risks of criminal activity by the probationers. Finally, policies regarding which types of criminal behavior should be deterred, investigated, arrested, and prosecuted demand decisions regarding allocation of human and material resources. Investigating and prosecuting organized crime, narcotics, and forcible rape require many times the resource allocations necessary to deal with larceny, robbery, and motor-vehicle violations. Unless resources are unlimited, a rare situation in criminal justice departments and agencies, a choice must be made between competing crime-control objectives.

Victimization as a Comprehensive Indicator

One of the comprehensive goals of the criminal justice system most apt to be forgotten by the public and practitioners is protecting the citizen against being victimized. Ironically, protection of the victim is not a central concern in criminal justice. In a sense, police do provide a fundamental service in protecting life and property. But the protective measures which police invoke must be carried out within a large body of complex rules for police administration and criminal procedure, and an even more complex set of rules informed by the "street sense" of the patrolman.

Moreover, police do not act on behalf of individual complainants, but must be primarily concerned with public order in an environment of danger,[21] perceived civilian hostility, shifting community values, and limited resources.[22] Police will use their discretion whenever possible to encourage private settlement of minor disputes when legal transgressions do not threaten public order. And the officer must be sensitive to private vengeance masquerading as public duty. For these and other reasons, Reiss and Bordua have characterized policing as a service without clients.[23]

Law enforcement and order maintenance are thus placed in a public framework of law, and not designed to reduce individual suffering, a fact which results in no end of confusion for policy analysis. The roots of the confusion are definitional and perceptual distinctions as to what the category "criminal law" refers to.

The general parameters of criminal law actually refer to three moral-jurisprudential categories. The first reference is to a moral quality: using drugs, engaging in egregious sexual practices, adultery, and stealing are considered social evils. However unfortunate it might be for social policy, "evil" behaviors such as homosexuality, gambling, and seeking pleasure or hallucinatory experience through drugs are often labeled as such by legislative proscription—sometimes even under circumstances where legislators publicly acknowledge the impossibility of enforcement. The second category of the meaning of criminal law refers to legal culpability or *mens rea,* and conceptually it is the peculiar province of the attorney and judge. The standard of culpability is a separate logical category which requires a demonstration, consistent with due process, of both intent on the part of the defendant to perform a legally proscribed act and commission of the act itself within the limitations of due process.

A third category can be deciphered from the perspective of the police officer and his concern for preventing trouble, for orderliness and decorum. Concern for public order may prompt the police to move against behaviors which are not technically criminal but, if ignored, may result, according to the perspective of the police officer, in administrative problems, in disorder, or in illegal behavior. Civil-rights demonstrations in the Deep South in the 1950's, and organized attempts by antiwar groups to "shut down" the nation's capital in 1970, are well-publicized events that resulted in order-maintenance conduct by the police. More commonplace disruptive events are traffic snarls and accidents, loitering, drunkenness, and family disturbances.

None of the above categories, of course, provide measures for victim suffering. To the extent that criminal justice policy analysis is to become comprehensive, it would do well to reduce its dependence on criminal law categories as reflected in arrests, reported crime, convictions, and riot control, and examine the impact policy has on reducing victimization. The Law Enforcement Assistance Administration has supported efforts for measuring stranger-to-stranger violence and burglary verified through survey data, as a comprehensive indicator for its impact programs.[24] The measurement of crime by moral-jurisprudential victimization indicators currently in use would be significantly improved upon by scaling victimization suffering in behavioral terms along the lines suggested by Sellin, Wolfgang, and Wilkins.[25] Both types of crime indicators would be complementary, the one measuring legal crime, the other measuring suffering. Quantifying victimization in monetary rather than legal terms would raise considerably our ability to analyze the impact of crime-control policies. Since victim costing would be unidimensional, the impact of alternative policies on a variety of crime types could be assessed, budget analysis would be enhanced, and the costs of diversionary programs more readily reviewed. Perhaps most important of all, victim costing might provide essential illumination for that politically volatile question discussed elsewhere in this volume, what behaviors to criminalize or decriminalize.

Certainly, we are not at present in a position to draw correlations between victimization reduction and policy initiatives, although this is an important area for research. But the victim's suffering, as a measure of the success or failure of an anticrime policy, might be the key to comprehensive planning and evaluation in an area of public policy replete with contending problem definitions.

Notes

1. John A. Gardiner, "Research Models in Law Enforcement and Criminal Justice," *Law and Society Review* 6 (November 1971): 223; James Q. Wilson, *Varieties of Police Behavior* (New York: Atheneum, 1973), pp. 227-236.

2. Malcolm M. Feeley, "Two Models of the Criminal Justice System: An Organizational Perspective," *Law and Society Review* 7 (Spring 1973): 407-425.

3. Daniel P. Moynihan, *Maximum Feasible Misunderstanding* (New York: Free Press, 1969), 190-203.

4. Leonard Merwitz and Stephen Sosnick, *The Budget's New Clothes* (Chicago: Markham, 1971), Ch. 9; Arthur Maass, "Benefit-Cost Analysis: Its Relevance to Public Investment Decisions," *Quarterly Journal of Economics* 80 (May 1966): 208-226; Aaron Wildavsky, "Analysis, Systems Analysis and Program Budgeting," *Public Administration Review* 26 (December 1966): 292-310.

5. William E. Connolly, "Theoretical Self-Consciousness," *Polity* 6 (Fall 1973): 5-35.

6. Richard Quinney, *The Social Reality of Crime* (Boston: Little, Brown, 1970), pp. 11-25.

7. Herbert Jacob, *Urban Justice* (Englewood Cliffs, N.J.: Prentice-Hall, 1973), pp. 1-3; James Eisenstein, *Politics and the Legal Process* (New York: Harper and Row, 1973), pp. 4, 307-323; James R. Klononsky and Robert I. Mendelsohn, eds., *The Politics of Local Justice* (Boston: Little, Brown, 1970); George F. Cole, *Politics and the Administration of Justice* (Beverly Hills, Calif.: Sage Publications, 1973), pp. 15-20.

8. David Easton, *The Political System* (New York: Knopf, 1960), Ch. 5.

9. Harold Lasswell, *Politics: Who Gets What, When, How* (New York: McGraw-Hill, 1936).

10. Anthony Turner, "Victimization Surveying—Its History, Uses, and Limitations," Unpublished paper, National Institute of Law Enforcement and Criminal Justice (July 1972).

11. Wilson, p. 228.

12. Substantially the same point is made in Martin A. Levin, "Crime and Punishment and Social Science," *The Public Interest,* No. 27 (Spring 1972), pp. 102-103.

13. Robert Martinson, "Can Corrections Correct," *The New Republic,* April 18, 1972, pp. 13-15.

14. Informatics, Incorporated, *Pennsylvania Community Treatment Services: An Evaluation and Proposed Evaluation Information Systems,* Pennsylvania Department of Justice, Bureau of Corrections (July 1972).

15. Grace Lichtenstein, "Rape Squad," *The New York Times Magazine,* March 3, 1974, p. 11.

16. U.S. Department of Commerce, National Bureau of Standards, *Compilation and Use of Criminal Court Data in Relation to Pre-Trial Release of Defendants: Pilot Study,* by J. Locke, R. Penn, J. Rick, E. Bunten, and G. Hare, Technical Note 535 (August 1970), pp. 2-12.

17. Richard H. Seeburger and R. Stanton Wettick, Jr., "Miranda in Pittsburgh—A Statistical Study," *The University of Pittsburgh Law Review* 29 (October 1967): 11-12. Seeburger and Wettick provide evidence that the confession rate was reduced by *Miranda* and, by inference, conviction rates were reduced. Other studies have disputed the impact of *Miranda* on "coercive" practices to obtain confessions at the precinct level. See Richard J. Medalic, Leonard Zeitz, and Paul Alexander, "Custodial Police Interrogation in Our Nation's Capital," *Michigan Law Review* 66 (May 1968): 1347-1422.

18. The literature is voluminous. For examples, see Jacob Belkin and Alfred Blumstein, *Methodology for the Analysis of Total Criminal Justice Systems,* Carnegie-Mellon University, Grant NI-026 (November 1970); Rand Corporation, *Prosecution of Adult Felony Defendants in Los Angeles County: A Policy Perspective* (March 1973).

19. Albert J. Reiss, Jr., and David J. Bordua, "Environment and Organization: A Perspective on the Police," in David J. Bordua, ed., *The Police* (New York: Wiley, 1967), pp. 25-55.

20. See *Carter v. Gallegher* 452 F2d 315 (1971); *Commonwealth v. O'Neill* 348 F. Supp. 1084 (1972). The difficulty of reconciling professionalism, leadership, and representativeness in bureaucracy is discussed by Herbert Kaufman, "Administrative Decentralization and Political Power," *Political Administration Review,* Vol. 29, No. 1 (January-February 1967).

21. Jerome Skolnick, *Justice Without Trial* (New York: Wiley, 1967), pp. 45-67.

22. See generally Wayne LaFave, *Arrest: The Decision to Take a Suspect into Custody* (Boston: Little, Brown, 1966).

23. Reiss and Bordua, p. 30.

24. Turner, pp. 1-3.

25. Thorsten Sellin and Marvin E. Wolfgang, *The Measurement of Delinquency* (New York: Wiley, 1964); Leslie T. Wilkins, "New Thinking in Criminal Statistics," *Journal of Criminal Law, Criminology and Police Science* 56 (September 1965): 277-284.

4

Sources and Limitations of Data in Criminal Justice Research

Roger B. Parks

To pursue systematically the many issues raised in this volume, it is important for researchers to be aware of the various sources of data bearing upon criminal justice systems, the range of data obtainable from such sources, and some of the limitations of these data. It will not be possible in a brief chapter to touch upon the full spectrum of sources, data types, or issues concerning the validity and reliability of criminal justice data. Rather, the intent of this chapter is to provide a point of departure for those whose interest in criminal justice research may be stimulated by the articles in this volume.

Widely varying quantities and qualities of data are found at different stages of criminal justice activities. Ideally one would like to have adequate, accurate data at all stages, from police activities through prosecution and judicial activities, short-term jail and longer-term penal and correctional activities, and probation and parole activities. Unfortunately, for some of these virtually no statistical information is currently available, and in some cases seems unlikely that such information will be forthcoming.

Following a proposal to the President's Commission on Law Enforcement and Administration of Justice, it would be desirable for researchers to have available both criminal justice agency statistics and criminal career records.[1] Agency statistics consisting of resource levels, workload, and performance data are necessary to address questions concerning which organizational and operational forms are better for the various types of agencies. These data are available to a greater or lesser extent at many levels and are the principal focus of this article. Criminal career records would allow the researcher to investigate the effects of interactions among agencies of different types as individuals are processed through them. They are currently being compiled in federal and state information systems such as the FBI's National Crime Information Center or New York's State Identification and Intelligence System. The maintenance and utilization of such records systems for either operational or research purposes is quite controversial, however. Critics have questioned whether adequate attention is paid to accuracy and security of such files so as to protect the rights of

I wish to acknowledge the very helpful comments of James C. McDavid and Dennis C. Smith.

31

individuals whose records are contained therein. While statistical series may be developed on the basis of criminal career records, it seems unlikely that researchers will gain access to individual files.

Data Sources

Most criminal justice agencies collect and maintain voluminous data pertaining to *some aspects* of their activities. As is the case with records maintained by many types of organizations, the data collected primarily for internal purposes are often not the data which a researcher studying these agencies would desire. The bulk of the data available pertain to either resources utilized, manpower, expenditures, and the like; or to workload, including offenses reported to the police, calls for service received, miles of streets patrolled, warrants applied for and issued, court caseloads, and numbers of prisoners in jails and other correctional facilities.

Federal agencies compile and publish data obtained from criminal justice agencies throughout the country. Probably the best known of such compilations is the *Uniform Crime Reports* (UCR) published annually by the Federal Bureau of Investigation. This report has without doubt the broadest coverage of any document presenting criminal justice data. In 1972, the UCR represented a compilation of data from approximately 10,000 distinct jurisdictions, serving 93 percent of the national population. The UCR contains data on crimes known to the police in seven basic (Part I) categories, with tabulations at national, regional, state, metropolitan, and local levels. It provides a wealth of information on the characteristics of those arrested for crimes in the Part I categories as well as for a number of other (Part II) categories. Of additional interest to the researcher is the fact that the UCR contains gross data on police employment for all reporting jurisdictions. While there have been many cogent critiques of the UCR, it does represent a very extensive effort over a number of years to obtain and publish accurate, consistent data on some aspects of criminal justice.

Another important compilation at the national level is *Expenditure and Employment Data for the Criminal Justice System,* published annually by the Law Enforcement Assistance Administration (LEAA) in cooperation with the Bureau of the Census. This volume provides data on the number of full-time and full-time-equivalent employees and on the expenditures of agencies at the federal, state, and local levels for police protection, judicial and legal services and prosecution, indigent defense, correction, and other criminal justice activities. The *Municipal Yearbook,* published by the International City Management Association, is another source of information on police manpower, salaries, and expenditures as well as on other administrative policy questions for cities with populations over 10,000. For a selected group of thirty large police departments, the *General Administrative Survey* of the Planning and Research Unit, Kansas City (Missouri) Police Department, lists manpower and expenditures and a wide range of additional data including salary levels, training, equipment, and pension information. The International Association of Chiefs of Police, with headquarters in Gaithersburg, Maryland, also compiles data on police agencies.

National Prisoner Statistics, published annually by the Bureau of Prisons, provides data on inmates of state and federal institutions as well as on the institutions themselves. Data on jails and their inmates are available in *Local Jails,* published by the LEAA, which draws upon data on jails obtained in the 1970 Census. The National Council on Crime and Delinquency has been experimenting with a system for producing Uniform Parole Reports based upon a common system of reporting by parole agencies nationwide.

The areas where the least information is available at the national and, indeed, at all other levels are those of prosecution and of judicial and probation activities. Many of the data that one would like to obtain in these areas are recorded in individual case records but not compiled into any statistical reports. These case records, while legally available for public inspection and used regularly by attorneys, pose many of the same questions of security and privacy as the criminal career records mentioned before; they are, in fact, an integral part of those records.

The prosecution stage of criminal justice activity is probably the most difficult area in which to obtain data. Over 75 percent of the cases which enter this stage from the police are substantially disposed of through plea bargaining or the prosecutor's decision not to continue the case (*nol-pros*) before reaching the judicial stage.[a] Much of this activity involves informal, unrecorded bargaining, however, and thus is not amenable to statistical reporting. Only the results of the process are recorded in the case records.

Moving from the national to the state level, one finds that several state governments have units charged with compiling data on criminal justice agencies within the state. These data include crime statistics similar to those compiled by the FBI (in 1972, 14 states had central collection systems for these statistics) and also may include such items as manpower

---

[a] In *The Challenge of Crime in a Free Society* (Washington, D.C.: U.S. Government Printing Office, 1967, pp. 262-263), the President's Commission on Law Enforcement and Administration of Justice provides estimates that only 38,000 of the 177,000 persons arrested and formally accused of Index (UCR Part I) crimes in 1965 ever came to trial. This represents only about 5 percent of those arrested for Part I offenses in that year. Over 75 percent of those arrested were not formally accused, and of those accused, 73 percent pleaded guilty.

and expenditure figures for criminal justice agencies in the state. State level reports often contain information on courts and corrections activities (e.g., manpower, expenditures, workload) within the state as well as data on police agencies. State councils on criminal justice and other state planning agencies organized to implement the Omnibus Crime Control and Safe Streets Act of 1968 and related federal programs are excellent sources of information on state and local agencies. Criminal justice plans and system descriptions published by these state councils provide good overviews of state and local criminal justice activities. State judicial councils often publish data annually on state court activities.

The number of potential data sources mushrooms at the metropolitan and local level, with a concomitant increase in the legwork required of the researcher. A good starting point is the local law enforcement assistance council or other local or areawide criminal justice planning unit organized under the 1968 and 1970 Omnibus Crime Control bills. Such bodies generally publish reports or at least maintain extensive files on the resources (manpower and expenditures) of the criminal justice agencies in their areas and may also have workload data for those agencies. Many metropolitan areas have one or more interested citizen groups which compile data on local criminal justice activities. The local bar association is often affiliated indirectly with such groups through member participation. For data on local police agencies, central records centers and planning and research units of large county or central-city police departments are excellent sources.

Most local criminal justice agencies maintain records pertaining to their activities, and many publish monthly and/or annual reports which summarize portions of those records. Larger agencies typically produce more elaborate reports, but even very small agencies generally prepare monthly activity reports, at the least in the form of a memorandum to local officials. These local agency reports and files are at the same time the most complete and the most problematic sources of information on criminal justice activities. They are the most complete in that they are the original sources of the information compiled at higher reporting levels and contain much additional information on the agencies not available in metropolitan, state, or national compilations. They are problematic because of the large variety of recording methods, with wide variations in complexity and detail of the information recorded. The researcher must attempt to identify common elements of data from these systems to ensure comparability for his analyses. This problem of commonality and comparability has been one of the most serious limitations on data series compiled at higher levels. Facing it at the local level, where many complicating factors may be invariant, will give the researcher a useful perspective on the limitations of national criminal justice statistics.

Most local criminal justice agencies are willing to allow the serious researcher access to their files for purposes of obtaining statistical data. Larger agencies with computerized records may provide special runs or may allow the researcher to borrow or copy data tapes to perform his own analyses. In smaller agencies, hand tabulation of all or of a sample of individual records is often the only means of data aggregation. However, the time spent doing so is often quite valuable in providing insight into agency operations and recording procedures. The author would encourage anyone planning to use statistics compiled from reports submitted by many local agencies to get "hands-on" familiarity with such data in this fashion.

This injunction leads directly to another data source, nonparticipant observation. Whether "nonparticipant" is the correct adjective is questionable, given the salience of an observer in many criminal justice milieus; however, what is intended is a usually nonquantitative but most enlightening research style. Riding along in police patrol cars over a period of time provides a knowledge of police operations and problems unobtainable from reports and data files. The same can be said for observing courtroom procedures firsthand. The possibility of some form of observation in jails and prisons should be explored. As events occur which are recorded in data systems, the observer has an opportunity to follow this process, ask questions, and gain important insight into the data he will be using in later quantitative research.

Finally, survey research techniques can be employed to collect data on the activities of criminal justice agencies. These techniques appear particularly relevant in studying the police, who tend to have the broadest contact with the public. Survey techniques for measuring the extent of crime were utilized in studies for the President's Commission on Law Enforcement and Administration of Justice in 1967, and have been since refined by the LEAA for the National Crime Survey.[2] Several police agencies utilize survey techniques to audit the accuracy of their reported crime statistics and to obtain independent information on police-citizen interactions.[b] At the University of Indiana, we have employed data from interviews with citizen-consumers of police services, and with police officers themselves, in a number of comparative studies of police performance.[3] Survey techniques might also be applied to collecting data on informal bargaining among police, prosecutors, and potential defendants, although consideration of privacy issues might prevent this. Similar con-

---

[b] The St. Louis Metropolitan Police Department has used the services of the Governmental Research Institute in that city for a number of years in conducting audits. Recently, the Baltimore Police Department has experimented with follow-up interviews for a sample of calls for service. See Frank F. Furstenberg, Jr., and Charles F. Wellford, "Calling the Police: The Evolution of Police Service," *Law and Society Review* 7 (Spring 1973): 393-406, for a description.

cern for individual privacy could limit the application of surveys in data-collection efforts bearing upon corrections, probation, or parole.

Data Limitations

In a discussion of some of the limitations of data in criminal justice research, the logical place to begin is the crime statistics maintained by police agencies and partially reported in the FBI Uniform Crime Reports (UCR). These are the most widely available and probably the most widely utilized data in the criminal justice field. Yet they have been seriously questioned recently with regard to both their accuracy and their consistency over time and different jurisdictions.

Crime statistics as discussed here are simply the count of offenses reported to the police in the seven Index (Part I) crime categories—murder, rape, aggravated assault, robbery, burglary, larceny over 50 dollars, and auto theft—and the count of arrests made by the police in other serious categories, which together comprise Part II crimes. Even though the vast majority of police agencies report these data to the FBI using the same forms and ostensibly the same definitions, state and local legal and operational crime definitions may vary significantly from the standards set for the UCR. Certainly local record-keeping procedures vary widely, and observations of changes in gross crime rate (crimes per 100,000 population) coincident with changes in records systems and procedures indicate that this is a significant source of variability.[4] The problem of legal variability is not limited to crime statistics data. Wide variations in state laws and policies regarding commitments to penal institutions or local jails mean that series such as the National Prisoner Statistics must be approached with some care.

Even if the UCR data were an accurate and consistent count of offenses reported and arrests over the 10,000 jurisdictions reporting, it would not be correct to use these data for a comparison of the amount of actual crime in those jurisdictions. As many recent surveys have shown, the majority of crimes are not reported to the police.[5] There is every reason to believe that there are wide variations in the extent of reporting to the police both within and especially between jurisdictions. This can lead to the situation where a police department that does a good job of following up reported crimes will face a rising (reported) crime rate due to increased citizen confidence in the efficacy of reporting. Comparisons over time are further limited by the built-in inflators for larceny over 50 dollars (items which were worth 49 dollars last year may be worth 51 dollars this year) and auto theft (a large increase in the number of cars on the road each year).[6] This latter consideration points to another pitfall in comparing crime rates: they are stated as the number of crimes per 100,000 resident population rather than as the number of crimes per target specific to that crime.[c] Finally, it should be noted that while the Index crime data receive the most attention and are believed to be more accurate than other crime data, many serious and prevalent crimes are not included. Perhaps the widespread view of crime as a principally lower-class phenomenon would change significantly if white-collar crimes were reported as regularly as the Index crimes.

Other crime-related statistics are available in national, state, and local compilations and files. Important data include the clearance rate—the proportion of reported crimes "cleared" by either an arrest or an "exceptional" clearance (often a failure of the victim to prosecute)—arrest rates for various crimes, and the value of stolen property recovered. These data have problems of accuracy, consistency, and comparability similar to those of the UCR crime statistics.[7] An important point to note in any of these crime-related measures is that if they are used as measures of performance either for between-jurisdiction comparisons or for within-jurisdiction evaluation of personnel, they can induce behavior which runs counter to expressed criminal justice goals. Excessive emphasis upon crime rates may result in juggling of reports.[8] Emphasis upon clearance rates to evaluate detectives may lead to considerable bargaining with professional criminals, with significant payoffs for those who cooperate by "clearing" (confessing to) many crimes.[9] A focus on arrest rates may lead to a high volume of low-quality arrests, and a focus on the value of property recovered may produce pressures for low initial valuations accompanied by revaluation upward of the property found.

A key consideration here is that any single measure, or group of measures of a single type, particularly when self-reported, is likely to lead to behavioral biases toward scoring well on the measures themselves. Such biases are particularly unfortunate since the measures are only imperfect reflections of the actual goals of the activity or organization.

Some measures are available which do not result from self-reporting.[d]

---

[c] Sarah L. Boggs, in her article "Urban Crime Patterns," *American Sociological Review* 30 (December 1965): 899-908, notes that auto theft rates would be more correctly based on the number of automobiles available for stealing, rape rates on the size of the female population, business robbery, nonresident burglary, and grand larceny rates on the number of business establishments, etc. In particular, this would tend to lower the often high crime rates reported for central business districts, which are characterized by low residential populations.

[d] The following paragraphs deal almost exclusively with problems in police data. This should not be construed to mean that there are not serious problems in other areas of criminal justice data. It is merely reflective of the author's relative familiarity with the several areas.

For police agencies, an example is the proportion of warrants applied for which receive favorable action from the local prosecutor. After careful adjustment for differences in prosecutor policies, this can provide a crude comparative quality-of-arrest measure. Further measures of this quality, such as the proportion of arrests leading to convictions on the original or a reduced charge, would be useful but are rarely, if ever, available. Because of inconsistencies among police, prosecutor, and court records, they are often unobtainable.[10]

Citizen reports of victimizations and police responses to calls provide another external source to be used in conjunction with police-reported data. Researchers have shown that citizen reports of police response time are quite accurate, and that police responsiveness in turn correlates highly with other citizen perceptions and evaluations of police service.[11] However, considerable care must be employed in the design and execution of surveys to ensure the validity and reliability of findings. In addition, many necessary police activities do not directly impinge upon the general public, and thus do not lend themselves to this form of data collection. Where surveys are applicable, though, they are a valuable tool, and should not be dismissed as mere opinion polls or public-relations gimmicks.[12]

Data accuracy, consistency, and comparability problems can also be found when manpower and expenditure figures are probed. One key distinction which is not always made when such data are reported is that between budgeted and actual manpower or expenditures. For many agencies this can be checked against audits of municipal accounts, but such audits tend to be one to two years in arrears and are not universally required. A lesser but still annoying problem with expenditures data is that many agencies' budgets are on a fiscal-year basis (often July to June), while most other data series are stated on a calendar-year basis.

Manpower data should be carefully examined to determine whether they contain all personnel. For example, civilian personnel in police agencies may not be included. Alternatively, police manpower may include school crossing guards and other auxiliary personnel in some data series. Authorized manpower is often reported in place of actual manpower.

In many cases, not all expenditures for policing are included in the police budget. Employer contributions for police officer pensions, fringe benefits, and social security are often found in separate accounts.[e] Expenditures for police service which are made from revenue-sharing or from various grant funds are often not listed with regular police expenditures, yet may constitute a large proportion of the total. Vehicles may be pro-

---

[e] But many police agencies are not included in the social security system and thus there are no employer contributions.

vided by a central garage and not charged to the police. A transmitter or communications center shared with other city departments may or may not appear in the budget or expenditures. Some police departments pay rent to the city for their police station, others do not. Equipment and other capital costs are treated in many different ways in municipal budgets. When comparing police budgets or expenditures across jurisdictions, it is important to be sensitive to such factors.

One approach to firming up manpower and expenditure data is to attempt to break them down into comparable functional categories. Police functions vary widely from city to city, and since many police activities are not directly related to criminal justice, it is quite important to sort out manpower and expenditure categories in analyzing these activities.[f] It should be noted, however, that this is not an easy task. Police and other agency budgets are typically "line item" in nature, without functional breakdowns. Police manpower assignments are made to broad categories such as patrol, investigation, and traffic. Functional assignments among various divisions vary from city to city, so that reliance upon similarly named divisions is often dangerous. The analyst who wishes to attempt functional breakdowns for manpower and expenditures is forced to supplement budget figures with field work in the departments studied in order to make a reasonably accurate allocation. As in dealing with any other multifunctional public-sector activity, in the end some of the allocation is essentially arbitrary.

A different type of breakdown of manpower and expenditures which is becoming quite important is the determination of manpower and expenditure allocations to various geographic areas within larger jurisdictions. This is especially difficult to do because it depends upon the functional breakdown discussed above and upon relatively detailed activity accounting, which is generally unavailable in even sophisticated police records systems. As noted above, only a small portion of police efforts are directly related to crime. However, the inordinate attention paid to that portion by the police themselves (who often refer to it as "real police work") and by many analysts has meant that little information is regularly recorded on other police efforts. Calls for service and radio dispatch data are often kept only as a radio log required by the FCC. Even when detailed crime and dispatch data are available, however, the analyst can

---

[f] As an example, in comparative studies of police efficiency in controlling street crimes, consideration should be given to the actual number of officers assigned to patrol activities. Of course, questions of overall organizational efficiency require consideration of total manpower and expenditures, but in examining subgoal performance, one needs to sort out the resources devoted to the achievement of that subgoal.

generally account for only 50 to 60 percent of most police efforts. This results in part from the nature of the police as a ready-response force.[g] Recent attempts to estimate police resource allocation both functionally and geographically have had a degree of success; yet such allocations must be treated as estimates, with analysis of the sensitivity of results to changes in the allocation rules used.[13]

Conclusion

The existence of multiple data sources and the limitations of data obtained from such sources suggest three useful research strategies. The first is to attempt to obtain multiple measures of desired information from multiple sources, and particularly to focus attention upon cases of conflicting data. The second is to observe wherever possible the original recording and compiling of the data of interest, so as to be sensitive to any incentives which might lead to biased or inaccurate data, or to any differences in definitions or recording techniques which might lead to incommensurability in the data. Finally, it would be well to perform a few deviant-case checks on the data. Where a particular jurisdiction or agency is found to differ considerably from other similar jurisdictions or agencies, the data may be reflecting a true difference, but more likely the difference is produced by discrepancies in data recording and collection. The employment of these three strategies, in concert where possible, should provide a strong base for criminal justice research.

Notes

1. See Peter F. Lejins in President's Commission on Law Enforcement and Administration of Justice, *Task Force Report: Crime and its Impact— An Assessment* (Washington, D.C.: U.S. Government Printing Office, 1967), pp. 178-206.

2. For the early studies see Albert D. Biderman, "Surveys of Population Samples for Estimating Crime Incidence," *The Annals* 374 (November 1967): 16-33; and P. H. Ennis, "Criminal Victimization in the United

---

[g] This does not mean that police are doing nothing during the remainder of their on-duty time, but rather that records are maintained at best for certain specified activities only. Often officer-initiated activities are not recorded. General patrol activities comprise the remaining time. See Roger B. Parks, for some examples of reporting systems in a modern, computer-equipped department. "Measurement of Performance in the Public Sector: A Case Study of the Indianapolis Police Department" (Bloomington, Ind.: Indiana University, mimeo, 1971).

States: A Report of a National Survey," *Field Surveys II* (Washington, D.C.: U.S. Government Printing Office, 1967). Recent refinements are discussed in Law Enforcement Assistance Administration, National Criminal Justice Information and Statistics Service, *Crimes and Victims, A Report on the Dayton-San Jose Pilot Survey of Victimization* (Washington, D.C.: U.S. Government Printing Office, 1974).

3. Discussions of these studies can be found in a series of recent articles. These include Elinor Ostrom and Gordon P. Whitaker, "Does Local Community Control of Police Make a Difference?" *American Journal of Political Science* 17 (February 1973): 48-76; Elinor Ostrom and Roger B. Parks, "Suburban Police Departments: Too Many and Too Small?" in Louis H. Masotti and Jeffrey K. Hadden, eds., *Urban Affairs Review VII: The Urbanization of the Suburbs* (Beverly Hills, Calif.: Sage Publishers, 1973), pp. 367-402; Elinor Ostrom, Roger B. Parks, and Gordon P. Whitaker, "Do We Really Want to Consolidate Urban Police Forces?" *Public Administration Review* 33 (September-October 1973): 423-432; Dennis C. Smith and Elinor Ostrom, "The Effects of Training and Education on Police Attitudes and Performance," in Herbert Jacob, ed., *Criminal Justice Annual III: Problems in the Criminal Justice System* (Beverly Hills, Calif.: Sage Publishers, 1974), pp. 45-81; and Roger B. Parks, "Complementary Measures of Police Performance," in Kenneth M. Dolbeare, ed., *Sage Yearbook in Politics and Public Policy: Public Policy Evaluation* (Beverly Hills, Calif.: Sage Publishers, forthcoming).

4. A recent article by Richard F. Rae, "Crime Statistics, Science or Mythology," *The Police Chief* 42 (January 1975): 72-73, reviews the experience in Chicago during O. W. Wilson's reorganization of that department. Reported crime in Chicago jumped from 57,411 in 1959 to 129,742 in 1960 and to 175,632 in 1961, presumably as a result of improved reporting and recording systems.

5. See the victimization studies cited in note 2. More recent figures are available in two LEAA publications, *Crime in the Nation's Five Largest Cities* (Washington, D.C.: U.S. Government Printing Office, 1974) and *Crime in Eight American Cities* (Washington, D.C.: U.S. Government Printing Office, 1974).

6. Problems of this nature are cogently discussed in Albert D. Biderman, "Social Indicators and Goals," in Raymond A. Bauer, ed., *Social Indicators* (Cambridge, Mass.: MIT Press, 1966), pp. 68-153; Elinor Ostrom, "Institutional Arrangements and the Measurement of Policy Consequences," *Urban Affairs Quarterly,* June 1971, pp. 447-474; and Michael D. Maltz, *Evaluation of Crime Control Programs* (Washington, D.C.: U.S. Government Printing Office, 1972).

7. Maltz provides a good summary of the difficulties with these measures.

8. See David Seidman and Michael Couzens, "Crime, Crime Statistics, and the Great American Anti-Crime Crusade," a paper delivered at the 1972 Annual Meeting of the American Political Science Association, Washington, D.C.

9. Jerome H. Skolnick illustrates this process nicely in *Justice Without Trial* (New York: Wiley, 1966); see especially pp. 174-179.

10. The Urban Institute reviewed some of the problems of data inconsistency in this area in its report for the National Commission on Productivity entitled "Measuring Police-Crime Control Productivity," Part III of *The Challenge of Productivity Diversity* (Washington, D.C.: The Urban Institute, 1972); see especially pp. A-5ff.

11. See Richard C. Larson, *Urban Police Patrol Analysis* (Cambridge, Mass.: MIT Press, 1972), p. 35; and Parks, "Complementary Measures of Police Performance."

12. For example, Clement S. Mihanovich, "Management Measures of Public Attitudes Towards the Police," *The Police Chief* 34 (May 1967): 28-30, argues that unfavorable responses represent "misconceptions" and show the need to "inform the uninformed," rather than possible indications of low performance levels.

13. Very similar means for estimating such allocations were derived independently by Donald C. Shoup and Arthur Rosett, *Fiscal Exploitation of Central Cities by Overlapping Governments: A Case Study of Law Enforcement in Los Angeles County,* MR-135 (Los Angeles: Institute of Government and Public Affairs, University of California, Los Angeles, 1969); and by Ostrom, Parks, and Whitaker, "Do We Really Want to Consolidate Urban Police Forces?"

5

Public Policy and Public Evaluations of Criminal Justice System Performance

Wesley G. Skogan

One of the major developments of the past decade of research and evaluation in crime control has been the emergence of a "consumer perspective" in plans to measure the efficiency and effectiveness of criminal justice agencies. This perspective has developed in response to dissatisfaction with traditional measures of institutional performance, the growing realization that those agencies touch our lives in many ways other than through the crime rate, and an emerging sensitivity to the differential distribution of safety and public satisfaction that criminal justice agencies foster. The consumer orientation toward performance measurement has been expressed in several ways: through the use of systematic interviews to evaluate the outcome of citizens' encounters with criminal justice organizations, through the incorporation of interviews with affected populations into designs for the evaluation of specific institutional reforms, and through the utilization of large-scale sample surveys to investigate the effect of existing variations in agency activity upon public attitudes and perceptions.

Research on citizen attitudes toward legal institutions was stimulated by the activity surrounding the Crime Commission and the Violence Commission during the 1960's.[1] Since then, a number of studies of institutional performance have been reported, with citizen assessments of police activity leading the field. For a variety of purposes, citizens have been asked to "rate the local police" from inadequate to outstanding, evaluate "how well the police do their job," and rank their "satisfaction with police service" on a scale from 1 to 9. Members of the public have also been asked to describe their experiences with some limited, but important, aspects of police activity: "how fast the police came when you called," whether the police "treat people like you fairly," and if they have observed any acts of official corruption. The local courts have been evaluated in a few studies tapping general satisfaction and perceptions of fair treatment. There appears to have been only one investigation of citizen evaluations of corrections, which revealed that most respondents did not fear the escape of

This chapter was written while the author was a Visiting Fellow at the National Institute of Law Enforcement and Criminal Justice, Law Enforcement Assistance Administration. The opinions expressed are those of the author and do not necessarily represent the positions of the National Institute or the Law Enforcement Assistance Administration.

prisoners and most encouraged rehabilitative, rather than punitive, efforts.[2]

The emergence of the consumer perspective has not precluded the use of other measures of system performance: many aspects of the operation of organizations cannot be observed even by contact populations, and cost-benefit calculations must aim at optimizing several desired outcomes of governmental activity, not just citizen satisfaction. And, as the corrections example illustrates, some agencies have only small interfaces with the public. But the incorporation of citizens' experiences into criminal justice performance measures provides feedback of a valuable kind to agencies which are facing the criticism that they are isolated from the public they serve, that their professional and bureaucratic norms insulate them from new or different values, and that they are failing to fulfill even their traditional mission. It may be that the widespread adoption of evaluation programs assessing citizen satisfaction would serve important political as well as analytic functions.

Thus it is probably not accidental that it is the police—the element of the law enforcement system most vulnerable to such charges—who have done the most experimentation with citizen evaluation programs, and whose activities have been the most closely monitored in this fashion by outside observers. Most of our experience with programs to evaluate citizens' experiences, test the effects of reform, and predict the effects of proposed policies on the basis of current patterns of public satisfaction and dissatisfaction has come from research on the police function. The models employed to analyze police operations are general ones, however. With some modification, they could be employed to evaluate the performance of other aspects of the criminal justice system. This essay reviews some of the applications of citizen evaluation techniques in the area of law enforcement, including projects measuring the effects of police-citizen encounters, the consequences of organizational reform, and the correlates of interjurisdictional variations in law-enforcement policy. It concludes that, while several provocative empirical propositions about citizen satisfaction have emerged, the research literature is conceptually deficient. Neither the theoretical nor the practical bases for the selection of performance indicators have been clarified.

Evaluating Citizen Encounters

The use of interview techniques to evaluate systematically the outcomes of interactions between the public and representatives of criminal justice agencies has potentially high payoffs, and correspondingly high risks. Research on the contact populations of most criminal justice agencies has been limited. There has been some suggestive work on prisoners' perceptions of the processes which brought them to justice, and the potential of such research for enhancing our understanding of the problems of witnesses and victims should be very attractive to court administrators.[3] Jacob's investigation of the perceptions and strategies of debtors who come into contact with the garnishment and bankruptcy proceedings is a model which should be followed up in the criminal courts.[4] Studies of the direct users of the services of the justice system are the most direct manifestation of the consumer perspective on performance measurement.

Most evaluations of encounters have been done in conjunction with police departments. Evaluations of this type involve follow-up interviews with samples of citizens who come into contact with the police under specified conditions. Usually those interviewed are the victims of crime, although the extension of the design to include the consumers of routine non-law-enforcement services or even offenders themselves would be of great value. These interviews may themselves be part of another task, the auditing of a department's crime-reporting system. Complementary studies include those which identify self-reported consumers in broader sample surveys and ask them a few additional questions about their experiences. However, since most have little or no contact with most criminal justice institutions, these pools of respondents are usually small and scattered, and it is difficult to squeeze any but a few of the most general questions into most ongoing, broadly focused survey projects.

Respondents who have been recent consumers of police services can provide valuable feedback into the law-enforcement system. Detailed descriptions of their encounter with an officer can be elicited. Their perceptions of such experiences can be used as independent variables to explain variations in their rating of police performance in the community, their support for the police, or their interest in police reform. Or these experiences may be related to variations in officer training, response time, or the type of contact involved. Through such analyses, data on citizen encounters can reveal patterns of individual and system performance.

One example of this kind of activity has been reported by Furstenberg and Wellford.[5] In cooperation with the Baltimore Police Department, they developed a questionnaire for use in evaluating the experiences of those requesting service. An analysis of interviews with 421 such consumers of police service revealed generally high levels of satisfaction with department performance, a nearly universal finding of surveys on citizen attitudes toward the police. Variations in the level of citizen satisfaction, measured by the respondents' rankings of police courtesy, understanding, and capability, were related to their perceptions of the kind and quality of the service they received. Satisfaction was higher when the officers who handled a call took adequate time to inform the caller of how they would handle a complaint and what could be expected to come of the case. Citizens who received follow-up telephone calls or visits from the police were even more favorably disposed toward the department. The same relationships held among blacks and whites, although mean levels of satisfaction were much higher among the latter. Finally, satisfaction levels were related to response time: callers who felt that the police responded rapidly to their summons were more pleased with their overall performance than those who felt that the police took too long to arrive on the scene. This is also a universal finding of general survey studies of the police.

Bordua and Tifft have reported similar findings from a small but intensive study of police-citizen encounters in an unnamed large city.[6] They interviewed contactees and directly observed police-citizen interactions from the vantage point of patrol officers. They found that by either measure, satisfaction was greatly affected by the manner in which responding patrol officers handled citizen complaints. Highly rated officers were those who were observed or reported to have made a thorough examination of a crime scene, informed victims of their situation, offered advice, listened to the parties involved, and showed concern for their plight. In the majority of encounters, officers acted in supportive fashion, contributing to the generally high levels of citizen satisfaction.

Bordua and Tifft indicate that the *type* of contact made between citizens and police is also an extremely important determinant of its outcome. Comparisons between levels of citizen satisfaction generated by police responses to calls for service and proactive, tactical-force traffic stops indicated that involuntary contacts raise hostility levels considerably. This was true regardless of race, although blacks were much more likely to take a negative view of both the specific incident and the police in general. This observation has been seconded by general population surveys. Walker et al. report that involuntary contactees tend to be more dissatisfied with the police than those who initiated contact, and the blacks are more likely to meet the police under involuntary circumstances.[7] This, plus the consistent finding that blacks report longer response times and more abrupt encounters, may go a long way toward explaining interracial differences in evaluations of the performance of municipal police departments.

This finding suggests an important payoff from this brand of performance evaluation: it can be used to test hypotheses about the improvement of police service, including those which are advanced as political demands upon criminal justice agencies. For example, surveys could be used to assess some of the consequences of meeting demands for a representative, racially integrated police department. It has been argued that only coethnics (or even officers of the same sex) generate the trust and provide the understanding necessary to foster perceptions of responsiveness and elicit needed police information among disadvantaged groups. This view is supported by surveys of *police* perceptions, which report higher levels of community participation among minority officers and smaller differences between their attitudes and the beliefs of black city residents.[8] Bordua and Tifft state (but do not provide supporting data) that racial matches between callers and their responding patrolmen did not increase satisfaction with the contact, although the same processes may not be at work among white and black citizens in this regard. Furstenberg and Wellford, on the other hand, indicate that the use of black interviewers for black contactees (and the use of civilian rather than police interviewers for all races) significantly increased the number of negative comments elicited about contact experiences. This tends to support the contention that information-sharing may be contingent upon the congruence of ascriptive characteristics. And in surveys of the *general* population, black respondents attribute bad relations with the police to the lack of black policemen, whatever their experiences. It may be difficult to separate concrete experiences from the symbolic dimensions of the problem.

Interviews with selected consumers of public services also could become effective (and probably more effective) surrogates for civilian review. In addition to information on modal behavior styles or the effect of general department policies, interviews with contact populations can provide specific feedback on individual events and officers. They may be used to gauge routinely the quality of service rendered by all officers, or to follow up complaints about individual patrolmen. This procedure has several advantages over more traditional review processes. It is not simply a reactive procedure, but represents positive determination on the part of a department to seek out instances of shoddy police work or outright individual misconduct. Carefully and systematically seeking out the consumers of agency services would enable departments to bypass the barriers of fear, uncertainty, and ignorance which currently block the flow of information from the street to police administrators. The use of standardized interviews would enable the results of these evaluations to be used routinely in departmental decision-making; survey measures of individual performance could be combined with traffic-ticket totals, arrests, and supervisors' evaluations to form new measures for use at promotion time.[9]

The opportunities for the development of such a review procedure are probably on the upswing. After decades of emphasis on the anonymous, radio-dispatched beat car, new strategies of policing are emerging which emphasize the development of extensive and intensive relationships between individual police officers and the communities they serve. This is integral to the concept of Neighborhood Team Policing, a plan which focuses 24-hour responsibility for a small geographic area upon a small band of permanently assigned patrol officers.[10] The reemergence of the foot patrol is also predicated, in part, upon a nostalgic reconsideration of what the relationship should be between a neighborhood and the cop on the beat. These policing strategies increase the opportunity for a broad variety of citizens to come into contact with individual officers. Surveys now indicate that most people do not know a policeman personally, and that the majority of those who do have developed this relationship outside of a professional context.[11] As the ability of ordinary citizens to form impressions of individual officers increases, citizen interviews can be conducted among a broad spectrum of contactees, including merchants along a beat, school-crossing guards, and other regular observers of public space.

Evaluating Organizational Reforms

A second important cluster of evaluation designs focuses upon organizational service delivery systems rather than the behavior of individual agency representatives. These treat reforms as experiments, attempting to discern the impact of changes in organizational structure or operating routines upon a variety of cost and effectiveness measures, including citizens' perceptions of the service they receive.[12] The evaluation of such "natural experiments" as reforms of judicial selection procedures, shifts in police manpower allocations, the introduction of schemes for the diversion of defendants from the criminal process, and changes in the criminal code provide an opportunity to reexamine the fundamental shibboleths of the law-enforcement professions.

The simplest experimental design, the pretest/posttest, requires but two measurements of citizen attitudes or perceptions and other evaluational criteria. Shifts in perceptions or opinions between the two measurements can be attributed only tangentially to the effect of the reform; alternative rival explanations for the shift must in effect be "argued away"—never a very satisfactory procedure. Furthermore, the initial measurement may heighten the respondents' awareness of the impending reform, making it difficult to generalize from them to the general public.[13]

More powerful evaluation designs introduce control groups or samples or populations which are *not* affected by the reform under investigation. Pretest and posttest changes in the control group enable us to estimate the magnitude of general changes in public opinion, which may be attributed to widely publicized events or common community experiences. Differing patterns of attitudinal change among the respondents affected by the reform may then be more confidently ascribed to institutional change. Since different kinds of people or neighborhoods of differing social composition are likely to react to reforms in the criminal justice system in different ways, the introduction of some randomness into the selection of experimental and control groups increases the strength of the argument.

The lack of such randomness, for example, seriously compromises an evaluational study of police reorganization by Rodgers and Lipsey.[14] They surveyed citizen opinion in two "matched" suburban communities in metropolitan Nashville, Tennessee, one of which was serviced by the Metropolitan Police while the other provided its own small-scale protective force. They found that citizens in the independent jurisdiction were more satisfied with the service their calls elicited, and that citizens there were generally more satisfied with and confident in their police. The difficulty is that the "control" group chose itself—it was independent because it opted out of the Municipal Services District by referendum. In this case of "selection-experimentation interaction," all we know is that people who were so pleased with their local services that they voted to keep them are still pleased with their services, while those who were not, are not.

A more complex methodological package for testing the effect of organizational change upon consumer experiences and evaluations was employed in the evaluation of the Kansas City Preventive Patrol experiment.[15] That year-long project involved testing the effects of two departures from the standard operating routines of urban police departments. Fifteen patrol beats were randomly divided into three experimental groups. One cluster, the "proactive" group, received two to three times its normal complement of men, enjoying extremely frequent police patrols. In the "reactive" cluster, routine patrols ceased; squad cars continued to respond to calls for service, but they did not cruise the streets seeking out enforcement opportunities. The third group of beats received normal service. Two central questions were to be addressed: does routine policing reduce crime and provide citizens with a sense of security, and can massive increases in the level of routine police work further reduce crime and increase security?

Citizens' responses to these changes in the types and levels of service they received were ascertained in a series of personal interviews. Twelve hundred pretest interviews were conducted in the 15 experimental beats; 600 follow-up re-interviews were conducted at the end of the experiment, along with 600 fresh posttest interviews. In addition, a panel of 110 businessmen were interviewed in each wave. During the experiment, interviews were also conducted with over 300 citizens who came into contact with policemen in the three areas, including both those who called for police service and those who were involved in an officer-initiated incident. About 1000 police-citizen contacts were recorded by observers riding in patrol cars in the experimental beats. A host of standard measures of police performance, including response time, traffic accidents, arrest totals, and reported crime rates, were evaluated as well.

Preliminary analyses of these data indicate strongly that citizens were unaffected by these innovations in policing. They were asked about the probability of becoming a victim of crime in their neighborhood and about their feelings of safety on the street; there were no differences across the beats. Neither reactive patrolling nor massive infusions of patrolling squad cars affected survey measures of actual victimization in the experimental neighborhoods. The kind of service provided did not affect the use of protective countermeasures (alarms, locks, dogs) by either householders or businessmen. Finally, neither the sample surveys nor the interviews with citizens who came into contact with the police revealed any consistent patterns of attitudinal change. Patrol types did not affect the quality of encounters with the police (this was confirmed by the observers' ratings), and attitudes toward the police were unaffected by the presence or absence of the experimental conditions. Nor were crime rates affected. Citizens were unable to detect any of these departures from established police practices, and the police could not detect any consequential variations in their own measures of organizational efficiency and effectiveness.

Since reactive policing is considerably cheaper than even present levels of proactive patrolling, and in light of increasing demands for intensive police presence on city streets, the Kansas City experiment contains some important lessons. It suggests that neither the concrete nor the symbolic payoffs of police work are manpower-responsive, and that the traditional modes of deploying manpower do not reap any particular benefits. The use of interview data buttresses the argument, for it can be argued that, for most kinds of crime, police work provides largely symbolic satisfactions. In light of low clearance rates and soaring crime rates, the primary function of the police at the individual level is to "cool the mark out," assisting citizens in coming to terms with their new status as victims.[16] This is reflected in Furstenberg and Wellford's findings on the attitudinal effects of kind and courteous police behavior. At the community level, convincing voters and opinion leaders that "something is being done" is perhaps the most important payoff of patrolling, for the general evidence on the deterrent effects of law enforcement is at best mixed.[17] Given the importance of the symbolic consequences of police work, evidence that innovation and cost-effective decision-making can be carried out without undue furor is the positive finding of this particular set of negative experimental results.

Evaluating Interjurisdictional Comparisons

The third approach to evaluating criminal justice policy through the eyes of consumers is *post hoc,* comparative, and statistical. It employs existing variations in system performance to explore the effects of policy upon consumer satisfaction. Data on citizen attitudes and perceptions are aggregated to the level of the institutional jurisdictions under investigation, usually neighborhoods or cities. Variations in the marginal frequencies of these data within each jurisdiction, such as "percent very satisfied," are related to policy indicators. Observations about the current covariation between organizational attributes and citizen evaluations are then projected into predictions about the effects of further changes in performance or the spread of certain policies into new jurisdictions.

Policy evaluations based on this design have been conducted in a variety of domains. In 1967, the National Advisory Commission on Civil Disorders sampled black and white opinions in 15 major cities. On the basis of the resulting data, Schuman and Grunberg reported that levels of citizen satisfaction were only weakly related to objective measures of service delivery: parks per capita, garbagemen per capita, police per capita.[18] Whatever the source of their attitudes, however, people within cities were in relatively high agreement about the services they received. In the 15-city study, correlations between mean ratings by blacks and whites within cities ranged from .36 (satisfaction with schools) to .90 (the police). A recent volume by Rossi, Berk, and Eidson (cited in note 8) utilized the Kerner Commission data to explore the city-level correlates of black and white perceptions of merchants, jobs, education, welfare, trust in public officials, and the responsiveness of municipal institutions.

The simplest designs of this type are descriptive and comparative: attitude surveys are conducted in two or three small communities which vary on some crucial dimension. The mean responses of citizens in each community are then compared, and related by inference to the interjurisdictional difference. This design was employed by Rodgers and Lipsey to evaluate metropolitan integration in Nashville. The effect of the congeries of variables which differentiate city from suburb—including size, race, class, and history—has been explored in studies by John Conklin and Sarah Boggs, who find that perceptions of crime, attitudes toward criminals and punishment, and the abstract "willingness" to report crimes to the police vary across pairs of jurisdictions.[19]

More sophisticated (and expensive) designs involve larger samples of communities, multiple indicators of citizen satisfaction and perceptions of performance, and the specification of multivariate causal models. Large samples of communities allow the introduction of statistical controls for a few of the myriad of variables which differentiate any pair of communities. Such statistical controls increase our confidence that the apparent consequences of policy differences between the communities are not artifacts of other covariations. The use of multiple measures of concepts to construct policy indicators with known reliabilities helps reduce the effect of measurement error. Single-item measures of attitudes are particularly prone to error, and correlational studies using them are improved greatly when multi-item scales (with smaller proportions of error) are employed and the observed relationships are corrected for attenuation. Causal models specify a network of relationships, making explicit the interaction between policy variables, which may be manipulated, and community attributes of a relatively fixed nature. If the causal paths reflecting the impact of the latter are strong, our expectation that changes in policy will yield dramatic benefits may be tempered.

The paradigmatic research of this type is reported by Ostrom and her students. They have conducted comparative studies of central-city police precincts and adjoining suburbs around Chicago and Indianapolis.[20] In their latest venture, surveys of citizen perceptions and opinions were conducted in 45 community areas in metropolitan St. Louis.[21] They have tested a number of causal models predicting the effects of policy and performance measures upon measures of citizen satisfaction. They find, for example, that communities in which the police respond rapidly to requests for assistance, in which victimization rates are low, and in which clearance rates for major offenses are high tend to view their departments more favorably.

Their efforts to isolate the effects of a major department characteristic —professionalism—have been less successful. In the abstract, police professionalism refers to something like competence, adherence to rules, lawful behavior, and bureaucratic formality in relationships with clients. It is both an organizational concept and an individual one, and the relationship between the two is problematic. At the organizational level, the professionalizing policies of a department are usually measured by such indicators as the employment of civilians in technical and support roles, the extent of rookie and in-service training programs, educational requirements, the adoption of innovations (the Master Patrolman rank, computers), or the early implementation of such organizational features as juvenile units or community-relations programs.

Some researchers indicate that these indices of professionalism are positively related to measures of citizen satisfaction or evaluations of the quality of police service in their communities.[22] Others, like the Ostrom group and Richard Chackerian, find them to be either unrelated or *negatively* related to citizen perceptions.[23] There are several plausible explanations for each set of findings, reflecting our still tentative knowledge about these affairs. One involves the problem of multicolinearity: professionalizing departments are not randomly distributed, but are found in cities which suffer from a variety of other ills. Chackerian reported that the most experimental departments were located in racially heterogeneous, high-conflict, high-crime cities, and that these factors appear to overshadow the effect of police organizational arrangements upon consumer satisfaction.

In a recent paper, Ostrom indicates that there are many forces at work within professionalizing departments which also may lower citizen evaluations.[24] Professional departments encourage impersonal, bureaucratic, formal relationships between police and citizens; they demand that officers ignore the plaints of a hostile citizenry, that they be nonparticularistic in their disposition of complaints, and that they work to rule. The trappings of professionalism include the rapid rotation of personnel across districts, the computerized deployment of manpower, and the rapid response of radio-dispatched cars to crime scenes. Professional departments may also rely upon formal intelligence systems to gather information about events, and they employ legalistic internal review procedures to punish their wayward members. Such practices may have a negative impact upon measures of citizen satisfaction.

The difficulty is that most police work does not involve crime control. All of these organizational arrangements are designed to improve the disposition of victimization complaints, not to guide officers in the settlement of intra-family disputes, tracking down runaways, and quieting senile senior citizens. As research on citizen encounters indicates, many of the demands of professionalism run counter to citizens' preferences: people want personalized, individual service geared to meet their self-defined needs, special consideration of their personal situation, and the intervention of the police to solve their lives' crises. Since police work is largely labor intensive, the primary determinant of citizen satisfaction should be the performance of police officers on the street; but the demands of professionalizing departments may be inconsistent with "satisfactory" police behavior.

An alternative explanation for the negative relationship between professionalism and satisfaction points to the problematic relationship between an organization's professionalizing efforts and the behavior of their representatives on the job. Organizational measures of police professionalism (like "percent employees civilian") are at best surrogate indicators of individuals' attitudes and behavior on the beat, and most of what we know about police departments indicates that the relationship between policies at the top and policing at the bottom of these agencies is probably not very clear-cut.[25] If we get reforms at the top of bad departments, and if these reforms fail to do much about the exercise of police discretion, the negative correlation between departmental professionalism and citizen satisfaction is perfectly understandable.

A great deal of research supports another hypothesis about communities: there are few economies of scale in police work, and some important diseconomies. A key assumption of metropolitan reformers has been that the fragmentation and dispersion of American police departments among the nation's thousands of local communities is both inefficient and ineffective. The profusion of small departments is believed to add greatly to the cost of law enforcement, for each agency duplicates facilities and maintains its own administrative offices. The lack of coordination over at least the metropolitan area is presumed to reduce the ability of the police to keep an eye on criminals and reduce crime.[26] The best evidence, however, fails to support the argument: there appear to be few payoffs from large size for measures of efficiency or effectiveness.[27] It is clear, however, that citizens' evaluations of their police are much more positive in smaller jurisdictions. Even when other factors are controlled for, residents of small communities fear crime less, feel safer on the streets, enjoy more positive relationships with patrolmen, feel that the police come faster when called, and are more likely to believe that their law-enforcement officials are honest.

These hypotheses about the effect of size are supported by the comparative studies by Boggs and Conklin, who interviewed residents of central cities and the suburbs surrounding them. They both report that suburban residents are considerably more satisfied with their police departments. Rossi et al. find that in larger cities the police know fewer people in their districts—merchants, residents, *and* troublemakers. Where the police do know district residents, the residents' perceptions of police abuse and hostility are lower. Ostrom has reported the results of three major comparative projects of her own, and has summarized the results of other replications and supporting reanalyses of existing data. All of these reveal that size is negatively associated with a host of measures of citizen attitudes and experiences, even when statistical controls are used to partial out the effects of other, size-related departmental and community characteristics.[28] She and her students have not been loath to suggest the policy implications of these findings, that the consolidation of metropolitan police services or the creation of larger, "more efficient" multijurisdictional forces may be a step in the wrong direction.

Research of this type also reinforces an observation of the Kansas City field experiment mentioned above: spending more may not generate further concrete or symbolic payoffs. In a comparison of citizen perceptions in a matched set of black suburbs and adjoining black Chicago neighborhoods, Ostrom et al. found that expenditure rates within the central-city jurisdictions were 14 times those enjoyed by the residents of the independent communities, but central-city residents were less satisfied with services rendered.[29] In a reanalysis of a 1966 National Opinion Research Center survey, they also found that police manpower levels were negatively correlated with perceptions of service, feelings of security, and confidence in the police among a national sample of citizens.[30] In general, comparative and statistical studies of citizen satisfaction indicate that it is not particularly responsive to the infusion of massive amounts of funds into police work, but rather to the reduction of the social and geographical distance between citizens and stationhouses.

The State of Performance Evaluation

Measurement of most of the key aspects of the performance of criminal justice systems is currently impossible. Police statistics are woeful, even though their disreputable state has been widely recognized for 40 years. Judicial statistics are little better. Even for individual cities, it is usually impossible to find meaningful measures of concepts as simple as "the conviction rate," and the continual reclustering of the units of analysis into "cases," "defendants," and "indictments," even within the same system, makes it impossible to put together a coherent picture of system performance.[31] The statistics on who is in individual jails are often quite good, but measures of how they are doing is another matter. The most widely discussed measure of correctional performance is the recidivism rate, but it is not clear that jails can be expected to be the major determinant of that figure.

Citizen-based measures of institutional performance promised to supplement these traditional indicators in a major way. They would provide pictures of system performance which were independent of the activities of the organizations involved; they would reflect the distribution of those activities among clients, rather than among branches of the agency, and provide measures of their quality as well as quantity; they would facilitate the measurement of institutional performance in new areas; they would be comparable across institutions and jurisdictions. However, the sum of the effort invested so far in the measurement of consumer perspectives on the criminal justice system has fallen far short of these goals. The reasons for this are conceptual, not methodological. There has been insufficient attention given both to the theoretical foundations of indicator development and to the applications of the indicators. Our inattention to conceptual considerations may mean that we are not measuring what we think we are measuring, while our lack of careful thought about the concrete applications of social indicators may mean that we cannot tell policymakers what to *do*.

The fundamental conceptual problem in performance measurement deals with what may be treated as "performance." It is important that we select measurement foci which are causally linked to agency activity. This problem is particularly acute in the literature evaluating the performance of local police departments. Perhaps the most commonly employed cluster of questionnaire items used to measure citizens' evaluations of the police are crime-related: questions tapping people's perceptions of city crime and neighborhood crime, their probability of becoming a victim of particular kinds of crime, or their fear of walking the streets. However, *it is not at all clear that the police are very important determinants of the environmental forces which shape these perceptions.* These include racial fears, neighborhood disorganization, the failure of community institutions, the proportion of young people in the local population, and the amount of wealth in the area, as well as the objective crime rate. Only one minor study (by Conklin, cited in note 19) appears to have attempted to establish the *subjective* linkage between citizen perceptions of crime and police work by asking, "Who is primarily responsible for controlling crime?" In the absence of any well-developed theoretical or empirical reason to expect variations in police activity to affect these evaluation items, their status as indicators of agency performance is dubious. Performance indicators must have clearly specified, direct causal connections with the activities they are evaluating.

The second conceptual difficulty relates to the validity of the measures of opinion and descriptions of events gathered in citizen interviews. Because measures of all types are only indirect, secondhand indicators of the "true" status of the object of interest, it is necessary to establish that the connection between the two is strong and that other forces which affect measurements are weak, random, and self-cancelling. There is some reason to doubt that this is the case for most of the measures reviewed here. The problem is summarized in Figure 5-1, using the police as an example.

As Figure 5-1 indicates, citizens' evaluations of the police are affected by several forces. As we have seen above, even the relationship between agency policy and citizen evaluations is problematic, linked as it is through the routine behavior of officers in the field. Without adequate measures of policy *implementation* at the street level—which are simply not obtainable from any police department—indicators of police department policy (expenditures, decisions, structural arrangements) are of little value.

More serious still are the "spill-over effects" depicted in Figure 5-1. These are forces at work in a community which will color citizens' perceptions of agency performance regardless of what that agency is or does. They include the history of the community's (and nation's) relationship between races, the structure of community power, local politics, the economy, and the level of alienation and anomie which characterizes the local populace. Evaluations even of specific services received may not be independent of one's position in the local community: reactions to policing are shaped by *expectations* about police performance, which may be high or low, and evaluations and descriptions of specific experiences will not be independent of these preconceptions. The model in Figure 5-1 may clarify the findings by Jacob and others which led them to conclude that citizens' attitudes toward their government (and especially the attitudes of blacks and middle-class whites, as different as they are in content) are not particularly responsive to their self-reported personal experiences with specific government agencies.[32] Attitudes toward particular agencies (or judges or

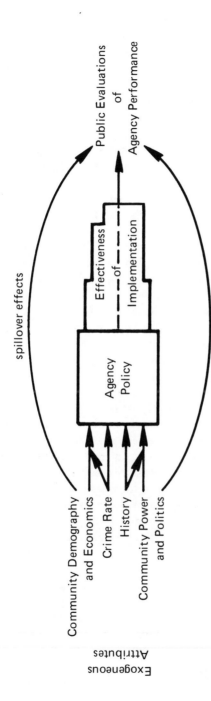

Figure 5-1. Forces Affecting Citizen Evaluations of the Police

policemen) do not develop apart from the context which surrounds both them and their clients.

The best that can be done is to attempt to partial out these exogenous forces. At the simplest level, this involves "matching" communities so that they will not vary along crucial dimensions which will cloud the effects of the policy variables of interest. But given the cacophony of causal forces at work in the world, we will always undermatch.[33] Larger samples of cities would enable us to substitute statistical controls for some of these forces, but this would run afoul of the multicolinearity depicted in Figure I: the same exogenous forces which independently shape perceptions of the police also directly shape agency policy. Controlling for the exogenous factors would artificially reduce the apparent impact of institutional variables. To tease out the impact of policy-and-its-implementation on citizen evaluations of performance calls for sophisticated analysis designs.

The final difficulty with the measures of citizen perspectives on system performance reviewed here is that they do not tell administrators what to do. In order to improve agency performance, if for no other reason than to improve their ratings the next time around, public officials need direct measures of those specific activities which are amenable to administrative manipulation. Most surveys of public opinion, however, have been worded in the most general fashion, calling for omnibus evaluations of overall institutional performance. For example, the attitude questionnaire recently administered to 600,000 large-city residents for the Law Enforcement Assistance Administration contained only one question tapping attitudes toward the police: "Would you say, in general, that your local police are doing a good job, an average job, or a poor job?" Richardson's survey of North Carolinians elicited similar responses to the question, "Based on your experience with the court, how satisfied were you with the way the courts operated?" [34] Such items measure a mélange of attitudes and experiences, some specific to the object of the question, and some not.

In determining levels of satisfaction with institutional performance, we also do not know the relative importance of crime control as contrasted to other activities of criminal justice agencies. The police provide ambulance service, perform rescues, clear the streets, direct traffic, and intervene in family disputes as well as search for burglars. Courts strip people of their belongings and relieve them of their debts, separate them from their spouses, and approve their wills, as well as try criminal cases. The manner in which this mix of activities determines levels of satisfaction may vary across individuals or reflect community variations in the variety of services offered by various agencies to the public.

Thus, at the most fundamental level, general evaluations do not tell administrators what actions to take in the face of low ratings from the population they serve. For all of the reasons outlined above, *post hoc*

attempts to ferret out statistically the policy correlates of intercity variations in omnibus ratings have not been fruitful. Rather, administrators
need to know the consequences of specific characteristics of their delivery
system: its race, speed, demeanor, and ability to resolve disputes or recover property. This suggests that follow-up interviews with the consumers
of specific services should be the most cost-effective source of such data,
especially when the goal is to evaluate relatively rare events such as the
intervention of the police in serious crimes. In the absence of such data,
officials can only cast about for public support in the traditional way:
evoking now-divisive symbols of law and order, or dressing their patrol
officers in blue blazers.

Notes

1. Philip H. Ennis, *Criminal Victimization in the United States: A Report of a National Survey,* The President's Commission on Law Enforcement and Administration of Justice, Field Surveys II (Washington, D.C.:
U.S. Government Printing Office, 1967).

2. John Galliher, "Attitudes of Missouri Citizens Toward the State
Prisons," *Criminology* 8 (November 1970): 239-250.

3. Jonathan Casper, *American Criminal Justice: The Defendant's Perspective* (Englewood Cliffs, N.J.: Prentice-Hall, 1972).

4. Herbert Jacob, *Debtors in Court* (Chicago: Rand McNally, 1969).

5. Frank F. Furstenberg and Charles F. Wellford, "Calling the Police:
The Evaluation of Police Service," *Law and Society Review* 7 (Spring
1973): 393-406.

6. David J. Bordua and Larry L. Tifft, "Citizen Interviews, Organizational Feedback, and Police-Community Relations Decisions," *Law and
Society Review* 6 (November 1971): 155-182.

7. Darlene Walker et al., "Contact and Support: An Empirical Assessment of Public Attitudes Toward the Police and the Courts," *North Carolina Law Review* 51 (November 1972): 43-79.

8. Peter H. Rossi, Richard A. Berk, and Bettye K. Eidson, *The Roots
of Urban Discontent: Public Policy, Municipal Institutions, and the Ghetto*
(New York: Wiley, 1974), Chap. 5.

9. For a discussion of traditional performance measures, see Roger B.
Parks, "Measurement of Performance in the Public Sector: A Case Study
of the Indianapolis Police Department," M.A. thesis, Department of Political Science, Indiana University (June 1971).

10. Peter B. Bloch and David Specht, *Neighborhood Team Policing*
(Washington, D.C.: National Institute of Law Enforcement and Criminal
Justice, Law Enforcement Assistance Administration, 1973).

11. Albert J. Reiss, Jr., *Public Perceptions and Recollections about*

Crime, Law Enforcement, and Criminal Justice, The President's Commission on Law Enforcement and Administration of Justice, Field Survey III, Section II (Washington, D.C.: U.S. Government Printing Office, 1967).

12. Donald T. Campbell, "Reforms as Experiments," *American Psychologist* 24 (April 1969): 409-429.

13. Donald T. Campbell and Julian C. Stanley, *Experimental and Quasi-Experimental Designs for Research* (Chicago: Rand McNally, 1963).

14. Bruce D. Rodgers and C. McCurdy Lipsey, "Metropolitan Reform: Citizen Evaluations of Performance in Nashville-Davidson County, Tennessee," Indiana University, Workshop in Political Theory and Policy Analysis, Department of Political Science (1974, mimeo).

15. George L. Kelling et al., *The Kansas City Preventive Patrol Experiment: A Summary Report* (Washington, D.C.: The Police Foundation, 1974).

16. Erving Goffman, "On Cooling the Mark Out: Some Aspects of Adaptation to Failure," in Arnold Rose, ed., *Human Behavior and Social Process* (Boston: Houghton Mifflin, 1962), pp. 482-505.

17. George Antunes and A. Lee Hunt, "The Impact of Certainty and Severity on Levels of Crime in American States: An Extended Analysis," *Journal of Criminal Law, Criminology, and Police Science* 64 (December 1973): 486-493; Harold Votey and Llad Phillips, "An Economic Analysis of the Deterrent Effect of Law Enforcement on Criminal Activity," *Journal of Criminal Law, Criminology, and Police Science* 64 (December 1972): 330-342.

18. Howard Schuman and Barry Grunberg, "Dissatisfaction with City Services: Is Race an Important Factor," in Harlan Hahn, ed., *People and Politics in Urban Society* (Beverly Hills, Calif.: Sage Publications, 1972), pp. 369-392.

19. John E. Conklin, "Criminal Environment and Support for the Law," *Law and Society Review* 6 (November 1971): 247-265; Sarah L. Boggs, "Formal and Informal Crime: An Exploratory Study of Urban, Suburban, and Rural Orientations," *The Sociological Quarterly* 12 (Summer 1971): 319-327.

20. For a summary of the Indianapolis study, see Elinor Ostrom et al., *Community Organization and the Provision of Police Services* (Beverly Hills, Calif.: Sage Professional Papers in Administrative and Policy Studies 03-001, 1973). The Chicago project is reported in Elinor Ostrom and Gordon P. Whitaker, "Community Control and Governmental Responsiveness: The Case of Police in Black Neighborhoods," in David Rodgers and Willis Hawley, eds., *Improving the Quality of Urban Management* (Beverly Hills, Calif.: Sage Publications, 1974), pp. 303-334.

21. Elinor Ostrom, Roger B. Parks, and Dennis Smith, "A Multi-Strata Similar Systems Design for Measuring Police Performance," Paper presented at the Annual Meeting of the Midwest Political Science Association, Chicago (May 1973).

22. Gary T. Marx, "Alternative Measures of Police Performance," Paper presented at the Annual Meeting of the American Sociological Association, New York (1973).

23. Elinor Ostrom, "Scale of Production and the Problems of Service Delivery in a Federal System," Paper presented at the Conference on Serving the Public in a Metropolitan Society, the Third "Toward '76" Conference of the Center for the Study of Federalism, Temple University (1974); Richard Chackerian, "Police Professionalism and Citizen Evaluations: A Preliminary Look," *Public Administration Review* 34 (March-April 1974): 141-148.

24. Elinor Ostrom, "The Design of Institutional Arrangements and the Responsiveness of the Police," in Leroy N. Reiselbach, ed., *People vs. Government: The Responsiveness of Institutions* (Bloomington, Ind.: Indiana University Press, 1974).

25. Wesley G. Skogan, "Policy-Making and Police Taking: Controlling Behavior on the Beat," *Urban Affairs Quarterly* 9 (June 1974): 520-528.

26. Elinor Ostrom, "Metropolitan Reform: Propositions Derived from Two Traditions," *Social Science Quarterly* 53 (December 1974): 474-493.

27. Elinor Ostrom and Roger B. Parks, "Suburban Police Departments: Too Many and Too Small," in Louis Masotti and Jeffrey K. Hadden, eds., *The Urbanization of the Suburbs* (Beverly Hills, Calif.: Sage Publications, 1973), pp. 367-402.

28. Ostrom and Parks, "Suburban Police Departments: Too Many and Too Small."

29. Ostrom and Whitaker, "Community Control and Governmental Responsiveness: The Case of Police in Black Neighborhoods."

30. Ostrom and Parks, "Suburban Police Departments: Too Many and Too Small."

31. James Eisenstein and Herbert Jacob, "Measuring Performance and Outputs of Urban Criminal Courts," *Social Science Quarterly* 54 (March 1974): 713-724.

32. Herbert Jacob, "Contact with Government Agencies: A Preliminary Analysis of the Distribution of Government Services," *Midwest Journal of Political Science* 16 (February 1972): 123-146.

33. Campbell and Stanley.

34. Richard J. Richardson et al., *Perspectives on the Legal Justice System: Public Attitudes and Criminal Victimization* (Chapel Hill, N.C.: Institute for Research in Social Science, University of North Carolina, 1972).

6

Political Issues in Labeling: Criminalization and Decriminalization
Carl Akins

The question of what behavior a society labels criminal is a political one, but one rarely examined by political leaders and even more rarely by political scientists. Labeling some behavior criminal—criminalization—and removing such a label from other behavior—decriminalization—are actions which touch upon many of the topics of other chapters in this volume. For example, correctional policies often are implicit in such labeling. In some of the substantive areas I consider below, the age of the person who behaves in a certain way, e.g., buys or attempts to buy an alcoholic beverage, is an explicit part of labeling, and thus considerations of the juvenile justice system come into play. Differential labeling, both formal because of different criminal jurisdictions and informal because of the attitudes of different participants in the criminal justice system, also raises issues more directly related to other chapters.

In the broadest terms, the issues of criminalization and decriminalization raise questions about the purposes of law itself. Even if the discussion is limited to the purposes of criminal law, the issues remain broad. Is the purpose justified as deterrence of some sort of behavior? Is it to uphold some moral principle? Or is it proclaimed to be for someone's own benefit? In the abstract, all of these raise philosophical questions concerning legitimacy, and in practice all of these raise empirical questions of effectiveness.

There are several more specific empirical questions about criminalization and decriminalization which help to provide a starting point for political scientists who are interested in the area. Will labeling certain behavior criminal or noncriminal have any impact at all on the frequency of such behavior, and what is that impact likely to be? What will be the broad impact on public attitudes toward the criminal justice system of criminalization or decriminalization? Is labeling certain behavior criminal or noncriminal simply a subtle way of discriminating against or in favor of some groups—discrimination which would not occur if it were more overt? What are the costs of decriminalization or criminalization in terms of resources which might be better used for other public purposes? Does criminalization or decriminalization have any impact on moral principles that can be expressed in some measurable way, as distinct from its impact on behavior? Can the proclaimed benefits of making one's behavior criminal or noncriminal for one's own good be demonstrated in any measurable way? What are likely to be the costs of the anticipated but unintended side-effects of decriminalization or criminalization?

There are also many value questions which might be of interest to political scientists who are less attracted to the empirical ones. Are there certain moral principles so important that they justify criminalization or decriminalization under any circumstances? If so, what are they? If not, are there certain circumstances which justify labeling, and what are they? What are the competing rights of the state and the individual in labeling actions criminal or in removing such labels? How are these rights to be reconciled? Is some behavior always criminal and is other behavior never criminal? If so, what? What should be the importance of intention in labeling action criminal or noncriminal?

In spite of these many questions which deal with issues very close to those of most political-science efforts, political scientists have left the examination of criminalization and decriminalization largely to lawyers, psychologists, sociologists, and criminologists. We have not examined the many questions of public administration that are often part of the issue, leaving them instead to systems analysts and management consultants as we often do other questions of court administration. The chief exception [1] to this lack of consideration by political scientists has been consideration of some of the basic questions of values by political philosophers, but their examination has emphasized the abstract rather than the empirical.

The value questions raised, e.g., the right of society to label a certain behavior criminal, often have an empirical component which political scientists might examine if they chose to do so. Political scientists could study comparatively across jurisdictions the deterrent effects of labeling an act criminal, but we leave deterrence studies to psychologists or criminologists and do so without noticing that our closely allied discipline of international relations has spent much effort on the study of deterrence. Only in impact studies of Supreme Court decisions [2] do political scientists study the deterrent effect of labeling behavior unconstitutional, and there we most often are interested only in special populations or the policy of school officials.

Possible Research Areas

There are many research areas in political science which illustrate the possibilities of exploring the issues raised above. Political scientists have the opportunity to contribute to the broad debate over criminalization versus decriminalization in several ways. We can sharpen the issues that raise value choices and we can contribute to deciding empirical questions through competent research efforts. There are many sources for information and ideas, and I briefly discuss some of them here as examples. The list is only a starting point and illustrative of specific questions which are minor parts of the much larger issue.

Political scientists have a good bibliographic starting point for studies of criminalization and decriminalization by the legal profession in the journal *Judicature,* though its articles are not limited to those by attorneys. Published by the American Judicature Society with its purpose, "to promote the efficient administration of justice," stated on the cover of each issue, the journal prints many articles which could stimulate political-science research. In the year 1973 alone, three articles raised questions for political scientists.

Victimless Crimes

One article [3] in *Judicature* proposes decriminalization for several categories of "victimless crimes" as means of reducing the criminal courts' caseload by as much as one-half. Vagrancy, gambling, alcoholism, drug use, some sexual behavior, and some juvenile behavior are the categories that the author briefly examines, and each one raises research questions for political science. Gambling, for example, is an area that a political scientist might examine to determine the extent of differential enforcement by class and race as a basis for addressing the question of decriminalization. The attempts in several states in recent years to increase their revenues by some form of a state-run gambling system—a type of decriminalization—provide a basis for comparative research on the merits and demerits of decriminalization and criminalization. Thus the usefulness of our federal system as a political laboratory could be taken advantage of, as only a few have done,[4] instead of simply being noted in passing.

The same article discusses briefly the alternatives to continuing criminalization:[5] Is behavior decriminalized by simply declaring it legally acceptable or labeling it mental illness or deviance, with the societal response becoming "treatment and rehabilitation" rather than "corrections"? Or perhaps is behavior decriminalized by making it subject to administrative regulation? The author gives only brief comments on these alternatives, and any attempts to examine them can surely benefit from political-science efforts. Political scientists have long studied administrative regulation and all its foibles, though of late much of the policy analysis in this area has been done by Ralph Nader, his co-workers, and his imitators. Even some of the work of political scientists has appeared in law journals, not political-science journals,[6] and it has most often dealt with matters of economic regulation with no examination of issues of criminalization and decriminalization.

Traffic Regulation

Two other articles from *Judicature,* the second a response to the first, examine the question of decriminalization and replacement with administrative regulation for most traffic offenses.[7] The first article is by a traffic-safety specialist who is also an attorney, and the reply is by an attorney who works in an American Bar Association program to improve traffic courts. The arguments of each are predictable, and study of them could be the first step in a study of the politics of decriminalization. Changes have already occurred in New York—and, under federal Department of Transportation leadership, are likely to occur in other states in the immediate future—which can be the basis for the raising of many interesting questions by those interested in state and local politics as well as intergovernmental relations. The work of political scientists could perhaps be of use in making a choice concerning decriminalization of certain traffic offenses and replacement of the traffic court with an administrative process. Clearly the competing goals and claims of traffic-safety specialists and of court-reform proponents are so at variance with one another that the choice between them must be a political one. Political scientists could assess the costs and benefits of the opposing positions with greater objectivity than the contending parties. The work of political scientists in examining police behavior, including traffic-law enforcement,[8] is a starting point for such efforts.

Other work by attorneys and articles by psychologists, sociologists, and criminologists raise questions that could stimulate fruitful research by political scientists in connection with important policy problems.[9]

Substance Abuse

The broad area of regulation of substance abuse is one which badly needs social-science research, including work by political scientists. There are basic questions which political scientists could help answer. Why, for example, are public attitudes toward legal drugs such as alcohol and nicotine so different from attitudes toward illicit ones such as heroin and marijuana that the former are not even thought of as drugs? One federal official who works in this area has speculated that the reason is partly that members of Congress are not willing to identify their favorite stimulant as a drug, and certainly similar speculation can be made about state legislators. The political-attitude surveys which we so commonly use for a variety of purposes might help test these speculations as well as others. Attempts at regulation of alcoholic beverages by all governmental units and increasing attempts to regulate tobacco smoking can provide us with enough information about the varying effectiveness of different controls to keep platoons of political scientists busy for years doing comparative work that could be the basis for future policy decisions. Given that neither criminalization (during Prohibition) nor decriminalization (current schemes of state sales and/or licensing) is very effective in dealing with the problems of alcoholism, what can we expect from regulatory schemes for other drugs? And why do political decision-makers continue to use similar methods of regulation? Careful research on both these questions might tell us much about the basic nature of our political processes, and also be of use in making better decisions.

Current Developments

Beyond these basic questions, there are other intriguing questions related to current policy developments. The United States Supreme Court stopped just short of decriminalizing alcoholism in 1968 when it rejected a constitutional claim that jailing for public drunkenness constituted cruel and unusual punishment for alcoholics.[10] The rejection came, in part, because the five-man majority was troubled that there was no realistic treatment alternative to jail in most jurisdictions. For those concerned with the impact of Supreme Court decisions on state and local governments, the decision is an interesting contrast to other decisions during that period in which the court was not so hesitant in making social policy. Is decriminalization of alcoholism a matter to be decided on the basis of local decisions to provide alternative treatment, and if so, what does the decision mean for other possible areas of decriminalization? Attempts to answer such questions can provide political scientists with yet another way to examine the interplay of governmental institutions in the making of social policy and can give policy-makers better information on how to make their decisions more effective.

Decriminalization of alcoholism in jurisdictions with alternative treatment facilities raises several policy questions of potential interest to political scientists. Should the treatment be compulsory? If so, should the police be the principal agents enforcing the treatment requirement? [11] Should treatment be compulsory only for those skid-row derelicts who previously ended up in jail or should it also include the middle-class intoxicated driver? One federally sponsored local experiment to require treatment for the intoxicated driver is currently under way in a Virginia suburb of Washington, D.C., and preliminary evaluation indicates that the program is successful in reducing traffic deaths caused by intoxicated drivers. Thus decriminalization of alcoholism and decriminalization of traffic violations are linked in at least this instance.

Decriminalization of marijuana use and possession of small amounts of it for personal use has been the subject of a statewide referendum in California, and marijuana use has been made a minor misdemeanor by legislative action in Oregon during the last two years. City governments, notably in towns dominated by large universities, have attempted to act similarly but have generally run afoul of state law. The State's Attorney in Chicago has, acting within his prosecutorial discretion, effectively decriminalized possession of small amounts of marijuana for first offenders who agree to attend five counseling sessions over a period of several weeks. These sessions are some ways similar to traffic schools, and the decriminalization is even more complete, for police mug shots and fingerprint records are returned to the person after completion of the sessions. Other prosecutors throughout the country have taken similar actions. A Presidential commission [12] and a lobbying organization, the National Organization for Reform of Marijuana Laws (NORML), have dealt with the same issue on the national level but have had impact only on state and local governments. Many other state legislatures have moved as far as holding hearings on marijuana decriminalization. Even those which have not moved that far have sharply reduced the criminal penalties associated with marijuana use and simple possession.

In the same time period, states have acted to make dealing in marijuana and possession and dealing in other drugs, notably heroin and LSD, subject to much stiffer criminal penalties—increasing criminalization, if you will. New York State has set up an especially harsh penalty structure, and other states and the federal government are considering similar action even though tough federal statutes during the 1950's seemed notably ineffective.

Standard techniques and questions of political science could be applied to much of this activity. For example, voting studies of the California marijuana referendum could be done and the impact of lowering the voting age in college towns could be studied. Comparative studies of state legislative activity on these issues could build on the many recent studies comparing states on other policy issues. Questions about the relation between science and public policy that have been raised in other policy areas could be used as the basis for similar questions regarding control of drug use. Several questions about the proper limits of prosecutorial discretion, which a few political scientists have studied in other contexts, could be examined. Analysis using the simple but crucial distinction between policy outputs and policy outcomes could be of critical importance in evaluating both decriminalization of drug use and increasing criminalization of dealing. Political scientists could do research on the alleged links between criminal activity and heroin use.[13] In addition, many of the questions asked about replacement policies in the decriminalization of alcoholism could be asked about similar replacement policies in drug use.

Current policy developments in decriminalization of many traffic offenses were mentioned above, and they raise research questions for political scientists beyond those of police behavior and the limits of administrative regulation. The basic political question of who will lose and who will gain from such a shift in public attitudes toward law enforcement in general because of a change in traffic-law enforcement could be examined by standard techniques of political-attitude surveys. Attitudes toward courts would be of particular interest. There are many other possible consequences not immediately apparent in such a shift, and political scientists could help policy-makers by doing research that attempts to predict what some of them might be before such a shift occurs.

Increased Criminalization?

Even though the United States is a country in which the statement "There oughta be a law" is common, criminalization of broad classes of activity not already under the criminal statutes is a rare occurrence. Given what we as political scientists have learned in our research efforts about the limits of administrative regulation, perhaps we should be proposing criminalization of certain activities that are now handled administratively. Current widespread public apathy and distrust toward all levels of government is based in part on realistic assessments of the failures of the system as well as of the people who run it. Any such shift would need study by people other than political scientists—attorneys, for example, on the different standards of proof required—but political scientists' efforts could be the beginning.

On the national level, there are several policy areas where the feasibility of increased criminalization might be explored because of the limits of current administrative regulation and already existing criminal statutes. Economic regulation is one, especially in the antitrust field, and protection of civil rights is another. The use of administrative regulation and only limited criminal sanctions in both these areas raises questions about both class and racial bias in our political system, questions which proposals for increased criminalization might bring out even more forcefully. The highly selective use of criminal sanctions in other policy areas on the national level, in tax-code enforcement for example, also presents opportunities for asking important questions about the basic nature of our system of politics.

On the state and local levels, there are similar questions for political scientists in such policy areas as housing and zoning-code regulations and enforcement and public-health protection. The self-regulation, under delegations of authority by state governments, of most professions, including law and medicine, provides an effective shield against criminalization of many of the activities of members of those professions. Political scientists examining the possibility of criminalization of some of the behavior of the members of self-regulated professional groups could use public-attitude surveys and comparisons of alternative means of regulation. The addition of criminal liabilities to the civil ones under which they currently operate might make state and local officials more careful in their behavior and more responsive to legitimate public demands.

Policy and Research Pitfalls

Let me emphasize that I am not calling for any sort of broadspread criminalization of behavior now controlled in other ways, but only for study of what the potential impact of such a change might be. Proposals for decriminalization should be examined by political scientists in the same way and with similar caution, for it too is no panacea. Reforms similar to decriminalization—a separate justice system for juveniles and indeterminate sentencing, to name two which are discussed in other chapters in this volume—have not had all the benefits their proponents claimed for them and have had many consequences that those proponents presumably would not have desired. Decriminalization reforms, unless done with more care and research beforehand, could produce all-too-familiar tales.

Just as proposals for criminalization and decriminalization can have pitfalls, so can research in this area. Some are obvious, such as the difficulty in using the notoriously dubious crime statistics which are generally available. There is also the problem of getting beyond our competence as political scientists by going into areas such as law or economics where we have only limited knowledge. Other problems are less obvious and more difficult to deal with. For example, what should be the political standards for evaluation of any proposed criminalization or decriminalization? Or what are the limits of validity for comparisons of programs in different jurisdictions or different policy areas? In spite of the limits, there are many fruitful research questions in criminalization and decriminalization which we as political scientists can explore both for the sake of increasing our own knowledge and in order to apply that knowledge to important policy questions.

Notes

1. J. Roland Pennock and John W. Chapman, eds., *The Limits of Law: NOMOS XV* (New York: Atherton, 1974).

2. One good source which will lead to many others is Theodore Becker and Malcolm Feeley, eds., *The Impact of Supreme Court Decisions* (New York: Oxford University Press, 1973).

3. Robert C. Bourchowitz, "Victimless Crimes: A Proposal to Free the Courts," *Judicature* 57 (1973): 69-78.

4. For examples, see the many recent works of Thomas Dye and Ira Sharkansky, among others.

5. Bourchowitz, p. 78.

6. Samuel P. Huntington, "The Marasmus of the ICC: The Commission, the Railroads, and the Public Interest," *Yale Law Journal* 61: (1952) 467-509.

7. George Brandt, "Improved Highway Safety through Improved Adjudication Procedures," *Judicature* 56 (1973): 358-362; and the reply, Stephen Goldspiel, "Let the Traffic Court Do its Job," *Judicature* 57 (1973): 26-29.

8. See James Q. Wilson, *Varieties of Police Behavior* (Cambridge, Mass.: Harvard University Press, 1968); and John A. Gardiner, *Traffic and the Police* (Cambridge, Mass.: Harvard University Press, 1969).

9. For several examples see the anthologies edited by Jackwell Susman in the AMS anthology series (New York: AMS Press).

10. *Powell v. Texas,* 392 US 514 (1968).

11. On this topic see Michael C. Musheno, "The Intake of Public Inebriates in the District of Columbia: A Policy Impact Study," Ph.D. dissertation, The American University (1974). It is worth noting that two of the four dissertation committee members are attorneys on the law school faculty and that one of them, who is also a political scientist, is chairman of the committee.

12. *Marihuana: A Signal of Misunderstanding,* First Report of the National Commission on Marihuana and Drug Abuse (Washington, D.C.: U.S. Government Printing Office, 1973).

13. James Q. Wilson, Mark H. Moore, and I. David Wheat, Jr., "The Problem of Heroin," *The Public Interest* 29 (1972): 3-28.

7

Policy Issues in Organized Crime and White-Collar Crime
Michael D. Maltz

Organized crime plays a paradoxical role in American criminology. On the one hand, it has been described as a "sinister criminal organization." On the other hand, it has been called a "stepladder of social ascent," a short-cut to success American style for groups without access to the legitimate means of power.[1] On the other hand, the practitioners of white-collar crime are normally considered to be those who *have* access to power but abuse it. Yet the role of white-collar crime is also paradoxical. While some look with "disgust at the favored treatment given the white-collar criminal,"[2] others have maintained that white-collar crime greases the economy's wheels, that "foul is useful and fair is not. Avarice and usury and precaution must be our gods for a little longer still."[3]

The observations expressed above are inconsistent. This is due in part to the way terms "organized crime" and "white-collar crime" are defined, in part to the different roles played by the observers, in part to the different aspects of the problem they see. In order to clarify these issues, the next section of this chapter discusses the problems in defining organized crime and white-collar crime and why they are treated together. Later sections discuss the laws that create them and the relationship between them; enforcement problems and strategies that are peculiar to organized crime and white-collar crime; problems in the measurement and evaluation of "success" in the campaigns to eliminate them; and the current trends in these areas of illegal endeavor.

Defining White-Collar Crime and Organized Crime

The terms "white-collar crime" and "organized crime" are too vague to be useful in criminal law.[a] There is very little agreement on what they constitute, as contrasted, say, with the specific terms "robbery" and "burglary." However, the concepts are useful from a criminological standpoint despite their vagueness. The following discussion is an attempt to shed some

---

[a] According to the *New York Times* of January 24, 1975 (p. 33), the New York State Supreme Court ruled that the law creating the State's Organized Crime Task Force is unconstitutional because "organized crime" is not defined.

light on the reasons for lack of agreement, and to suggest an alternative structure for categorizing them which eliminates some of their present vagueness.

Act or Group?

Central to the lack of consistent definitions is a semantic problem. The word "crime" is usually taken to mean the aggregate of specific "crimes"; i.e., *a crime* is a specific behavior or act, and *crime* is the set of behaviors encompassing all crimes. In like manner we can call *an organized crime* a specific behavior or act. Yet when we talk of *organized crime* in the *generic* sense we usually refer, not to a *set of behaviors,* but to an *entity,* a group of (unspecified) people, a disease, a bogeyman. For example, we read headlines such as "Organized Crime Controls the Scavenger Industry in Westchester," "The Penetration of Legitimate Business by Organized Crime," [4] "Why Organized Crime Thrives," and other anthropomorphisms.

Definition of White-Collar Crime

A similar situation exists with respect to the two formal definitions of white-collar crime that have been attempted. In 1949 Sutherland defined it as "a crime committed by a person of respectability and high social status in the course of his occupation." [5] In 1970 Edelhertz called it "an illegal act or series of illegal acts committed by nonphysical means and by concealment or guile, to obtain money or property, to avoid the payment or loss of money or property, or to obtain business or personal advantage." [6] The first definition relates primarily to the offender, the second to the act.

Definitions of Organized Crime

The greater concern given to organized crime by criminologists has led to a number of definitions. Some of these are listed in the appendix to this chapter. The only attempt to define organized crime in a federal statute is found in the Omnibus Crime Control and Safe Streets Act of 1968: "Organized crime means the unlawful activities of the members of a highly organized, disciplined association engaged in supplying illegal goods and services, including but not limited to gambling, prostitution, loan sharking, narcotics, labor racketeering, and other unlawful activities of members of such organizations." The Law Enforcement Assistance Administration uses this definition for developing action programs, but it is too vague to be used in a criminal code.

Some common characteristics of these definitions include (1) the commission of crimes, (2) the type of organization (in some cases rigid, hierarchical, and disciplined), (3) violence or the threat of violence (muscle, fear, or need for an enforcer), and (4) corruption. Yet the term "organized crime" can be applied with validity only to the first two characteristics (and to the second only without presuming organizational rigidity). The last two factors may be necessary for certain types of organized crime but not for all "crimes that are organized."

For example, violence is not a necessary concomitant of organized crime. Rather, it can be viewed as a substitute for economic and political power for those who lack access to these subtler means of coercion.[b] As the criminal enterprise matures, it usually gains access to and begins to use these more sophisticated, covert, and powerful forms of persuasion. For those who start their criminal careers with such access, we normally reserve the term "white-collar criminals." [7]

A Tentative Definition/Typology of Organized Crime

In reading the various definitions of organized crime and white-collar crime, it is tempting to search for unifying concepts. This is even more tempting in view of the "penetration of legitimate business by organized crime" (discussed below), in which the crimes are white-collar crimes although the perpetrators are usually considered to be "in organized crime."

Rather than a single definition, a typology may be more appropriate. As Clinard and Quinney point out,[8] the construction of a typology should be determined by the purpose at hand. Most existing typologies are related to the *offender* or the social system in which he is imbedded. Typologies of *crimes* are normally based on legal definitions, although it is well known that the variation *within* a legal category is frequently as great as the variation *between* categories.

When most people think of organized crime, they conjure up visions of 1934 Duesenbergs racing across city streets spitting machine-gun bullets from side windows. This type of organized-crime activity still goes on, but not to the same extent it did 40 years ago. But this image does make clear

---

[b] This point is being made not because violence-based organized crime is unimportant or because the author condones violence. Violent crime is abhorrent whether organized or unorganized. But the term "organized crime" should not be taken to refer only to this manifestation when so many other types exist, and are hidden from sight because all attention is focused on this one type.

that one characteristic of our typology, if we are to take preconceptions into account, should be whether or not violence is employed as a means of achieving the criminal objectives.

A typology based only on the *means* of committing crimes is inadequate. To use violence as an example, a store can be bombed by professional robbers, by an extortion gang, by a political extremist group, or by a building owner who wants to collect on the building's insurance. The *objective* of the organized crime, and the manifestation this objective takes, should also be factors in the typology.

Our tentative definition/typology, then, consists of the following elements:

A crime consists of a transaction proscribed by criminal law between offender(s) and victim(s). It is not necessary for the victim to be a complainant or to consider himself victimized for a crime to be committed.[c] An organized crime is a crime in which there is more than one offender, and the offenders are and intend to remain associated with one another for the purpose of committing crimes. The *means* of executing the crime include violence, theft, corruption, economic power, deception, and victim collusion or participation. These are not mutually exclusive categories; any organized crime may employ a number of these means.

The *objective* of most organized crimes is power, either political or economic.[d] These two types of objectives, too, are not mutually exclusive and may coexist in any organized crime.

There are a number of *manifestations* the objectives may take. When the objective is political power, it may be of two types: overthrow of the existing order, or illegal use of the criminal process. When the objective is economic power, it may manifest itself in three different ways: through common crime (*mala in se*), through illegal business (*mala prohibita* or "vices"), or through legitimate business (white-collar crime).

As can be seen from Table 7-1, a single type of illegal activity can encompass many organized crimes. For example, playing the numbers is an illegal business based on victim collusion. If payoffs are made to the po-

---

[c] The customer of a narcotics dealer normally is not a complainant, because he does not see himself as a victim. But neither is the patient of a swindler advertising a fake cancer cure a complainant; in fact, the patient may even testify for the defense.

[d] Some of those convicted in the Watergate cases attempted to justify their actions by stating that they had derived no financial gain from their actions. But money is not the only currency in use; political power is a more commonly used medium of exchange in Washington.

lice, it is also corruption-based. If force or violence is used to prevent competition from moving in, it is also violence-based. Similarly, the Watergate activities included theft-based, corruption-based, and deception-based political organized crime. Although more labels may be needed to characterize a subcategory of one general activity such as numbers, they serve to distinguish the above-mentioned kind of numbers business from other numbers rackets where violence and/or corruption are not employed.

These distinctions are very important. When the police launch "an all-out attack on organized crime" by going after a numbers racket, is it a benign "ma and pa" numbers operation (i.e., a victim-participation-based illegal business), is it also corruption-based, and does it contain elements of violence as well? Distinctions of this type must be made to determine how effectively our enforcement resources are being allocated.

It should be stressed that this typology of organized crime is not exact. It will, however, permit us to distinguish among many disparate activities now lumped together under the rubric *organized crime* or *white-collar crime,* and to introduce the various aspects of these activities and their different manifestations.

The rest of this chapter concentrates on those types of organized crime that are normally considered "organized crime" or "white-collar crime." Thus the crimes with political objectives and the common crimes that are organized are not included. The next section discusses the illegal-business aspects of organized crime. A subsequent section analyzes crimes within the framework of legitimate business.

Organized Crime and the Vices

A vice, in the context of organized crime, is a behavior indulged in by a sizable fraction of the population which is prohibited by the criminal law. These prohibitions have been undergoing change in the twentieth century: Prohibition (of alcoholic beverages) had a short lifetime (1920-1933); laws prohibiting abortion have recently been declared unconstitutional; laws against homosexuality are being repealed; laws prohibiting criminal usury (loan sharking) have had to be revised recently to permit banks to charge interest rates formerly considered usurious; pornography laws are in a state of flux, but the lack of a guiding definition of "pornography" from the U.S. Supreme Court has made their enforcement difficult; prostitution, at present legal in only one state (Nevada), appears to be gaining acceptance as a necessary evil; marijuana use is being decriminalized in some states (Oregon, Michigan), although the sale of large quantities is still criminal; heroin or methadone use (but again, not their sale) is no longer being treated as a criminal offense; and budgetary problems in a

Table 7-1
Typology of Organized Crime

| | Manifestation | | | | |
| | Economic Objective | | | Political Objective | |
Means	Through Common Crime (Mala in se)	Through Illegal Business (Mala prohibita)	Through Legitimate Business	Through the Existing Order	Against the Existing Order *
Violence	Juvenile gangs Hijacking	Gang wars for control of narcotics, etc. Extortion racket Loan-sharking enforcement	Strike-busting Enforcing strike on non-strikers by force	Threatening (or killing) election opponents Roughing up opposing voters	Revolution Kidnaping government officials
Theft	Burglary ring Stolen-car ring	Theft of rival organizations' goods (e.g., alcohol during Prohibition)	Burglary for insurance purposes Stealing trade secrets, industrial espionage	Watergate burglary	Ellsberg's theft of the Pentagon papers
Corruption	—	Gambling and narcotics payoffs to police, judges, etc.	Paying kickbacks to purchasing agents, union officials, politicians, in return for contracts	Pardoning a convicted felon in return for political support Offering patronage jobs to election judges in return for help at the polls	CIA actions in Chile
Economic	—	Betting heavily on a fixed sports event to bankrupt a bookie	Price-fixing Restraint of trade Closing down a factory with an illegal strike	Obtaining political support by selective enforcement of the antitrust law	U.S. embargo of Cuba Arab oil embargo
Deception	—	Fixing a sports event	Planned bankruptcy Fencing stolen property Siphoning off corporate funds through a dummy corporation	Watergate coverup	Espionage

		Falsifying auto emission data to comply with EPA rules Underreporting oil and gas reserves
Victim Participation	Prostitution Narcotics Gambling	—	Phony cancer cure Home-improvement schemes Polluting a town dependent on the polluter for its livelihood	—

* Note that these are crimes only within the existing political framework; if a revolution succeeds, the "crimes" have been legitimated.

number of states have caused them to start competing with illegal lottery, numbers, and book-making operations. The rationale for these changes has been discussed in several sources.[9]

The Consequences of "Crime Tariffs"

Vices such as these are created not by a demand, but by criminal laws prohibiting the fulfillment of that demand. As Packer points out,[10] these laws can be seen as "crime tariffs." Just as a tariff is designed to protect a commodity from outside (usually foreign) competition, these criminal laws are, in effect, crime tariffs that protect the illegal business from competition by those unwilling to break the law.

Other consequences arise from the use of the criminal law to prohibit these behaviors. Among the more salient are those relating to product quality, to violation of business norms, and to official corruption.

Product Quality. The public is protected to a great extent in its purchases of legitimate goods and services: The Food and Drug Administration, U.S. Department of Agriculture, Securities and Exchange Commission, and Federal Trade Commission, to name but a few of the governmental regulatory commissions, are charged with ensuring the quality of the products offered for sale to the general public. No such protection exists for prohibited goods and services, and as a result we find people dying of heroin overdoses (or as a result of injecting other substances into their veins), getting cheated in illegal gambling operations, smoking oregano rather than cannabis, and contracting venereal diseases from careless prostitutes. We can contrast this situation with the reduction in cases of alcohol poisoning after Prohibition was repealed in 1933, and with the reduction in abortion-related deaths after the prohibition of abortion was declared unconstitutional. Legalization of a good or service permits regulation of its quality.

Business Norms. Business and the public are also protected against unfair competition that adversely affects the price or quality of the product sold, or the market for the product. If the product is illegal, the businessman is under no obligation to adhere to business norms. Whereas "price wars" occur in the upperworld when competition becomes fierce, *actual* wars take place between underworld rivals for a monopoly in an illegal product. Many of the books and movies alluded to earlier glorify these gang wars. Thus there are no standards of business to protect an illegal businessman.

Corruption. A third major consequence of criminalizing a product is that it fosters official corruption. If the business is not considered harmful by much of the population (e.g., gambling, drinking), the police are inclined to use their discretion to permit it to continue, "as long as it doesn't get out of hand." However, if the business is lucrative and attracts competition and gang wars, it does get "out of hand" and the police must step in to control it. But control means regulation rather than elimination, and thus *the police become the regulators of criminal activity.* The Knapp Commission report [11] describes some aspects of this activity; it distinguishes between the "grass eaters" (those who accept some forms of graft) and "meat eaters" (those who actively extort bribes from criminals).

On Removing the "Crime Tariffs"

Of all laws relating to vice, the ones prohibiting gambling are the most inconsistent. Consider New York: One can gamble legally on horse races in certain locations run by private enterprise (tracks), but placing a bet over the telephone is illegal unless the state is the bookie.[12] The state-run lottery is legal, but private lotteries and numbers operations are illegal. The question then arises: If laws prohibiting the good or service are of questionable value, would some form of legalization be better? With legalization, a number of new conditions appear. They relate to changing the laws, legalization alternatives, and generating revenues.

Changing the Laws. A major stumbling block in eliminating a prohibition is the problem of who will bell the cat. Few politicians will sponsor legislation legalizing a previously illegal practice if they feel they will be subjected to criticism on the grounds that the activity is immoral, that legalizing it is tantamount to condoning crime, that it promotes the decay of society, and that legalization will encourage more participation and thus increase the revenue of illegal business. Since gambling is considered a lesser evil than most other vices, arguments in favor of legalization are winning out: it is an activity accepted by most people; although the penalties are high, they are rarely meted out; even if it is harmful, the state should not intervene in a person's own decision to harm himself; if it is legalized, the state can obtain revenue from it, revenue which otherwise would have "gone to organized crime"; if it is legalized, the state can police it; if it is legalized, a major factor in police corruption will be removed.

Regulation. Legalization can take two forms, either regulation of private enterprise or creation of a public agency to monopolize the trade. The state of Nevada regulates gambling through the Nevada State Gaming Commission. By licensing the activity, it controls those who can obtain licenses. It also maintains surveillance on casinos and continually audits gambling establishments. Yet "skimming" (hiding a part of the profits so that no tax need be paid on it) is still alleged to be taking place. Nevada also regulates prostitution through public-health laws. (Although some maintain that legalized prostitution will reduce the incidence of sex offenses, there is no evidence to support this hypothesis.) And when the sale of alcoholic beverages was legalized, some states decided to regulate (license) private stores, while others opted for state monopolization of the business.

State Control. State lotteries in the U.S. are run by state agencies, either agencies in existing treasury tax departments or independent agencies whose boards are appointed by the governor and/or legislature. New York City's Off-Track Betting (OTB) Corporation is run by a board appointed by the mayor. Although the main reason for establishing these organizations appears to have been the raising of revenue, in most cases a secondary objective was to reduce the revenue of illegal business. Many people feel that only by full state control can this objective be realized, but it seems to depend upon the type of gambling.

It appears that lotteries have little effect on the illegal numbers operations, but rather create a new class of bettors. Yet the OTB Corporation may have made a dent in bookie operations, at least to the extent that their clients bet on horse races.[13] It has been suggested that the OTB Corporation expand its operations by taking bets on other sporting events, but thus far little movement has been made in this direction.

Of course, legalization of an activity, either by regulation or by state monopolization, does not automatically solve all the problems created by its former prohibition. There are still opportunities for graft and other forms of corruption; there is no assurance that "organized crime" will not continue to compete with the state monopoly, or to "infiltrate" the activity, if it is regulated. But the problems then become problems faced by other legitimate activities, discussed in the next section.

Organized Crime and Legitimate Business: The Transition to White-Collar Crime

Diversification and Respectability

Much has been written about the penetration of legitimate business by "organized crime," [14] that is, by those involved in illegal businesses. This movement is explainable in economic and sociological terms. From an economic standpoint, most organizations mature as they prosper, and diversify their activity so as not to keep all their eggs in one basket. This is also true for an illegal business, which may be threatened by legal competition. And from a sociological standpoint, as a "family" prospers, it feels the need to acquire respectability. The illegal money is the key that opens the doors to legitimate professions and business.

The transition to respectability is not necessarily an easy one. A criminal enterprise is not a good training ground for junior executives; the organization is not accustomed to legal competition, to controlling costs, to filling out forms, to obeying the many rules that protect competitors and customers alike. For an industry penetrated by such an organization, the transition period can be very difficult.

However, the alternative to penetration of legitimate business is the reinvestment of the ill-gotten gains into the same criminal enterprises, which may cause greater social harm. Just as these enterprises can be viewed as "the queer ladder of social mobility," the penetration can be seen as another rung up the ladder to legitimation of the family fortune. This legitimation has come harder to Italians and blacks than it has to other ethnic groups: descendants of the Anglo-Saxon robber barons of the nineteenth and early twentieth centuries appear not to have suffered by being linked to the depredations of their ancestors; and the son of a major Jewish gambling figure in the 1920's was appointed to an ambassadorship during the Nixon administration.

Fencing

Another form of "penetration" into legitimate business has little to do with social mobility. When a truckload of television sets or razor blades or meat is hijacked, obviously a fence is needed to unload the merchandise. Reputable wholesalers and retailers who purchase goods "no questions asked" are of necessity part of the "organization"; without ready outlets, these large quantities of merchandise would be very hard to dispose of.[15]

It is interesting to note that the Knapp Commission felt that most hijackings in New York City took place with police involvement. Yet the federal Interagency Committee on Transportation Security has requested that money be spent to paint numbers on trucks, equip them with emergency radios, and patrol with helicopters to prevent hijackings, all of which would be useless if the police are involved in the hijackings. There is clearly a need to study the problem more thoroughly before proposing expensive, albeit glamorous and technologically up-to-date, solutions.

Crime and Business

The need for a distribution system for stolen goods, and the consequent complicity of so-called legitimate businessmen, underscores the difficulty in distinguishing between a criminal act (i.e., receiving stolen property) and a poor business practice (buying goods from people of unknown or questionable reputation). Drawing the line between the two is even more difficult when no stolen property is involved, but rather a fraudulent or deceptive practice. An additional complication is caused by the redefinition of previously legal acts as criminal. New criminal laws relating to the sale of securities, to pollution, to occupational safety and health, or to antitrust matters, for example, may cause some people to break the law unknowingly (or at least, claim that the violation was unknowing). In such crimes it can be extremely difficult to prove criminal intent, without which there can be no crime. (In one publicized case, price-fixing of electrical equipment,[16] proving intent was fairly easy. The participants in the conspiracy met in distant cities and used pseudonyms when gathering to discuss rigging the bids on prospective contracts.)

White-Collar Crime Categories

Although there is a great deal of overlap with organized crime, not all white-collar crimes are organized crimes. Edelhertz has categorized white-collar crimes into four types. As can be seen, the categories overlap the ones used for organized crime.

Personal crimes are "crimes by persons operating on an individual, *ad hoc* basis, for personal gain in a nonbusiness context." Such crimes include credit-fard frauds, individual income-tax violations, or welfare cheating. They may be looked upon as "ripping off the system," where the system is either the government or big business.

Abuses of trust are "crimes in the course of their occupations by those operating inside business, government, or other establishments, or in a professional capacity, in violation of their duty of fidelity to employer or client." An example of this is a kickback scheme, whereby a buyer for a firm or a government contract evaluator agrees to accept a bid only upon payment of a bribe. Or an official of a union pension fund may make a loan to himself (or, to disguise it, to a firm he controls or from which he receives a bribe). A director of a corporation (i.e., an "insider"), hearing of a possible merger with another company, may buy stock in the other company or tell a relative or friend to do so, in violation of the SEC's rules governing insider transactions.

Business crimes are "crimes incidental to and in furtherance of business operations, but not the central purpose of such business operations." The price-fixing case mentioned previously was the first major example of the perpetrators of such crimes (including a vice-president of the General Electric Company) being sent to jail. In another kind of business crime, a firm may "pad the bill" to a customer in order to pay for costs otherwise unrecoverable; some defense contractors have been accused of doing this to pay for cost overruns.

Con games are business operations whose central activity is a fraud or swindle. A recent example of a "ponzi scheme" is the Home-Stake Production Company. Investors poured over $100 million into the firm, which was supposed to be discovering oil wells. The ponzi scheme relies on an expanding base of investors (for this reason it is also referred to as a pyramid scheme), and the later investors' funds are used to pay off the earlier investors. Thus early investors may make a profit while the later investors are left holding the bag. Although it didn't start out that way, the Investors Overseas Service had similar characteristics.

Another example is a home-improvement scheme whereby a homeowner is talked into signing a contract to pay for home improvements which are done shoddily or in some cases not at all. The contract is sold as a promissory note to a bank, which collects the money regardless of the quality of workmanship; the "holder in due course" doctrine means that the homeowner cannot stop payments on the note because of inadequate work, but must keep paying the bank. The only recourse the homeowner has is to sue the original home-improvement contractor.

White-Collar Crime as a Diseconomy of Scale

Since concealment and guile are at the heart of white-collar crime, the increasing anonymity of business transactions in contemporary society has helped to increase its prevalence. The individual thinks nothing of "ripping off the system" when the system is faceless; the stockholders push for increased corporate profitability at the expense of corporate ethics and responsibility toward employees and clients. As organizations grow in size, this anonymity increases; thus white-collar crime can be looked upon as a diseconomy of scale, a direct concomitant of the bureaucratization and depersonalization of business and society.[17]

Enforcement Problems

There are many problems associated with investigating organized crimes. Because of the nature of the crimes, investigators often rely on undercover activity or on wiretapping or other forms of eavesdropping to obtain evidence and to prove conspiracy. Evidence is also obtained by giving a witness immunity, but since he is often a criminal himself, this puts the prosecutor in the position of forgiving one criminal to catch another. Other problems relate to the use of conspiracy statutes, the need to prove criminal intent, restitution, the *nolo contendere* plea, and the negotiated settlement.

Undercover Activity

Obtaining evidence in vice cases is very difficult because neither party in the (illegal) transaction wants the police involved. So the police go undercover and pose as either buyers or sellers to obtain evidence. Prostitution cases are usually based on the solicitation of an unwary prostitute by an undercover policeman, or the solicitation of an undercover policewoman by an unwary "john."

In narcotics cases the going gets a little rougher. Cases have been documented in which undercover narcotics agents from one agency bought narcotics from undercover narcotics agents from another agency, the former trying to apprehend sellers and the latter buyers. In addition, no-knock raids made by undercover federal agents have been severely criticized; without a police uniform it is difficult for the raided party to ascertain that the agents are actually law-enforcement officers.

Eavesdropping

Law-enforcement officials long maintained that they needed wiretapping and bugging legalized to obtain evidence against "the leaders of organized crime." Congress provided them this tool in 1968: a law was passed legalizing "the interception of electronic or oral communications" for obtaining evidence about various federal crimes, provided a court order was obtained which specified the nature of the evidence sought. Most of the high-level personnel, the putative targets of this statue, still seem to escape prosecution despite this tool—forewarned is forearmed. But it has been used extensively against lower-level gamblers and narcotics peddlers.[18]

Some people maintain that the statute has given rise to more illegal wiretapping than legal wiretapping. Assisted by compliant telephone companies, law-enforcement officials reputedly place taps on people's telephones without the necessary legal formalities. If any evidence is found, a subsequent legal tap can be requested by court order with great specificity. And, unlike other abuses of police power, there is no way of knowing that one's telephone has been tapped, legally or illegally.

As a result of the widespread illegal eavesdropping by the Nixon administration, and of reports of illegal wiretapping in Texas, wiretapping and bugging have lost much of their popularity. With the current emphasis on maintaining the privacy of the individual, it is not unlikely that eavesdropping will again be made illegal, or that stronger safeguards will be enacted to prevent abuses in this area.

Immunity and Conspiracy

Because the upper echelons in the criminal organizations are often insulated from complicity in substantive crimes by lower-level personnel, immunity laws have been passed to assist in prosecuting them. A person can be immunized in different ways. General or *blanket immunity* permits a witness to tell all, regardless of its relevance to a particular case. With blanket immunity a person could confess to homicide with impunity, even if the case in question had nothing to do with the murder. This type of immunity is rarely used any more. *Use immunity* prevents law-enforcement officials from using the witness's testimony in making a case against the witness. It cannot be used directly, or as a source of leads for finding evidence. However, the witness can be tried for a crime if law-enforcement officials develop a case (before or after immunization) in a way totally unrelated to the witness's testimony. *Transaction immunity* furnishes full protection against prosecution, but only for a specified crime or set of crimes.

A conspiracy statute permits a person to be charged with a felony if it can be proved that he took part in planning the felony. By granting immunity, a prosecutor tries to work his way up from the low-level actors who committed the substantive crimes to the upper-level people who conspired to cause the crimes to be committed. Care must be taken that the immunized persons are not the "big fish," since their testimony will protect them from imprisonment. Very often a person under law-enforcement pressure tries to make a deal with the prosecutor by offering testimony against others. It is a moot point whether justice is served when a millionaire contractor is granted immunity from prosecution on bribery charges, for giving evidence about the bribes he gave state legislators; or when, of 40 people involved in price-fixing, 38 are given immunity.

An interesting case in point about the use of these laws occurred in the Watergate trials. Messrs. Dean and Magruder were allowed to plead guilty *inter alia* to lesser offenses than they were originally charged with, in return for testifying against their superiors. It is ironic that one of those convicted by their testimony, former U.S. Attorney General John Mitchell, urged Congress (successfully) to enact such laws to combat organized crime; they are embodied in the Organized Crime Control Act of 1970.

Proving Criminal Intent

A major problem in the investigation and prosecution of white-collar crimes is the difficulty of proving criminal intent. If a government regulation is involved, for example, it must be proved that the individual was aware of the regulation; ignorance of the law *is* an excuse, and in some circumstances it is a valid defense against criminal charges in white-collar crime.[19]

Restitution

Another problem with white-collar crime cases in which the victims have lost money is the possibility that a prosecution may be undercut by the defendant's offering to make restitution. When the victims face a one- or two-year delay while the case is being tried, with the prospect that the defendants' money may be exhausted by lawyers' fees, they will often opt for guaranteed restitution of a fraction of their losses rather than a possibility of gaining nothing but vengeance. In this way a defendant can escape prison. It should be noted, however, that in many states, if such a restitution is made in private, e.g., between an employer and an embezzling employee, the employer is guilty of compounding the crime by concealing it.

The Nolo Contendere Plea

The *nolo contendere* plea is also a problem in white-collar crime investigations. Very often in a white-collar crime case there is a collateral civil suit to recover damages. By pleading *nolo contendere,* the defendant ensures that the evidence generated by the prosecution stays secret. Recently, however, former Vice President Spiro Agnew was allowed to plead *nolo contendere* on reduced charges in a construction kickback case, with the proviso that the government's case against Agnew would be published.[20]

The Negotiated Settlement

A frequent concomitant of the *nolo contendere* plea is the negotiated settlement, a settlement worked out between the prosecution and the defendants in lieu of a trial. Because of some abuses that were brought out in the settlement of an antitrust case against the International Telephone and Telegraph Corporation, a new law was passed relating to prior negotiated settlements, to bring out into the open this formerly closed procedure. All contacts on behalf of the defendant must be recorded; the negotiated settlement must be published by the government, with a detailed explanation of why the settlement is believed to be beneficial; and the settlement becomes effective only after other parties have commented on its provisions and any necessary revisions have been made.

Recent Federal Action

In addition to the creation of national commissions to recommend policy changes related to wiretapping, narcotics, and gambling, a law was passed in October 1974 which affects the enforcement of state laws prohibiting gambling. Public Law 93-499 reduced the federal wagering tax on bookies and lottery operators from ten percent of gross to two percent of gross. It also increased the cost of the wagering tax stamp from $50 to $500.

The most important provision of the new law relates to the disclosure of information. Two recent Supreme Court decisions held that the previous law's provision requiring public display of the tax stamp was self-incriminating, since compliance with the federal law subjected a commercial gambler to state prosecution in states where gambling is illegal. The new law forbids disclosure of who pays the tax, and restricts use of the information to the administration of the law.

Although billed as "a powerful weapon to combat organized crime," its main effect will be to increase the revenue the federal government obtains from taxing gambling. A secondary effect is that we will have a better estimate of the nature and extent of gambling in the United States; the estimate made in 1967 of $7 to $50 billion [21] is both unsubstantiated and outdated.

Evaluating Programs to Counter Organized Crime and White-Collar Crime

Lack of Statistics

Although much has been written on evaluating programs in health, education, poverty, and criminal justice, little of its applies to evaluating programs aimed at most types of organized crime. First, there are no statistics at present, although this situation is changing: the National District Attorneys Association, under a grant to fund economic crime prosecution projects in 15 jurisdictions, is developing a Uniform Economic Crime Reporting System. No such system exists for reporting political crimes.

Second, for most of these crimes there is no way of knowing the total number of crimes, both reported and unreported. For statistics of *common* crimes we rely on the victim to report the crime to the police (or to an interviewer in the National Crime Survey); in many types of *organized* crime, the victim may not think he is victimized.

Third, the crimes should not simply be added together to calculate a meaningless statistic. One credit-card fraud plus one antitrust violation may equal two crimes, but the former may amount to hundreds of dollars and the latter may amount to millions of dollars. A scheme for weighting each crime according to the harm it causes should be developed.

Trends and Predictions

This past decade has seen the emergence of black and latino criminal groups which have inherited or wrested the control of illegal businesses from their predecessors further up the ladder of social legitimacy.[22] Although the businesses are doing well, they are faced with major threats to their existence: legalization (or, at least, decriminalization or regulation) and legal competition, which threaten to drive the customers to legal outlets to obtain the goods and services.

However, while the laws relating to illegal-business activities are weakening, those relating to crimes by legitimate business are being expanded and strengthened. Regulations concerning pollution and trading in commodities, among others, have recently been enacted, and the penalties have been increased for antitrust violations. In other words, in the legitimate-business area more activities are being criminalized rather than decriminalized.

These two seemingly opposite trends are not inconsistent. The criminal law is being used less and less to protect a person's morals and more and more to protect a person's money. Or, looked at in another way, decriminalizing vices strengthens the hand of the individual vis-à-vis the state; and criminalizing white-collar crimes strengthens the hand of the individual vis-à-vis the corporation.[e] This trend toward strengthening the role of the individual can be seen in other areas of criminal justice as well: the federal "no-knock" law has been repealed, and regulations protecting the privacy and confidentiality of an individual's criminal record are being promulgated.

As has been discussed, an illegal business is created whenever a law forbids an activity considered proper by a significant minority of the

---

[e] As Edelhertz points out, *"Caveat emptor* loses meaning when we buy closed packages."

public. It is interesting to speculate on the future of organized crime. To what extent will new criminal business ventures be created by laws prohibiting the use of criminal-record information, or the sale of fire-crackers, or the hides of endangered species, or the sale and ownership of handguns by the general public?

Notes

1. Both of these descriptions are found in G. Tyler, ed., *Organized Crime in America* (Ann Arbor, Mich.: University of Michigan Press, 1962). The first is from the Kefauver Committee (p. 11), the second by Daniel Bell (p. 175).

2. R. W. Ogren, in "A Symposium on White-Collar Crime," *American Criminal Law Review* 11 (1973): 959.

3. This was written by John Maynard Keynes in 1930. It is quoted in E. F. Schumacher, *Small Is Beautiful: Economics as if People Mattered* (New York: Harper and Row, 1974).

4. M. K. Bers, *The Penetration of Legitimate Business by Organized Crime,* National Institute of Law Enforcement and Criminal Justice, Law Enforcement Assistance Administration, U.S. Department of Justice (1970).

5. E. H. Sutherland, *White Collar Crime* (New York: Dryden Press, 1949).

6. H. Edelhertz, *The Nature, Impact and Prosecution of White-Collar Crime* (Washington, D.C.: U.S. Government Printing Office, 1970).

7. G. Geis, *White-Collar Criminal* (New York: Atherton, 1968).

8. M. B. Clinard and R. Quinney, *Criminal Behavior Systems: A Typology,* 2nd edition (New York: Holt, Rinehart and Winston, 1973).

9. V. G. Cook, *Gambling: A Source of State Revenue* (Lexington, Ky.: Council of State Governments, 1973); G. Geis, *Not the Law's Business?* (Washington, D.C.: U.S. Government Printing Office, 1972); *Legal Gambling in New York: A Discussion of Numbers and Sports Betting* (New York: Fund for the City of New York, 1972); *Legalized Numbers in Washington* (Washington, D.C.: Washington Lawyers' Committee for Civil Rights Under Law, 1973).

10. H. Packer, *The Limits of the Criminal Sanction* (Stanford, Calif.: Stanford University Press, 1968).

11. M. F. Armstrong, *The Knapp Commission Report on Police Corruption* (New York: Braziller, 1973).

12. See Cook; *Legal Gambling in New York; Legalized Numbers in Washington;* and *Easy Money: Report of the Task Force on Legalized Gambling* (New York: Twentieth Century Fund, 1974).

13. *Legalized Numbers in Washington.*

14. See Bers; D. R. Cressey, *Theft of the Nation* (New York: Harper and Row, 1969); ITT Research Institute and Chicago Crime Commission, *A Study of Organized Crime in Illinois* (1971); and President's Commission on Law Enforcement and Administration of Justice, *Task Force Report: Organized Crime* (Washington, D.C.: U.S. Government Printing Office, 1967).

15. See D. Chappell and M. Walsh, "Receiving Stolen Property: The Need for Systematic Inquiry into the Fencing Process," *Criminology* 11 (1974): 484-497; and C. B. Klockars, *The Professional Fence* (New York: Free Press, 1974).

16. Geis, *White-Collar Criminal.*

17. For a discussion of other diseconomies of scale, see Schumacher (cited in note 3).

18. E. J. Lapidus, *Eavesdropping on Trial* (Rochelle Park, N.J.: Hayden Books, 1974).

19. See Edelhertz for more detail on proving criminal intent and on restitution.

20. J. A. Gardiner and D. J. Olson, eds., *Theft of the City* (Bloomington, Ind.: Indiana University Press, 1974).

21. President's Commission on Law Enforcement and Administration of Justice, *Task Force Report: Organized Crime.*

22. F. A. J. Ianni, *Black Mafia* (New York: Simon and Schuster, 1974).

Appendix 7A
Definitions of "Organized Crime"

The following is a sample of definitions or descriptions that have been applied to the term "organized crime."

1. "While this criminal group is not by any means completely organized, it has many of the earmarks of a system. It has its own language; it has its own laws; its own history; its traditions and its customs; its own methods and techniques; its highly specialized machinery for attack upon persons and particularly upon property; its own highly specialized modes of defense. These professional criminals have interurban, interstate and sometimes international connections." (Report of the Chicago City Council on Crime, 1915)

2. "Organized crime is the product of a self-perpetuating criminal conspiracy to wring exorbitant profits from our society by any means—fair and foul, legal and illegal. Despite personnel changes, the conspiratorial entity continues. It is a malignant parasite which fattens on human weakness. It survives on fear and corruption. By one or another means, it obtains a high degree of immunity from the law. It is totalitarian in its organization. A way of life, it imposes rigid discipline on underlings who do the dirty work while the top men of organized crime are generally insulated from the criminal act and the consequent danger of prosecution." (Oyster Bay Conference on Combating Crime, 1965)

3. "The Department of Justice, in its operations, considers organized crime to be twofold: first, a criminal syndicate consisting of families operating as criminal cartels in large cities across the Nation, banded together in an organization with what corresponds to a board of directors at the top to settle problems, such as jurisdictional disputes, and to enforce discipline; and second, any large continuous criminal conspiracy which has significant impact upon a community, a region, or an area of our country." (House Government Operations Committee, *Federal Effort Against Organized Crime,* 1968)

4. "An organized crime is any crime committed by a person occupying, in an established division of labor, a position designed for the commission of crime, providing that such division of labor also includes at least one position for a corrupter, one position for a corruptee, and one position for an enforcer." (D. R. Cressey, *Theft of the Nation,* 1969)

5. "[W]e can define organized crime as any criminal activity involving two or more individuals, specialized or nonspecialized, encompassing some

93

form of social structure, with some form of leadership, utilizing certain modes of operation, in which the ultimate purpose of the organization is found in the enterprises of the particular group. . . . [A] continuum of different types of organized crime . . . includes *political-social, mercenary, in-group* and *syndicated* organized crime." (J. L. Albini, *The American Mafia: Genesis of a Legend,* 1971)

6. Organized crime consists of the participation of persons and groups of persons (organized either formally or informally) in transactions characterized by:

(1) An intent to commit, or the actual commission of, substantive crimes;

(2) A conspiracy to execute these crimes;

(3) A persistence of this conspiracy through time (at least one year) or the intent that this conspiracy should persist through time;

(4) The acquisition of substantial power or money, and the seeking of a high degree of political or economic security, as primary motivations;

(5) An operational framework that seeks the preservation of institutions of politics, government and society in their present form." (ITT Research Institute and the Chicago Crime Commission, *A Study of Organized Crime in Illinois,* 1971)

8

Flexibility and Uniformity in Criminal Justice
Lief H. Carter

The "flexibility and uniformity" issue can prove perplexing for several reasons. First, both words connote conditions that many of us value positively. Flexibility connotes adaptation and, ultimately, survival uniformity connotes justice, equal treatment, and objectivity. Yet juxtaposing these words implies a value conflict (indeed, many of our greatest stories hinge on such a conflict), and science cannot rescue us from this ubiquitous antinomy.

Second, we may choose from at least two plausible definitions of the word "uniformity." Uniformity can mean *commonality*—does the criminal justice system treat similarly situated individuals similarly? It can also mean *legality*—do the decisions of system personnel "follow the law"? These two questions do not necessarily overlap. We may find circumstances in which defendants in similar circumstances receive identical illegal treatment; we may find "institutionalized" violations of law.[1] Conversely, law may authorize or permit such wide discretion that uncommon, idiosyncratic, and nonuniform practices are legal.

Finally, problems of measurement compound the perplexity. We do not have sufficient confidence in measurement of crime incidents or organizational outputs to produce convincing cross-jurisdictional comparisons or convincing evaluations of the effectiveness of different programs. Hence we cannot establish clearly what we may gain (or if we can gain) from flexibility. We also have no convincing methods for showing when two individuals are or are not similarly situated *legally,* and hence we cannot verify the degree of uniformity the system now embodies.

Juxtaposing uniformity with "flexibility" calls for emphasizing the role of discretion in criminal justice, a convenient choice both because law in fact confers wide discretion and because it postpones a collision with the measurement difficulties. The emphasis on discretion suggests these principal policy questions: (a) To what extent do rules—constitutions, statutes, judicial decisions, administrative rules—attempt to predetermine the decisions of legal actors? To what extent do they, conversely, confer discretion? (b) To what extent do criminal justice actors evade rules that predetermine behavior? (c) Do system participants use their legally conferred discretion in ways that reliably promote the policy goals of the system? Do legally irrelevant factors about suspect and case regularly affect dispositions? (d) In what respects should we seek to increase (or decrease) the "programming" of criminal justice decisions by rules? [2]

How Much Flexibility Does the Law Permit?

Rules of law specify in considerable detail the procedures for determining a suspect's guilt or innocence at trial. Common law and statutory rules govern the admissibility of evidence and the proper and improper uses of evidence when admitted, and constitutions provide procedural safeguards. If we routinely determined guilt through trials, the uniformity problem would be simplified; the adversary system, coupled with the public character of trials, would reveal, and hence discourage, evasions. The discretionary element would arise largely in the sentencing process. But trials do not dispose of the majority of cases. The literature, derived largely from major urban centers, commonly reports the percentage of nontrial dispositions to be near 90 percent. Rules of evidence and procedural safeguards do not play a major part in nontrial dispositions, but these dispositions are not illegal. Law confers wide discretion respecting decisions to arrest, to file charges, to reduce or dismiss charges, to enter pleas, and to sentence. Even when law seeks to program nontrial behavior, as it does with respect to police searches and interrogations, the law speaks in fact to the question of admissibility of evidence at trial, a policy that weakens the sanction.[3] Criminal justice actors, similarly, see the presumption of innocence as a trial rule. They do not, indeed cannot, presume innocence in informal case dispositions.

Thus, in the case of police behavior, law imposes only outside limits: Police should not themselves engage in criminal behavior, and police should arrest (without unnecessary force) only suspects about whom plausible inculpatory evidence exists. The literature contains examples of both of these kinds of law violations.[4] However, police more frequently choose not to arrest those whose guilt is clear.[5] Neither law nor police rules reliably program nonenforcement decisions. The relevant constitutional principle, the "equal protection clause" of the Fourteenth Amendment, prohibits those forms of discrimination that bear no relationship to reasonable policy goals, e.g., discrimination according to skin color in public education. In terms of current legal doctrine, police have abundant defensible policy reasons—conservation of resources, individualized justice —to justify such nonenforcement decisions.

The legal framework for nontrial dispositions fits the same pattern.[6] "Underforcement" dominates.[7] Courts have upheld the practice of plea bargaining (*Brady v. United States,* 397 U.S. 742, 1970) even where the suspect pleads guilty to a crime which he did not legally commit. Judges have traditionally exercised considerable discretion in sentencing, particularly in the case of misdemeanors, those offenses that may receive local jail sentences but which do not carry prison sentences. (These cases also constitute the bulk of all criminal convictions.) In some, but not all, jurisdictions the judge has little discretion regarding the nature of prison sentences for felony convictions, and the Supreme Court has prohibited capital punishment as currently administered (*Furman v. George,* 408 U.S. 238, 1973). In most cases, however, the judge may, in the name of individualized justice, choose among varying lengths of jail terms, lengths of probation, conditions of probation, and combinations thereof.[8] Again, the legal limits apply primarily to in-court procedures. A judge must, for example, interrogate the suspect to ensure that he has entered his guilty plea voluntarily without pressure or offer of reward. But this procedure, like the procedural requirement for a hearing prior to revocation of parole, often has little impact on substance.

Do Discretionary Decisions Reliably Promote Policy Goals?

Thus the bulk of criminal justice decision-making falls in the zone of legally conferred discretion, and we must turn to the next question, how is this discretion used in fact? Does it reliably promote policy objectives? How uniform are such practices in fact? The descriptive literature, given the difficulties of measurement and the problem of gaining the access necessary for reliable observations, does not consistently reveal frequencies of certain modes of decision. We know, for example, that some police officers will arrest and search a known drug pusher when they observe him committing a minor traffic violation they might otherwise ignore (and that prosecutors may file unusually weak charges against the pusher), but we have little evidence of frequency.

Research has not yet thoroughly settled a number of more accessible empirical questions, such as the impact of race on sentence, although some important contributions have been made.[9] At the gross empirical level, the literature does substantiate the existence of considerable variation among jurisdictions in styles of police administration, patterns of sentence length, workloads, and resource allocations to and within the system. When we address the problem of arbitrary treatment of individuals within a jurisdiction, i.e., differences in case outcomes explainable by the characteristics of individuals and the circumstances of cases that do not bear on the goals of crime control and due process, the literature suggests the following conclusions. Whether these patterns of discretionary behavior constitute arbitrariness as defined above remains, however, a normative and hence unsettled question.

1. Police are particularly likely to behave suspiciously toward the activities of young black males. These encounters are most likely to produce mutual and escalating hostility.[10]

2. Wealth, the capacity to make bail, to procure experienced legal counsel, to obtain the full range of evidence supporting the defendant and to present it, if necessary, at trial, relates statistically to lower likelihood of conviction and shorter sentence if convicted.[11]

3. The full range of decisions regarding case disposition, from bail decisions to plea bargaining to probation, is significantly affected by factors unrelated to the specific case in question. Bail decisions do not regularly reflect the likelihood of appearance at trial, nor do they regularly serve as a form of preventive detention.[12] The workload of the prosecutor and defense attorney, their repertoire of role experiences and personal attitudes, their mastery of the skills of interpersonal persuasion, and their friendship and trust in one another can affect the outcome of guilty plea negotiations. So can the judge's sentencing attitudes and his propensity to intervene at the informal stage to engineer a result. The defendant's prior experience in the system may also give him skills with which to manipulate it.[13] For example, a prosecutor, concerned about his or his office's record of defeats at trial, may offer such an attractive sentence to a defendant likely to win at trial that the defendant will plead guilty (and place the conviction on his record) to an unprovable charge. The private attorney of a low-income defendant may not seek bail for his client in order to preserve the client's limited funds to pay his fee. Prosecutors may file the most severe charges to gain bargaining leverage over the suspect.

4. In the juvenile area particularly, the adjudicator will dispose of the case partly in terms of his own subcultural values.[14] He may respond differentially to facts about the defendant—his family stability, his school performance, his demeanor—that do not necessarily dictate the appropriate choice among correctional alternatives. Experienced participants in the system seek to influence case outcomes by manipulating the superficial indicia of repentance.

5. Criminal justice actors tend to define the seriousness of different forms of criminal behavior in terms of physical injury or threat of physical injury. The tendency to rate white-collar, "paper" crimes as less severe than others is compounded by the lack of resources to pursue these complicated cases effectively.

Is Greater Uniformity Either Desirable or Achievable?

It is safe, in summary, to conclude that criminal justice actors do not exercise their discretion in ways that reliably promote clearly stated system goals. Neither penological nor evidentiary and constitutional considerations dominate the decision-making process. The personal values of actors do matter. While some patterned variation among jurisdictions exists, personal variation within a jurisdiction is also great. *Which* officer observes an incident, *which* prosecutor files the case, *which* judge and *which* probation officer help resolve it, do make a difference. Yet this conclusion does not for several reasons necessarily call for policies that seek by rules to make decision-making more uniform. First, democratic values complicate the issue. Size, wealth, political traditions, and regional values help explain differences among jurisdictions.[15] Furthermore, much of the potentially arbitrary discretionary decisions described above may themselves reflect dominant community attitudes. The subcultural-variation hypothesis is particularly troublesome. Popular democratic values do not undercut the principle of procedural "equality before the law," but prevalent values do endorse the seriousness of personal injury, the sanctity of property rights, and the legitimacy of the work ethic. Wealth and family stability may be, therefore, appropriate substantive criteria to employ in choosing among penological alternatives. So may a history of violent behavior be an appropriate criterion. If these values are indeed dominant, rule-making will not easily alter their impact.

The jurisprudential writing of Lon Fuller suggests a second reason for hesitation. The criminal justice system seeks conviction for violations of rules that are publicized, rules that are not applied retroactively, rules that are in most instances clear, rules that are not mutually contradictory, rules that do no call for impossible conduct, and rules that are relatively stable. The defendant under our system has notice of the possible consequences of certain behavior choices, the sanctions imposed upon him do not exceed those publicly announced, and he is informed that he need not abandon the formal procedures prescribed by law unless he believes it rewarding to do so. Thus present arrangements arguably do no violence to the "morality of law."[16]

The most serious cause for hesitation arises from organization theory, for criminal justice organizations may possess characteristics that doom attempts to predetermine decisions by rules. Put briefly, nonuniformity in criminal justice can be viewed as a failure of organizational control. Three characteristics of the system make control difficult. It operates with a highly ambiguous technology in an unpredictable environment, and much of its personnel is professionalized.[17] The technology is ambiguous in the sense that men have incomplete and ambivalent beliefs about the cause-effect relationships that will produce desired outcomes. How much incarceration will deter or rehabilitate, whether incarceration will produce a net increase or decrease in crime, is a judgment many in the system do not confidently make. John Griffiths has put the point this way:

> I am thoroughly convinced that the traditional jurisprudence of criminal law has reached essential sterility. This is particularly true of the most basic level of all . . . : No one is presently capable of giving an adequate, intelligible and coherent account of why it is useful and right to punish men, and *a fortiori,* no one can explain which men ought to be punished in which circumstances.[18]

At this point we collide with measurement difficulties. The ambiguity of criminal justice technology not only makes it difficult to decide what the rules ought to be, it makes it difficult to enforce chosen rules because performance and goal attainment under the rule cannot be measured and defended on persuasive rational grounds.[19]

The prevalence of shifting and unpredictable environments in criminal justice compounds the difficulty. The police environment, as Skolnick and Wilson point out, exposes the officer to unpredictable danger and multiple plausible meanings of citizen behavior. The prosecutor's environment is unstable for other reasons. He serves as a middleman who must juggle the inconsistent expectations of police, judges, defense attorneys, and the public. Both prosecutors and defense attorneys must treat with some skepticism the facts of the cases before them. They know the suspect may misrepresent his case to his attorney; the "victim" may in fact seek prosecution to work out a grudge.[20]

Finally, the structure of incentives governing criminal justice personnel does not easily produce rule compliance. Many prosecutors and public defenders are young attorneys seeking litigation experience and contacts to prepare them for private practice. Expertise in penology has not been a requirement for judicial appointment. The pressures to handle the caseload and the infrequency of review by appellate courts, dictated largely by the financial position of most defendants, isolate the system from frequent supervision and correction.[21]

In these circumstances, policy choices for criminal justice raise unusually difficult normative questions. The finding that criminal justice personnel behave incrementally to serve a mix of ill-defined and partially inconsistent personal and collective goals should not surprise us. Most public and private organizations operate that way most of the time. The finding interests us because we believe that distinctively high legal norms ought to apply and because the system has a greater than average potential for class bias.[22] Much recent organization theory has suggested that in conditions of technological ambiguity and environmental unpredictability, organizational effectiveness requires nonhierarchical, decentralized, problem-specific decision-making. Yet increasing system uniformity would appear to call for a form of bureaucratization that would undercut both the capacity to adapt to new information in specific cases and to seek out, over the longer run, less ambiguous technologies.

In some areas of criminal justice we are, given available public financing, already prepared to adopt widely some structural reforms. Bail reform is the best example. Increasing the resources invested in public defense and in probation and presentencing investigations is another. But if the postulates of organization theory above correctly describe the system, the costs of seeking rule uniformity may prove high. Before doing so, we may wish to mount a considerable research effort to examine the relationship between the method of determining guilt, defendants' perceptions of fairness, and recidivism.[23] We may wish to experiment with the diversion of suspects into probation before the process of determining guilt begins, or with reducing rather than reinforcing the hierarchical command structure of police departments. Indeed, regarding behavior which is neither physically nor financially seriously harmful, democracy may dictate greater variation among communities rather than less. In the area of morals offenses, the city, or conceivably communities within the city operating through lay community courts, might best determine legality and sanction. Whether our present level of mobility makes the state the smallest unit of government capable of dealing with this problem deserves further examination. At least, the current state of criminal justice requires law schools to increase the sophistication of young attorneys to the social-science dynamics that affect penological decision-making.

Whether "the morality of law" permits a policy approach that does not seek swiftly to eliminate discretion must remain, for now, a matter for lively debate, intensive research, and personal judgment. Students of policy processes should assume some responsibility for the present state of criminal justice, for its participants fail to promote system goals primarily because no one, including ourselves, has succeeded in telling them how.

Notes

1. Abraham Blumberg, *Criminal Justice* (Chicago: Quadrangle, 1967).

2. Herbert Packer, *The Limits of the Criminal Sanction* (Stanford, Calif.: Stanford University Press, 1968).

3. Dallin Oaks, "Studying the Exclusionary Rule in Search and Seizure," *University of Chicago Law Review* 37 (1970): 665-753.

4. Paul Chevigny, *Police Power* (New York: Pantheon, 1969); Albert Reiss, Jr., *The Police and the Public* (New Haven: Yale University Press, 1971); Johnathan Rubinstein, *City Police* (New York: Farrar, Straus and Giroux, 1973).

5. Joseph Goldstein, "Police Discretion Not to Invoke the Criminal Process: Low-Visibility Decisions in the Administration of Justice," *Yale Law Journal* 69 (March 1960): 543-589; Wayne R. LaFave, *Arrest: The Decision to Take a Suspect into Custody* (Boston: Little, Brown, 1964).

6. William Chambliss and Robert Seidman, *Law, Order, and Power* (Reading, Mass.: Addison-Wesley, 1971).

7. John Kaplan, "The Prosecutorial Discretion: A Comment," *Northwestern Law Review* 6 (1965): 180; Frank W. Miller, *Prosecution: The Decision to Charge a Suspect with a Crime* (Boston: Little, Brown, 1969).

8. Marvin Frankel, *Criminal Sentences* (New York: Hill and Wang, 1972); John Hogarth, *Sentencing as a Human Process* (Toronto: University of Toronto Press, 1970).

9. Julian C. D'Esposito, Jr., "Sentencing Disparity: Causes and Cures," *Journal of Criminal Law, Criminology and Police Science* 60 (1969): 183-194; Edward Green, "Inter- and Intra-Racial Crime Relative to Sentencing," *Journal of Criminal Law, Criminology and Police Science* 55 (1964): 348-359.

10. Jerome Skolnick, *Justice Without Trial* (New York: Wiley, 1966); Carl Werthman and Irving Piliavin, "Gang Members and the Police," in David Bordua, ed., *The Police* (New York: Wiley, 1967), pp. 56-98.

11. Ann Rankin, "Effects of Pretrial Detention," *New York University Law Review* 39 (1964): 642.

12. Frederic Suffet, "Bail Setting: A Study of Courtroom Interaction," *Crime and Delinquency* 12 (1966): 318-331.

13. Albert W. Alschuler, "The Prosecutor's Role in Plea Bargaining," *University of Chicago Law Review* 36 (1968): 50-112; Donald J. Newman, "Pleading Guilty for Considerations: A Study of Bargain Justice," *Journal of Criminal Law, Criminology and Police Science* 46 (1956): 780-790; Jerome Skolnick, "Social Control in the Adversary System," *Journal of Conflict Resolution* 11 (1967): 52-70; David Sudnow, "Normal Crimes: Sociological Features of the Penal Code in a Public Defender Office," *Social Problems* 12 (1965): 255-276.

14. Robert M. Emerson, *Judging Delinquents* (Chicago: Aldine, 1969).

15. Martin Levin, "Urban Politics and Policy Outcomes: The Criminal Courts," in George Cole, ed., *Criminal Justice* (North Scituate, Mass.:

Duxbury Press, 1972), pp. 330-363; James Q. Wilson, *Varieties of Police Behavior* (Cambridge, Mass.: Harvard University Press, 1968).

16. Lon Fuller, *The Morality of Law* (New Haven, Conn.: Yale University Press, 1964).

17. Herbert Kaufman, *The Forest Ranger* (Baltimore: Johns Hopkins Press, 1960); James D. Thompson, *Organizations in Action* (New York: McGraw-Hill, 1967).

18. John Griffiths, "The Limits of Criminal Law Scholarship," *Yale Law Journal* 79 (1970): 1390; reprinted by permission of the Yale Law Journal Company and Fred B. Rothman and Company.

19. John Gardiner, *Traffic and the Police* (Cambridge, Mass.: Harvard University Press, 1969).

20. Lief H. Carter, *The Limits of Order* (Lexington, Mass.: Lexington Books, D. C. Heath and Company, 1974).

21. Anthony Amsterdam, "The Supreme Court and the Rights of Suspects in Criminal Cases," *New York University Law Review* 45 (1970): 785-815.

22. Kenneth C. Davis, *Discretionary Justice* (Baton Rouge, La.: Louisiana State University Press, 1969).

23. Jonathan Casper, *American Criminal Justice* (Englewood Cliffs, N.J.: Prentice-Hall, 1972; David Matza, *Delinquency and Drift* (New York: Wiley, 1964).

**Part II
Participants in Crime and Criminal
Justice Policy-Making**

9

Public Participation in the Criminal Justice System: Volunteers in Police, Courts, and Correctional Agencies

Thomas J. Cook and Frank P. Scioli, Jr.

Volunteerism as a form of public participation in the social and political system of the United States has become increasingly widespread in recent years. It has been estimated that there are over 500,000 voluntary organizations in the United States.[1]

The voluntary movement in the criminal justice system traces its history back to 1841 when a Boston shoemaker, John Augustus, became the first probation officer in our country's history. John Augustus was an unpaid volunteer.

Despite this initial effort, volunteerism in the criminal justice system was largely displaced in the early 1900's by the advent of professionally trained, paid probation officers. It wasn't until the early 1960's that volunteerism began to reemerge as a mode of public participation in the criminal justice system.[2] Since that time there has been a steady increase in the extent, and diversity, of volunteerism. It has been estimated, for example, that there are now more than 200,000 volunteers donating their time and efforts in some 2000 court systems throughout the United States.[3]

In this article, we will examine volunteerism in the criminal justice system in terms of the variety of services offered by different types of programs. We will also point out some of the prominent research issues associated with this area.

Types of Programs

It is, perhaps, incorrect to speak of *a* volunteer *program,* suggesting the delivery of a single service to clients, for most programs represent a "mixed bag" of services and delivery modes. Within any one program, a variety of "subprograms" such as Guidance and Counseling, Academic Tutoring, Job Placement, Recreation, etc., may also be operative. For example, in the Hennepin County (Minneapolis, Minnesota) volunteer program, in addition to working on a one-to-one volunteer-probationer basis, volunteers have been used in the following capacities: to recruit foster parents; as juvenile and adult marriage counselors; as therapy-group leaders; as supervisors of parent child visitations; etc. More recently, volunteers have been utilized in preparing presentence investigations and custody study reports as inputs to court decision-making on case dispositions.

Another example of the diversification of volunteer services within a program can be seen in the privately operated Partners Program, located in Denver, Colorado. The Partners Program, which began in 1968 in the Denver Juvenile Court, offers a variety of recreational and cultural activities within the context of its core one-to-one, senior-junior partner relationship. Support activities include fishing and camping trips, free airplane rides, free access to the YMCA, a multifunction sports center, and other activities. Senior partners are people who have volunteered to spend at least three hours per week for a twelve-month period with a youth, i.e., "junior partner," placed on probation by the Denver Juvenile Court.

As was pointed out above, volunteers provide a variety of services, both within court jurisdictions and under private auspices. The range of services is as potentially diverse as the community resources available at a given program location: clerical aides, case aides, court watchers, volunteer dentists, data analysts, insurance and legal consultants, psychiatrists, optometrists, speech therapists, speakers' bureau, transportation, etc. The core program activity, within this range of diversity, continues to be the one-to-one, volunteer-offender relationship, that is, the assignment of a volunteer to an offender to serve as a friend and companion for the offender in a relationship of mutual trust, support, and self-respect. In a sense, the volunteer serves as an important reference point for the offender within the community to aid him or her in adjustment to the community and to provide support and advice in various problem-solving situations.

In addition, volunteers are active in numerous correctional institutions serving a variety of needs. Visitation programs, job and family counseling programs, educational programs, etc., are currently operating within numerous correctional institutions. The PACE (Programmed Activities for Correctional Education) program is illustrative of this type of program. Founded in 1967 in the Cook County, Illinois, Jail, the program is physically located within the jail itself. The professional PACE staff is augmented by a core of volunteers made up of business and professional men and women, housewives, teachers, and students who give an afternoon or evening a week for tutoring, counseling, seminars, and dialogue groups. In one six-week night volunteer program, seminars were offered in basic reading, civil law, advanced mathematics, money management, metal trades, automotive skills, electronics, television, etc. The basic concept is to deliver the program services directly to the jail inmates at their place of confinement. This type of program, involving direct participation within the confines of a correctional institution, continues to be a prominent kind of volunteer activity.

While the bulk of volunteer activity in the criminal justice field has centered on the courts and probation, there is an increasing demand for volunteer citizen participation as an aid to the police in carrying out their law-enforcement responsibilities.[4] In Chicago, for example, programs such as Operation Identification and Operation Whistlestop encourage citizen involvement in the criminal justice area. Operation Identification is a program pioneered in 1963 in Monterey Park, California, whereby citizens can obtain tools from local police departments to mark their personal property (e.g., with their social security number) as an aid to the recovery of stolen property by those victimized by burglary or theft. Operation Whistlestop is a program which began in the Hyde Park-Kenwood area of Chicago as a citizen response to an increase in on-street assaults in the area. Citizens are encouraged to carry a whistle at all times and sound this as an alarm should they either be accosted or observe another person being victimized. The whistle alarm serves as a signal to other area residents to immediately call the police.

In a similar vein, the term "Urban Vigilante" has been used by some authors to label the resurgence of an old American tradition—the policing of communities by private citizen groups.[5] These self-styled "self-defense" groups have emerged in diverse communities such as Boston, Cleveland, Baton Rouge, Minneapolis, and Oakland. Under titles such as the Jewish Defense League, Watts Community Alert Patrol, and the Louisiana Deacons for Defense, these private defense groups have drawn mixed reactions from the regular police departments. Gary Marx and Dane Archer distinguish between groups which serve to supplement (and hence identify with) regular police operations and those groups which serve in more of an adversary role vis-à-vis the regular police. The latter groups function primarily to detect and thwart potential *police* abuse or neglect. Both types of groups perform a variety of functions such as observing and reporting police operations, foot and car patrols, escort service, etc. In a sense, all of these activities involve a form of voluntary citizen participation, but in a somewhat different mode than that discussed in connection with court-related volunteer programs.

In a more conventional sense, volunteers have been recruited and trained to handle telephone services, i.e., "hot lines," which offer 24-hour referral information to both police and court-related services. Another mode of volunteer participation, closely related to the police function, has been the establishment of youth service bureaus. More than 100 bureaus have been set up in cities throughout the United States. In addition to the referral function, the youth service bureaus use volunteers in halfway houses and foster homes for boys who have come under court jurisdiction. Many of the volunteers are off-duty policemen who donate time to the various projects.[6]

Research Issues

The establishment and operation of a volunteer program raise a host of research issues.[7] These issues relate to both the administrative or managerial aspects of the program and the extent to which the program is successful in meeting its goals or objectives, i.e., program effectiveness. Program effectiveness is, of course, contingent upon the success of the various operational components endemic to a volunteer program. For example, the success of a program may be largely a function of the types of people recruited to serve as volunteers. The research issue here concerns the selection of a recruitment strategy to obtain the optimal mix of volunteer types consistent with program goals or objectives. A commonly cited shortcoming of many volunteer programs, for example, is the under-representation of males and various minority groups (e.g., blacks and Latins) within the volunteer population. One important research issue, therefore, concerns the development of a recruitment program to increase the effectiveness of recruitment among these underrepresented groups.

In addition to recruitment, a series of potential research issues confronts the volunteer program administrator. Volunteers must be screened to meet program needs, placed in the appropriate volunteer role (i.e., job classification), and, in the case of direct service, matched with a counselee in, for example, a one-to-one situation. Furthermore, the volunteer will be expected to participate in an orientation and training program as well as, perhaps, in-service training sessions during participation in the program. Thus research questions dealing with the efficacy of such matters as alternative methods of recruiting, screening, matching, orienting, and training permeate the operation of a volunteer program. Moreover, volunteer turnover is a continual problem in many programs. Thus the question of volunteer incentive and support is also an important research issue for the maintenance of program continuity.

All of the above operational questions are relevant to the performance of the volunteer coordinators. Similar types of questions could be addressed to the paid program staff in their supervisory and administrative roles.

A related series of research issues concerns the area of program effectiveness.[8] These issues may be approached through an analysis of the impact of program operation upon different groups within the program's environment: the clients of the program, the program staff, other service-centered agencies, the volunteers themselves, and finally, the community at large. The crucial issue, of course, is the extent to which a volunteer program effectively delivers a needed social service to the clients of the program.

A recently completed research project funded by the National Science Foundation (RANN) has addressed the volunteer effectiveness question from a nationwide perspective. The investigators critically evaluated research reports on program effectiveness from over 200 different volunteer programs across the United States. In general, the investigators found that research in the volunteer field is consistent with the general thrust of research on correctional rehabilitation as discussed in Chapter 14 of this volume. For example, the research reports were very mixed in terms of their technical quality. Only 43 out of approximately 250 reports met minimum criteria for systematic program evaluation.[9] Moreover, there was no clear-cut pattern of success when one compared volunteer program treatments with nonvolunteer assigned comparison groups. Part of this noncomparability was due to the fact that none of the reports used exactly the same set of effectiveness criteria. One notable finding was that, of those programs which had sufficient technical quality, the investigators found no instance of a volunteer program performing in a less effective manner than a comparison treatment alternative (e.g., regular probation). The problem with interpreting this type of finding is the fact that data on program cost were not available and, therefore, an assessment of the relative effectiveness, from a cost-effectiveness perspective, was not possible. While these initial evaluative efforts are suggestive, much more in the way of systematic comparative evaluation is necessary before any conclusive statements on the relative effectiveness of volunteer programs can be made.

Conclusion

The above discussion has focused on volunteerism primarily in terms of the provision of support services to the official agencies of the criminal justice system, the point being that volunteers serve to complement, rather than supplant, the existing activities of the criminal justice system. Another viewpoint is that the increase in volunteerism is evidence of a desperate search for workable alternatives to the present criminal justice system, alternatives that are effective in reducing crime and the probability of criminal recidivism. It is our hope that this increase in volunteer activity will be coupled with the systematic evaluation of volunteer program effectiveness. Only in this way will the utility of volunteerism as a means of reducing crime be firmly established. We feel that the importance of the problem more than justifies the effort.

Notes

1. For a comprehensive listing of the major national volunteer organizations, journals, and newsletters, see "Clearinghouse Green Sheets, Ad-

ministration and Organization in Volunteerism," National Center for Voluntary Action, 1735 Eye Street NW, Washington, D.C. 20006.

2. See June Morrison, *The Use of Volunteers in Juvenile Courts in the United States* (Tucson, Ariz.: Institute of Public Administration, University of Arizona, 1971).

3. *Volunteers in Law Enforcement Programs* (Washington, D.C.: Law Enforcement Assistance Administration, Division of Program and Management Evaluation, 1972), p. 17; see also Ivan H. Scheier and Judith Lake Berry, *Guidelines and Standards for the Use of Volunteers in Correctional Programs* (Boulder, Colo.: National Information Center on Volunteerism, 1972).

4. For a discussion of this point, see National Advisory Commission on Criminal Justice Standards and Goals, *A National Strategy to Reduce Crime* (Washington, D.C.: U.S. Government Printing Office, 1973), especially Ch. 4, "Community Crime Prevention."

5. See Gary T. Marx and Dane Archer, "The Urban Vigilante," *Psychology Today,* January 1973, pp. 45-50. Also see *Community Police Patrols: An Exploratory Inquiry* (Springfield, Va.: National Technical Information Service, U.S. Department of Commerce, n.d.).

6. For other examples of citizen involvement, see *Opportunities for Improving Productivity in Police Services,* Report of the Advisory Group on Productivity in Law Enforcement (Washington, D.C.: National Commission on Productivity, 1973), pp. 41-43.

7. Candace Peters, "Research in the Field of Volunteers in Courts and Corrections: What Exists and What is Needed" (Boulder, Colo.: National Information Center on Volunteerism, n.d., mimeo).

8. See Ernest Shelley, *An Overview of Evaluation Research and Surveys* (Boulder, Colo.: National Information Center on Volunteerism, 1971; see also the 1972 Addendum); David H. Smith, ed., *Voluntary Action Research* (Lexington, Mass.: Lexington Books, D. C. Heath and Company, 1973).

9. Thomas J. Cook and Frank P. Scioli, Jr., "Evaluating the Effectiveness of Volunteer Programs in Courts and Corrections," National Science Foundation (RANN)-funded Grant GI-39277.

10 Police Policy
Leonard Ruchelman

The rising crime rates and social turmoil of the last decade have subjected the law-enforcement capabilities of America's cities to more intensive examination than ever before. Because they are the most visible part of the criminal justice system, much of the discussion has centered on what the police should or can do in preserving order and stability. Taking interest in this phenomenon, social scientists have been contributing a stream of studies on the police jurisdiction. Since the field has lacked empirical definition, the greater part of such research has attempted to identify the full range of problems. Thus the literature contains a number of works on such subjects as police abuse of citizen rights,[1] police-community relations,[2] police culture and discretion,[3] and police accountability.[4]

But if we now have a firmer grasp of where the difficulties lie, there is the additional obligation to broaden the framework of analysis. Most important at the present time is the need to clarify police policy objectives, to identify various alternatives likely to lead to those objectives, and to assess impacts more systematically than has heretofore been done.

Defining Objectives—The Police Mission

Until we come up with a clearer understanding of what we expect our police to do, effective standards of police performance will continue to hang under a cloud of ambiguity. Meaningful evaluation, moreover, cannot be expected to proceed until there is a realistic identification of objectives. By and large, this has not been forthcoming in the police policy area.

To the man on the street as well as to the policeman himself, the apprehension of criminals is usually stressed as a major goal. This means responding to crime-related calls and carrying through with such activities as criminal investigations, collection of evidence, and interrogating and arresting suspects. Another objective of police work which overlaps the former is crime deterrence. The most important activity here is street patrol to detect incidents of crime or situations with crime potential. A third objective is community service. Here the police provide a variety of services to the community such as interceding in family quarrels, pro-

113

viding emergency rescue or medical assistance, and generally acting as a social agency of last resort.

While the last objective has received little attention in the professional police literature,[5] recent studies have noted that the service function takes up an inordinate amount of the average patrolman's time. For example, in his study of the Chicago Police Department, Albert J. Reiss found that about eight of every ten incidents handled by police patrols were regarded by the police as noncriminal matters.[6] Most of these kinds of contacts, moreover, took place in lower-class neighborhoods.

At the same time, there is a growing questioning of the traditional police objective of crime deterrence. We do not know, for example, the extent to which the police are capable of fulfilling this function. A research experiment set up to monitor the effects of patrol in Kansas City has shown that the number of patrols assigned to a district has little effect on the crime rate. In his Chicago study, Albert Reiss illustrates the low productivity of preventive patrol for criminal matters—only about two-tenths of one percent of the time spent on preventive patrol is occupied in dealing with criminal matters.

The criminal apprehension function also presents ambiguities. A study by Philip H. Ennis for the President's Commission on Law Enforcement and the Administration of Justice shows that in only about 25 percent of the instances in which a person believes he has been a victim of a crime do the police label the incident as a crime; and, what is perhaps more important, victims do not call the police in about half the cases. In a surprisingly high number of instances—237 out of 1024—the police did not respond when notified. Consequently, in only about five percent of the total instances in which a crime may have been committed do the police actually make an arrest.[7]

While such gaps can be attributed to the ineffectiveness of police methods (this is discussed below), the objectives themselves may be unrealistic. Short of total police saturation, some high-crime neighborhoods may simply be immune to law enforcement because of prevailing conditions. What often seems like a police "clean-up" is really a scattering of crime to other places. It would seem, furthermore, that there is at least some misapprehension about the relative importance of the community-service function. Consequently, as revealed in a study of Miami, policemen are prone to role conflict which can lead in turn to frustration and demoralization.[8]

Assessing Results—Police Productivity

If objectives are not being realized, this should be determined through diagnosis. Poor productivity should raise questions about either police objectives or activities designed to achieve those objectives. To illustrate, patrolmen may be poorly deployed given certain crime patterns; or they may be poorly trained in specific areas such as investigatory work.

In the past, the subject of police productivity has been treated rather simplistically by reliance on such criteria as the crime rate per capita or the number of policemen per capita.[9] Staff members of the Law Enforcement Task Force of the National Commission on Productivity have attempted to move beyond this by proposing measures of efficiency, effectiveness, and quality.[10] *Efficiency* measures are based on the ratio of police activities to resources expended in performing these activities. All other factors being equal, those departments which require more resources to provide the same amount of activities performed by other departments with less resources are less efficient. *Effectiveness* measures relate the volume of activity to the fulfillment of an objective. For example, a department that consistently achieves more arrests with a lower number of responses to crime calls is more effective than a department that achieves fewer arrests with more responses. *Quality* measures are intended to indicate changes in quality of law enforcement that could result from efforts to improve numerical productivity. For example, increases in arrests that result in court dismissals or failure to get convictions would indicate poor quality. Another important indicator of quality would be surveys which measure citizen perceptions and estimates of police services. Though difficult to apply, the special benefit of such techniques is that they allow expression to those who are usually unheard from, e.g., the poor.[11]

While police productivity measures are feasible for assessing crime apprehension and crime deterrence objectives, this is generally not the case for assessing community services. For the most part, statistics on non-emergency services, e.g., family disputes or arguments between neighbors, are rarely collected by police agencies. Nor is there any special awareness among the police of the full range of activities which could serve as a basis for evaluating the community-service function.

Alternative Police Strategies: Three Illustrations

In light of police objectives, what are the various strategies for achieving them? The following limited discussion attempts to identify research needs in three important areas: police patrol, police organization, and police-community relations. In considering these, it should be kept in mind that police performance is only one of many factors which affect the security of a community. For example, irrespective of police activities, high-status low-density neighborhoods populated by older people are likely to be safer than low-income high-density neighborhoods populated by relatively youthful persons. It is possible to control for such factors by comparing police departments applying different strategies in neighborhoods which are otherwise similar.

Police Patrol

The effectiveness of this most basic of police functions has never been adequately tested. Consequently, the subject is fraught with ambiguities. To what extent does patrol prevent crime? To what extent does it lead to the apprehension of criminals? Under what kinds of conditions do different patrol techniques seem either more effective or less effective?

Examples of different techniques are special-purpose units, neighborhood team policing, citizen involvement to serve as "eyes and ears," proactive patrols (rather than reactive) based on crime pattern analysis, and patrol dispatch by call rather than random deployment. How effective each one of these strategies may be must be assessed not only in terms of particular results for particular programs, but also in terms of secondary and unintended effects. One common complaint, for example, about team policing in specially designated neighborhoods is that it reduces flexibility in the use of police manpower to meet other needs. Complaints from ghetto dwellers about the activities of special tactical patrol units of big-city police departments are another example. In spite of some success as a decoy operation (as measured by the number of arrests), the special anticrime "Stress" squad in Detroit was recently disbanded when blacks blamed it for 19 fatal shootings—all of the victims were black.

Perhaps the most ambitious project to date which attempts to test patrol methods has involved the Kansas City Police Department in a series of experiments. In matched areas of Kansas City with no regular patrol cars, one patrol car, and four or five patrol cars, there were virtually no changes in levels of reported crime during the one-year test period. If valid, these findings would seem to suggest that the police have been misled about the best way to allocate resources for crime control.[12]

Police Organization

Proposals for changing the organization of police departments are usually made without any evidence of the expected benefits. An issue that illustrates this is the debate over the extent to which police systems should be centralized or decentralized.

Persons who argue for the consolidation of police departments contend that large-scale police units are more effective and efficient than small units. Persons who support schemes of decentralization contend that citizen participation at the grass-roots level improves police relations with residents—particularly ghetto residents—and this reduces the number of community flare-ups and arrests.

This issue is related, in turn, to concepts of police professionalism, i.e., the need to insulate the police from politics in order to preserve standards of honesty and efficiency. In this context, advocates of neighborhood control are seen as anathema to the requisites of merit, objectivity, and neutrality in the administration of the law.

Answers to these important questions must be treated less simplistically than has been the case in the past. In his book *Community Control,* Alan Altshuler states that "community control should be conceived as a continuum rather than an absolute" and that the degree of such control may vary from one dimension of a given policy arena to the next. Thus it may be that supervision of the police from some central authority should be greater with respect to fiscal matters than with respect to determining tolerable levels of street disorder.[13]

Part of the problem in deciding on different alternatives is a general lack of empirical data. In their appraisal of police consolidation, Ostrom, Parks, and Whitaker conclude that certain assumed benefits of efficiency and effectiveness are not necessarily realized through the integration of police agencies.[14] Comparing three independent communities with three Indianapolis neighborhoods of comparable size, population, and socio-economic characteristics, they found that small police departments can deliver higher levels of services than larger departments. Furthermore, high degrees of specialization and professionalization are not required for effective police services. These findings are based on a sample survey which examined citizens' experiences with their local police and their evaluation of services provided.

In this light, citizens' surveys which assess certain qualitative aspects of police performance would appear to have special utility in the design of police strategies. Elinor Ostrom warns: "Using producer-oriented measures can lead us into the trap of assessing police departments highly efficient when citizens consider the output they receive to be public bads rather than public goods." [15] It can be further argued that cultural relativism in the administration of police services should not be ignored: what leads to good will in white middle-class neighborhoods may lead to ill will in black ghetto neighborhoods.

Police-Community Relations

Since the violent confrontations of the 1960's, there has been much open discussion about strategies of strengthening police-community relations.

For the most part, proposals have centered on police-citizen contacts and the ways and means of reducing the tensions and hostility which can result from such contacts. Described in this way, the subject tends to be rather narrowly defined. Rather than focus on programmatic aspects alone, researchers must strive to widen their scope of analysis.

In addition to the attitudes and behavior exhibited by citizens and policemen toward each other, the following factors all have some effect on police-community relations: (a) ineffective courts and corrections systems, (b) unenforceable laws, (c) inequities in city services, (d) biased news reporting, (e) racism and discrimination, (f) poverty, (g) poor parental supervision, (h) unemployment, and (i) the stakes of special interests.

How to account for the impact of such factors is very much the problem. The political scientist must be prepared to view police-community relations as a sociopolitical phenomenon in the broad sense as well as an aspect of intergroup relations. Reflecting special values of their own, the police may in some instances be quite willing to expand their community role for purposes of asserting influence and control. At the same time, there may be those who resist such efforts because they fear police power as being counterproductive.

Compounding such concerns is the fact that police systems tend toward insularity. William A. Westley's classic case study reveals how sensitive the police are toward anything that might downgrade their self-respect.[16] Police administrators tend to look to themselves and their fellow officers for answers—if they look for answers at all.

In light of all this, community-relations programs (e.g., "Officer Friendly" school visitations, neighborhood centers) must be seen as essentially intervening variables. In a community where prejudice, bad housing, or job inequalities are manifest, such programs by themselves are not likely to be very effective. Nor are they likely to work where the police system is a closed system, immune to outside influences.[17] Through experimental-design techniques, research must strive to identify those combinations of societal and programmatic factors likely to achieve desired objectives.

Conclusion

In addition to strategies of patrol, police organization, and police-community relations, other vital subjects deserve recognition for future research. For example, what are the alternatives to arrest, particularly when victimless crimes are committed? What are effective investigative strategies and how can they be distinguished from the ineffective ones?

Do recruitment and promotion standards reflect the realities of the contemporary policeman's roles?

As discussed in this paper, a necessary first step in the search for answers is to define measures of police performance in order to evaluate output. Evidence of limited or adverse effects in relation to activities or resources committed is a sign that programs are working poorly or that objectives may have to be reconsidered. Not to be ignored in a democratic society is the potential utility of qualitative measures as derived from citizens' evaluations of police services.

Notes

1. See, for example, Paul Chevigny, *Police Power: Police Abuses in New York City* (New York: Pantheon Books, 1969); Jerome H. Skolnick, *Justice Without Trial: Law Enforcement in a Democratic Society* (New York: Wiley, 1966).

2. See, for example, Michael Banton, *The Policeman and the Community* (New York: Basic Books, 1965); Terry Eisenberg, Robert H. Fosen, and Albert S. Glickman, *Police-Community Action* (New York: Praeger, 1973).

3. See, for example, William A. Westley, *Violence and the Police* (Cambridge, Mass.: MIT Press, 1970); James Q. Wilson, *Varieties of Police Behavior* (Cambridge, Mass.: Harvard University Press, 1968).

4. See, for example, Leonard Ruchelman, *Police Politics: A Comparative Study of Three Cities* (Cambridge, Mass.: Ballinger, 1974).

5. See, for example, George D. Eastman and Esther M. Eastman, eds., *Municipal Police Administration* (Washington, D.C.: International City Management Association, 1969).

6. Albert J. Reiss, Jr., *The Police and the Public* (New Haven, Conn.: Yale University Press, 1971), p. 97.

7. Philip H. Ennis, *Criminal Victimization in the United States,* Field Surveys II, The President's Commission on Law Enforcement and the Administration of Justice (Washington, D.C.: Government Printing Office, 1967), p. 48.

8. Bernard L. Garmire (Miami Chief of Police), "The Police Role in an Urban Society," in Robert F. Steadman, ed., *The Police and the Community* (Baltimore: John Hopkins Press, 1972), pp. 2-4.

9. See "Measuring Police Crime Control Productivity," in *The Challenge of Productivity Diversity* (Washington, D.C.: The Urban Institute, June 1972); George Barbour and Stanley Wolfson, "Productivity Measurement in Police Crime Control," *Public Management,* April 1973.

10. Gary B. Hirsch and Lucius J. Riccio, "Measuring and Improving

the Productivity of Police Patrol," *Journal of Police Science and Administration,* June 1974, pp. 169-184.

11. See Gary T. Marx, "On the Inter-Relationship of Police Organization and Operations, Crime, City Characteristics, and Citizen Attitudes: Data from 10 Cities," paper presented at the Annual Meeting of the American Political Science Association, 1972.

12. See *Kansas City Preventive Patrol Experiment: A Summary Report* (Washington, D.C.: The Police Foundation, 1974).

13. Alan A. Altshuler, *Community Control: The Black Demand for Participation in Large American Cities* (New York: Pegasus, 1970), p. 44.

14. Elinor Ostrom, Roger B. Parks, and Gordon P. Whitaker, "Do We Really Want to Consolidate Urban Police Forces? A Reappraisal of Some Old Assertions," *Public Administration Review,* September/October 1973, pp. 423-432.

15. Elinor Ostrom, "On the Meaning and Measurement of Output and Efficiency in the Provision of Urban Police Services," *Journal of Criminal Justice,* Vol. 1 (1973), p. 108.

16. William A. Westley, *Violence and the Police* (Cambridge, Mass.: MIT Press, 1970). Published as a doctoral dissertation in 1951.

17. See Donald F. Norris, *Police-Community Relations: A Program that Failed* (Lexington, Mass.: Lexington Books, D. C. Heath and Company, 1973).

11

Adjudication as the Administrative Procedures of Charging and Plea Bargaining: The Roles of Prosecution and Defense

Michael A. Mulkey

The quality of justice in local criminal courts of the United States is to a large extent determined by the patterns of behavior of prosecutors and defense counsel and their characteristic modes of interaction. Prosecutors, through their dominance of the decision to charge suspects with crimes and through plea bargaining with defense counsel, largely control the direct, day-to-day administration of criminal justice, rivaling and perhaps surpassing even judges in their impact on the criminal justice system. This is not to say that judges, the police, and others involved in the criminal justice system do not exercise both direct and indirect influence upon charge decision-making and plea bargaining, for they do. Nor is it to say that the administration of criminal justice involves nothing more than prosecutors charging suspects with crimes and bargaining with defense counsel to dispose of charges via guilty pleas, for certainly more is involved at times, and prosecutors and defense attorneys do at times play roles quite different from those to be discussed below. Nevertheless, charging and plea bargaining by prosecutors account for most of that process which is termed "adjudication," and which is our focus in this chapter.[a]

In discussing adjudication, ample reason to focus on the decision to charge and on plea bargaining is provided by data on the disposition of arrests in which the police seek prosecution. As early as the 1920's, studies of the administration of justice in Missouri and Cleveland found, much to the dismay of the researchers, that prosecutors refused to proceed

Opinions expressed in this essay are those of the author only and do not necessarily represent positions of the National Institute of Law Enforcement and Criminal Justice or the Law Enforcement Assistance Administration.

[a] One major policy issue relating to prosecution and defense in criminal cases which will not be covered in this essay is the provision of counsel to the indigent. This issue appears to have been resolved with regard to criminal trials by the recent Supreme Court ruling, in *Argersinger v. Hamlin*, 407 U.S. 25 (1972), that a defendant in any criminal trial which may result in incarceration has a constitutional right to counsel. An as yet unsettled policy issue in this area is the right to *effective* counsel, i.e., whether perfunctory or inept representation entitles a defendant to some form of judicial relief. See Leo J. Flynn, "Adequacy of Counsel: An Emergent Fair Trial Issue," paper delivered at the Annual Meeting of the Western Political Science Association, Denver, Colorado, April 6, 1974.

with a substantial number of the felony cases brought to them by the police, and of those which were accepted for prosecution, the overwhelming majority were disposed of by guilty plea, not at trial.[1] Recent studies have found that this situation remains unchanged today.[2] Clearly, justice is not typically produced by the struggle of dedicated adversaries at trial; rather, the allocation of justice normally proceeds through the administrative processes of charging and plea bargaining.

The Decision to Charge

Once the police have decided to seek prosecution of a suspect, they are dependent upon other authorities for initiation of that prosecution in the courts. In some jurisdictions, such as Chicago, courts make the initial decisions concerning prosecution of cases brought by the police;[3] in most jurisdictions, however, this decision is dominated by the prosecutor.[4] The law liberally recognizes the discretion of the prosecutor to initiate and terminate prosecution,[5] although it also provides authority, which is only rarely exercised, for varying degrees of judicial intervention in the decision to charge.[6,b] In general, however, the law does not articulate standards and guidelines to be used by prosecutors in exercising their charging discretion, despite the fact that many cases are disposed of at the charging stage of the criminal justice process. Although sketchy at best, what data do exist indicate that in those cases in which the police seek prosecution, from 10 to slightly more than 50 percent, depending upon the jurisdiction, are refused by the prosecutor's office.[7]

Students of the prosecutorial function have identified a number of factors which seem to guide prosecutors in their charge decision-making. The single most important of these appears to be the strength of the state's case in terms of the "convictability" of a suspect, that is, the probability that the case will result in a conviction on some charge.[8] The existence of such a criterion is not surprising in light of the fact that a prosecutor's conviction record or "batting average" appears to be the universal standard of excellence among prosecutors.[9] Considerations pertinent to "convictability" include the strength and admissibility of evidence, the willingness of complainants and witnesses to cooperate in prosecution, the general reputation of the complainant, and the evaluation of the police officer bringing

---

b This statement applies strictly to the initiation of prosecution. The judiciary is much more highly involved, of course, in the continuation of prosecution at subsequent decision points prior to trial or the entry of a guilty plea, such as preliminary hearings and pretrial motion hearings.

the case as to its strength.[10] Independent of considerations of the evidentiary strength of a case, the propensities of juries and particular judges in dismissing, acquitting, and sentencing certain types of offenders may affect the decision to charge, as may the possible defenses available to the defendant.[11] In addition, the prior criminal record of a suspect may influence the decision to charge, both because the existence of a prior record enhances a suspect's "convictability" and because it labels a suspect as a more serious threat to the community.

Other factors can also enter into the charging calculus. As an administrator concerned with maintaining the flow of cases through the court system, the prosecutor frequently may attempt to screen out cases as a means of conserving system resources.[12] He may also refuse cases out of concern for avoiding undue harm to the suspect and/or because he doubts the appropriateness or utility of using criminal sanctions to deal with the offense and to prevent any recurrence.[13] Relevant to both types of considerations is the seriousness of the offense; the more serious the offense or offender, the more likely the prosecutor is to bring charges. As mentioned above, a suspect's prior criminal record, if any, is one indicator of the threat he represents to the public. Other indicators of seriousness utilized by prosecutors are the value of property stolen and the extent of any physical injuries inflicted upon the victim.[14] Indeed, the use by prosecutors of such indicators may structure the charging decision to an amazing degree. For example, Subin reports that in one jurisdiction prosecutors utilize a "stitch rule" in deciding between misdemeanor or felony assault charges against a suspect: if the victim of an assault required fewer than 30 stitches to mend his wounds, a misdemeanor is charged; but if 30 or more were required, felonious assault is usually the charge.[15] In evaluating the seriousness of a case, the prosecutor is likely to be influenced by community attitudes toward the general type of offense involved, by anticipated public opinion toward the specific offense, and by the attitude of the victim.[16] In less serious cases, the charging decision is to some extent structured by the alternatives to criminal prosecution available to the prosecutor, including civil commitment of the mentally ill, restitution by the suspect in exchange for nonprosecution, mediation, and conciliation.[17]

To this point, we have discussed the criteria used by the prosecutor in deciding whether or not to initiate prosecution. These same criteria also operate in his decision on the nature of charges to be brought against a suspect. An additional factor in choosing specific charges may be the anticipation of subsequent plea negotiation in the case. In order to establish a favorable bargaining position, the prosecutor may "overcharge" by bringing the most serious charge or as many charges as the facts of a case can conceivably support.[18]

Plea Bargaining

Plea bargaining, as the term is used in this essay, refers to negotiation between a prosecutor and defense attorney over the entry of a guilty plea by the defendant in exchange for a specific sentence recommendation to the court or reduction of charges (or both) by the prosecutor.[c] In most urban jurisdictions, 80 to 90 percent of the criminal cases are disposed of through guilty pleas,[19] although in some cities, such as Philadelphia, Pittsburgh, and Los Angeles, a far larger percentage go to trial.[d] It is not at all clear what portion of these guilty pleas involve bargaining between prosecutors and defense counsel, although the percentage is assumed to be high, at least in felony cases.

In general, the same considerations which influence prosecutors' charging decisions also influence their decisions in plea bargaining. For the institutionalized participants in the criminal justice process, the most powerful incentive to encourage guilty pleas from defendants is the conservation of scarce resources, many more of which are presumably consumed by a trial than are consumed by a guilty plea.[e] Both prosecutors' and public defenders' offices handle such large caseloads that they can try no more than a small percentage of their cases. Resource conservation is also a preeminent consideration for private attorneys regularly practicing criminal law, since they maximize their incomes through rapid turnover of a large number of low-fee cases.[20] An additional major incentive for both prosecutor and defense attorney is the avoidance of the uncertainties of trial and the attendant possibility of losing.[21]

Plea bargaining is also encouraged by the frequency of contact between prosecutors and defense attorneys. This frequent interaction breeds familiarity, close working relationships, and common understandings as to the informal rules of plea bargaining, particularly between the prosecutor and the public defender.[22] Close relationships may develop to such an extent that prosecutors and defense counsel, far from being adversaries, often

---

[c] Whether plea bargaining focuses on sentence promise or charge reduction depends largely upon the degree of sentencing discretion available to the court under the applicable state statute. For a discussion of the effects of statutory maximum and minimum sentences on plea bargaining, see McIntyre, *Law Enforcement in the Metropolis* (cited in note 4), Ch. 4; and Newman, *Conviction* (cited in note 18), Ch. 6.

[d] Many of these "trials," however, may in reality be what Lynn Mather refers to as "slow pleas." The slow plea is a brief, jury-waived trial of varying formality in which the defense attorney explicitly or implicitly admits the guilt of his client but attempts to influence the judge in favor of a lenient sentence. See Mather, "Some Determinants of the Method of Case Disposition" (cited in note 21), p. 190.

[e] As yet, there have been no studies showing how much "savings," if any, are achieved through guilty pleas relative to trials.

work as a team to promote their mutual interest in the efficient processing of cases and the avoidance of trial. This may lead to institutionalization of routine plea bargains for "normal" crimes, that is, crimes which closely resemble common definitions shared by prosecutors and defense attorneys as to what constitutes the typical burglary, robbery, assault, etc., in their particular jurisdiction.[23] In such circumstances, the major task of defense counsel is not to assess the defendant's guilt, for this is assumed, but to assess the accuracy of the prosecutor's charges, to determine whether or not the crime is a "normal" one (and thus eligible for the typical reduction), and to play a brokerage role for the criminal justice system by persuading the defendant to accept the proffered bargain.[24]

The defendant is motivated to accept a plea bargain, of course, by his desire for a more lenient sentence than he anticipates, or is led to believe he would receive at trial. However, as noted above, many "bargains" may be more apparent than real inasmuch as they are routine and involve no special concession to particular defendants.[25] Real benefits do accrue to defendants who plead guilty, however, simply through the avoidance of trial. Clearly the plea-bargaining system is predicated upon the practice of penalizing, through harsher sentences, those defendants who insist upon exercising their right to trial even though the facts of the case "clearly" establish their guilt and/or they have no credible defense.[26]

Critics point out that the prospect of a harsher penalty upon conviction at trial may encourage some defendants to plead guilty even though they are innocent. This is but one possible criticism of plea bargaining, however.[f] Critics also assert that plea bargaining leads to incomplete development of the facts in cases. Underdevelopment of the facts may lead to defendants pleading guilty to inaccurate charges; restriction of the opportunity for the judiciary to review the legal propriety of law-enforcement activities; nondiscovery of legitimate defenses and mitigating circumstances; and the partial or total determination of sentences without consideration of the individual rehabilitative needs of each defendant. Furthermore, it is argued that plea bargaining leads to irrational sentence disparity and allows illegitimate considerations, such as the strength of the state's case and the concern for maintaining the flow of cases through the system, to enter into the determination of sentences. In short, critics of plea bargaining maintain that reliance upon bargaining involves an emphasis upon administrative convenience which subverts achievement of criminal justice goals, including the suppression of crime, the rehabilitation of offenders, and the maintenance of procedural due process.

The most commonly cited advantage of plea bargaining is conservation

---

[f] The following discussion of the advantages and disadvantages of plea bargaining is based on the sources cited elsewhere in this section.

of the limited resources of the criminal justice system for use in priority activities. Plea bargaining, it is asserted, also allows the courts to mitigate the harshness of the law and facilitates the individualization of justice. Furthermore, it allows defendants the opportunity to avoid both the uncertainties and the stigmatizing effects of trials. Lastly, plea bargaining enables law-enforcement officials to exchange leniency for the cooperation of defendants in convicting other offenders and providing information helpful in suppressing crime.

Policy Issues Relating to Plea Bargaining

Inasmuch as the widespread practice of plea bargaining is a radical departure from the criminal justice process as portrayed in our codes of criminal procedure, in law-school classrooms, and on our television screens, the policy issues surrounding the topic are numerous and important. Many of these issues relate to the criticisms of plea bargaining outlined above.

Two of the more important issues relating to plea bargaining which have received considerable attention in terms of proposals for reform are the low visibility of the practice and the widespread lack of explicit policy concerning its procedures and standards. Both legislatures and courts have failed to prescribe standards of fairness and due process in plea bargaining, in sharp contrast to the establishment of well-articulated standards for the investigatory, pretrial, and trial stages of contested cases.[27] The United States Supreme Court, while validating plea bargaining, has formulated few guidelines for its practice.[28] The only standards the Court has set relate to the intelligence and voluntariness of guilty pleas [g] and due-process requirements in cases where defendants enter such pleas in reliance upon a prosecutor's promises which are subsequently not honored.[29]

Lack of explicit legislative and judicial policy has by default vested in prosecutors great discretion in the control of plea-bargaining practices. Efforts by prosecutors, however, to centralize management control over plea bargaining or to promote intraoffice guidelines for bargaining have been sporadic and incomplete at best, with the result that plea-bargaining standards and practices may vary greatly among assistant prosecutors in the same office. Recent proposals have devoted considerable attention to formulating measures to make plea-bargaining practices more uniform and

---

[g] The court has recently shown a willingness to broadly construe as voluntary and intelligent guilty pleas entered by defendants represented by "competent" counsel. See *Brady v. U.S.*, 397 U.S. 742 (1970); *McMann v. Richardson*, 397 U.S. 759 (1970); and *Parker v. North Carolina*, 397 U.S. 790 (1970).

to increase the visibility and judicial review of bargaining activities.[30] These proposals speak to the *reform* of plea bargaining, and in doing so give recognition, willingly or otherwise, to plea bargaining as a legitimate mechanism in the administration of justice. This position represents but one policy option, however. More recently, the National Advisory Commission on Criminal Justice Standards and Goals, while advocating similar reforms as interim measures, recommended the eventual abolition of plea bargaining altogether.[31]

Such policy recommendations as these, particularly when they are so radical as that of the National Advisory Commission on Criminal Justice Standards and Goals, suffer from lack of sufficient empirical grounding and could benefit greatly from further research on plea bargaining. At present, we do not have even a reliable estimate of the extensiveness of plea bargaining, much less a sufficient understanding of the reasons for its variance among jurisdictions and the consequences of that variance. Useful research also should be undertaken on the costs and benefits of plea bargaining relative to trial. Also needed is an accurate identification of the criteria which guide the formation of plea bargains under varying conditions, and an empirical estimation of the weights given those factors which are found to influence the outcomes of bargaining. Research on questions such as these is essential to rational development of and choice among alternative policies toward plea bargaining.

Notes

1. Alfred Bettman and Howard Burns, "Prosecution," in Roscoe Pound and Felix Frankfurter, eds., *Criminal Justice in Cleveland* (Cleveland: The Cleveland Foundation, 1922), pp. 85-228; G. E. Gehlke, "A Statistical Interpretation of the Criminal Process," in Raymond Moley, ed., *The Missouri Crime Survey* (New York: Macmillan, 1926), pp. 269-345; and Arthur V. Lashly, "Preparation and Presentation of the State's Case," *ibid.,* pp. 113-162.

2. See, for example, The President's Commission on Law Enforcement and Administration of Justice, *Task Force Report: The Courts* (Washington, D.C.: U.S. Government Printing Office, 1967), p. 9; also Peter W. Greenwood et al., *Prosecution of Adult Felony Defendants in Los Angeles County: A Policy Perspective* (Washington, D.C.: U.S. Government Printing Office, 1973).

3. Dallin H. Oaks and Warren Lehman, *A Criminal Justice System and the Indigent* (Chicago: University of Chicago Press, 1968), pp. 28-35; and Donald M. McIntyre, Jr., "A Study of the Judicial Dominance of the

Charging Decision," *Journal of Criminal Law, Criminology and Police Science* 59 (December 1968): 463-490.

4. Donald M. McIntyre, Jr., ed., *Law Enforcement in the Metropolis* (Chicago: American Bar Foundation, 1967), Ch. 3; Frank W. Miller and Lawrance P. Tiffany, "Prosecutor Dominance of the Warrant Decision: A Study of Current Practices," *Washington University Law Quarterly* 1 (February 1964): 1-24; Frank W. Miller, *Prosecution: The Decision to Charge a Suspect With a Crime* (Boston: Little, Brown, 1969), pp. 11-19; and David W. Neubauer, *Criminal Justice in Middle America* (Morristown, N.J.: General Learning Press, 1974), pp. 113-137.

5. Comment, "Prosecutorial Discretion in the Initiation of Criminal Complaints," *Southern California Law Review* 42 (1968-1969): 519-545.

6. Miller and Tiffany, "Prosecutor Dominance of the Warrant Decision."

7. Cf. George F. Cole, *Politics and the Administration of Justice* (Beverly Hills, Calif.: Sage Publications, 1973), p. 149; Greenwood et al., *Prosecution of Adult Felony Defendants;* Donald M. McIntyre, Jr., and David Lippmann, "Prosecutors and the Early Disposition of Felony Cases," *American Bar Association Journal* 56 (1970): 1156; Harry C. Mellman, "The System of Criminal Justice in St. Louis," University of Missouri-St. Louis, Administration of Justice Program (August 31, 1971, mimeo), pp. 19-23; and Neubauer, *Criminal Justice in Middle America,* p. 124.

8. Albert W. Alschuler, "The Prosecutor's Role in Plea Bargaining," *University of Chicago Law Review* 36 (1968-1969): 50-112; McIntyre, *Law Enforcement in the Metropolis,* Ch. 3; Miller and Tiffany, "Prosecutor Dominance of the Warrant Decision"; Miller, *Prosecution,* p. 27; and Neubauer, *Criminal Justice in Middle America,* pp. 117-118.

9. Abraham S. Blumberg, *Criminal Justice* (Chicago: Quadrangle, 1967), Ch. 3; Cole, *Politics and the Administration of Justice,* Ch. 4; John Kaplan, "The Prosecutorial Discretion: A Comment," *Northwestern University Law Review* 60 (March-April 1965): 174-193; but cf. Miller, *Prosecution,* Ch. 3.

10. George F. Cole, "The Decision to Prosecute," *Law and Society Review* 4 (February 1970): 331-343; and McIntyre, *Law Enforcement in the Metropolis,* Ch. 3.

11. Cole, "The Decision to Prosecute"; and Miller, *Prosecution,* Ch. 3.

12. Miller, *Prosecution,* Chs. 9 and 12.

13. Miller, *Prosecution,* Chs. 11, 13, and 19.

14. McIntyre, "Judicial Dominance of the Charging Decision."

15. H. F. Subin, *Criminal Justice in a Metropolitan Court* (Washington, D.C.: U.S. Government Printing Office, 1966), p. 36.

16. Cole, "The Decision to Prosecute"; Cole, *Politics and the Administration of Justice,* Ch. 4.

17. Miller, *Prosecution,* Chs. 14-16; and McIntyre, *Law Enforcement in the Metropolis,* Ch. 3.

18. The literature is conflicting as to the extensiveness of this practice; cf. Alschuler, "The Prosecutor's Role in Plea Bargaining"; Blumberg, *Criminal Justice;* Cole, "The Decision to Prosecute"; McIntyre, *Law Enforcement in the Metropolis,* Ch. 3; and Donald E. Newman, *Conviction: The Determination of Guilt or Innocence Without Trial* (Boston: Little, Brown, 1966), p. 79.

19. Blumberg, *Criminal Justice,* p. 54; McIntyre, *Law Enforcement in the Metropolis,* Ch. 4; Mellman, "The System of Criminal Justice in St. Louis"; McIntyre and Lippman, "Prosecutors and the Early Disposition of Felony Cases," p. 1156; Newman, *Conviction,* p. 3; Oaks and Lehman, *A Criminal Justice System and the Indigent,* p. 46; The President's Commission on Law Enforcement and Administration of Justice, *Task Force Report: The Courts,* p. 9; and David Sudnow, "Normal Crimes: Sociological Features of the Penal Code in a Public Defender's Office," *Social Problems* 12 (1965): 255-276.

20. Albert W. Alschuler, "The Defense Attorney's Role in Plea Bargaining," unpublished report submitted to the National Institute of Law Enforcement and Criminal Justice, Law Enforcement Assistance Administration, U.S. Department of Justice (March 1973), pp. 43-74; and Blumberg, *Criminal Justice,* Ch. 5.

21. Blumberg, *Criminal Justice,* Ch. 2; and Lynn M. Mather, "Some Determinants of the Method of Case Disposition: Decision Making by Public Defenders in Los Angeles," *Law and Society Review* 8 (Winter 1973): 187-216, p. 187.

22. Alschuler, "The Defense Attorney's Role in Plea Bargaining," pp. 90-95; Blumberg, *Criminal Justice,* Ch. 5; Jonathan Casper, *American Criminal Justice: The Defendant's Perspective* (Englewood Cliffs, N.J.: Prentice-Hall, 1972), pp. 77-92, 100-125; Jerome Skolnick, "Social Control in the Adversary System," *Journal of Conflict Resolution* 11 (March 1967): 52-70; Sudnow, "Normal Crimes"; and Paul Wice and Peter Suwak, "Current Realities of Public Defender Programs: A National Survey and Analysis," *Criminal Law Review* 10 (March 1974): 161-183.

23. Newman, *Conviction,* p. 79; Sudnow, "Normal Crimes," p. 317; but see the caveat by Alschuler, "The Prosecutor's Role in Plea Bargaining."

24. Blumberg, *Criminal Justice,* Ch. 5; and Sudnow, "Normal Crimes."

25. Newman, *Conviction,* p. 98.

26. Alschuler, "The Defense Attorney's Role in Plea Bargaining," p. 73; Blumberg, *Criminal Justice,* p. 31; and Newman, *Conviction,* pp. 60-66.

27. Blumberg, *Criminal Justice,* p. 21; Arnold Enker, "Perspectives on Plea Bargaining," in *Task Force Report: The Courts,* The President's

Commission on Law Enforcement and Administration of Justice, pp. 108-119; and Newman, *Conviction,* Chs. 1-3.

28. See *Brady v. U.S.,* 397 U.S. 742 (1970).

29. See *Santobello v. New York,* 404 U.S. 257 (1971).

30. American Bar Association, *Standards Relating to Pleas of Guilty, Approved Draft* (Chicago: American Bar Association, Project on Minimum Standards for Criminal Justice, 1968); and The President's Commission on Law Enforcement and Administration of Justice, *Task Force Report: The Courts,* pp. 4-13.

31. National Advisory Commission on Criminal Justice Standards and Goals, *Courts* (Washington, D.C.: U.S. Government Printing Office, 1973), pp. 42-65.

12

Courts Policy: The Recommendations of the National Advisory Commission
George F. Cole and David W. Neubauer

In a famous speech given in 1906, Roscoe Pound warned that a criminal justice system created within the framework of a rural America could not meet the needs of an urban society.[1] In spite of this notice, little modernization of the courts has occurred in this century. One highly visible result is the heavy caseloads in metropolitan courts, whose harassed and overworked staffs must try to handle the products of the rising crime rate. In 1967 the President's Commission on Law Enforcement and Administration of Justice expressed shock at what it found in the criminal courts:

> It has seen cramped and noisy courtrooms, undignified and perfunctory procedures, and badly trained personnel. It has seen dedicated people who are frustrated by huge caseloads, by the lack of opportunity to examine cases carefully, and by the impossibility of devising constructive solutions to the problems of offenders. It has seen assembly line justice.[2]

In addition to these conditions, the type of justice meted out is being questioned by many. Some say courts coddle criminals; others believe the courts have failed to protect the rights of the defendants. Most agree, however, that the time to do something about the criminal courts is now.

But while a consensus has developed that the criminal courts require change, there is no consensus on the direction. Herbert Packer has described two competing schemes for the administration of justice. These constructs, the Crime Control Model and the Due Process Model, are ways of looking at the goals and procedures of criminal justice.[3] Packer likened the Crime Control Model to an assembly line whose primary function is the repression of criminal conduct. To achieve its goal, major attention must be paid to the efficiency with which it operates to screen suspects, determine guilt, and secure appropriate disposition of persons convicted of crime. Given the scarcity of law-enforcement resources, a premium must be placed on speed and finality. This means that there has to be a high rate of apprehension, administrative sifting out of the innocent, and conviction of offenders. The Crime Control Model depends on informality, uniformity, and the minimizing of occasions for challenge.

If the Crime Control Model is similar to an assembly line, the Due

Process Model resembles an obstacle course. It predicates the administrative fact-finding of the police station and prosecutor's office to be inadequate, believing that evidence should be tested in the formal (but also slower) court process. Quality control is emphasized over volume production, since the accused should be deprived of his freedom only after the evidence has been tested through an adversarial proceeding. Hence the Due Process Model assumes that a person is innocent until proved guilty, that he has an opportunity to discredit the case brought against him, and that an impartial judge and jury are provided to decide the outcome. The Crime Control Model finds such restrictions unpalatable because they divert the system from its primary task of efficiently processing the guilty.

Packer's models serve the important function of allowing us to contrast the idealized version of criminal justice—to which most Americans have been socialized—with the reality of day-to-day administrative practices. "Assembly-line justice" has been recognized by social scientists as the way the system operates.[4] Particularly in the misdemeanor and traffic courts of large cities, dispositions are usually made with lightning speed by overworked judges who seem more interested in moving the steady stream of cases than in weighing facts on the scales of justice. Cases are disposed of through negotiation: defendants trade their admission of guilt for reduced charges, dismissal of multiple counts, and/or a light penalty. Because of the central role played by plea bargaining, trials are a relative rarity (but important in setting standards nonetheless). Finally, the bulk of criminal cases are effectively beyond the purview of the appellate courts.

A corollary of the administrative justice system is the importance of the organization. Although we usually think of criminal justice in terms of a conflict at trial, a more realistic appraisal is one of limited cooperation among the major participants. What many fail to understand is that the actors on the courtroom stage (judge, prosecutor, defense attorney, accused, clerks, bailiffs) are members of a social organization with interests and goals that may differ from those of due process.[5] Although there is some shifting from courtroom to courtroom, most of the same actors appear daily on the same judicial stage, where they engage in exchange or collaborative relationships. Stated another way, defendants come and go through the system but the participants remain and develop a stake in maintaining the basic outlines of the system. Thus those who work within the system can expect to receive benefits, while those who challenge the system can expect sanctions. Some researchers—like Blumberg, Casper, and Sudnow—believe this cooperation is too extensive, and that as a result defense attorneys sometimes sacrifice the best interests of their clients.[6]

Undergirding this administrative system is discretion. The textbook image of justice is one of mechanical jurisprudence apparently devoid of human hands or minds; a closer examination shows that each of the participants possesses ample discretion—the police in arresting, the prose-cutor in charging and plea bargaining, the judge in sentencing. Several studies have suggested that, in the aggregate, the exercise of discretion by officials of the criminal justice system is shaped by the values of the larger community.[7]

The National Advisory Commission

The recent report of the Courts Task Force of the National Advisory Commission on Criminal Justice Standards and Goals is significant in that, for the first time, an official body has recognized the administrative nature of the criminal justice process and the role played by discretion.[8] Its picture of the reality of the system coincides with that of most social scientists. Its recommendations, however, seem to be based on a fundamental misunderstanding of the literature of social organization.

The task force wants to try to regularize and formalize administrative justice. The report notes the usefulness of the informal administrative processes that affect the flow of most criminal cases, but suggests that they become regularized by way of formal standards; the assumption that the adverse effects of discretion can thus be minimized runs throughout. Going beyond these concerns, the task force recommends the elimination of plea bargaining by 1978. Although these standards are not only challenging and useful in that they prompt a rethinking of the entire criminal court process, we believe that the recommendations neglect two important aspects of organizations. First, the emphasis on efficiency, speed, and economy overlooks the organizational needs of the criminal justice system. As the literature of social organization documents, bureaucracies expend resources to maintain the organization, to ensure cooperative social relations, and to continue stability—needs that are inconsistent with efficiency, speed, and economy. Second, a primary goal of the report is to reduce conflict among participants in the criminal justice process; given the very different perspectives on criminal justice held by the police, prosecutor, defense attorney, judge, and probation personnel, it seems unlikely they will approach a consensus. Nor would lessened tension necessarily be a good in and of itself, for in practice it acts as a check on the participants.[9]

Efficiency

The goals of the National Advisory Commission are very similar to those of court reformers in general: increase speed and efficiency, upgrade prosecution and defense, and ensure a high-quality judiciary.[10] The first is given particular stress. Critics have said that the huge caseload brings delay, which infringes on the defendant's right to a speedy trial. Delay is measured both by the age of the case and by the amount of courtroom time devoted to its resolution. Levin found that the median age of the cases in the five criminal courts that he analyzed ranged from 14 to 160 days.[11] Courtroom time may be several minutes (when a guilty plea is offered), several weeks (when a jury trial is required), or anything in between. Given the poverty of most defendants in American criminal courts and the preponderant use of money bail, the time spent waiting for one's case to be called is usually time spent in jail.

Citing these conditions, many policy recommendations have been based on the assumption that additional courtrooms, judges, and prosecutors would bring about a return to a system more in keeping with the values of the Due Process Model. Often it is argued that what may have been suitable in a simpler yesterday cannot cope with the "law explosion" of today—the tendency of modern society to use the criminal law for an increasing variety of purposes. As Chief Justice Burger has said, "In the supermarket age we are trying to operate the courts with cracker-barrel corner grocer methods and equipment—vintage 1900." [12] Besides the focus on bigger facilities and better personnel, it has been proposed to bring the tools of management to court administration; the Law Enforcement Assistance Administration has funded a number of training projects toward that end.

Improved management of the court's docket extends to attempts to reduce, through screening and diversion, the number of cases brought to it. The Commission recommends greater prosecutorial screening of police arrests, thus eliminating from the system legally weak cases and allowing more resources to be concentrated on those that are legally sound. In nonserious cases where the guilt of the defendant is not disputed, the Commission advocates diversion programs under which prosecution is held in abeyance until the defendant successfully completes a rehabilitation program or makes restitution, and then charges are dropped. The Commission largely avoids a discussion of more controversial ways to lower court volume, such as the decriminalization of vice crimes. Efforts to lighten the court's caseload are of major policy interest because they can result in a significant alteration of who gets what from the criminal justice process. In particular, diversion will probably aid the middle-class defendant more than the truly poor.

Fairness

The Commission's concern with making the courts more efficient, however, relegates other concerns to lesser status. Thus the fairness of the system and protection of the defendant's rights are not stressed. For example, while disparities based on economic status, race, or geography are treated, they are treated somewhat tangentially.

The Warren Court produced a major increase in the rights of defendants at trial, a trend roundly criticized by some as the coddling of criminals. But these procedural rights have not necessarily altered the basic cutting edges of the system. Economic and racial discrimination are still principal areas of concern. The clientele of the criminal courts is largely people in poverty or near poverty. Further, court procedures like bail and counsel require money. A basic reform is "Release on Recognizance" (ROR), where defendants are released without posting cash bail on their promise to show up in court when required. Many communities are reluctant to use ROR because of the political risks involved. Not only do judges seek to avoid the stigma of permitting a "known burglar" to be on the street before trial, but there is also the possibility that the released suspect will be re-arrested for another offense in the interim.[13]

Counsel for indigents is provided either through a public-defender program, where an attorney represents all indigents on a regular basis in return for a salary, or the assigned-counsel system, where a judge appoints an attorney on an ad hoc basis to represent an individual client and he may or may not be compensated. A current policy question centers on which is the more adequate method.[14]

Closely intertwined with the issue of economics in justice is race. Because blacks tend to be poorer than whites, it is often hard to determine whether blacks receive fewer of the "goods" of the system because of poverty or because of race.[15]

Sentencing

Nowhere has the dominance of the idealized version of criminal justice directed attention away from the realities of the system more than in sentencing. While most of us identify the courts with the determination of guilt or innocence, that is less compelling in the majority of cases than the issue of what should be done with the guilty. While more study is needed of the criteria used in sentencing, research does indicate several important features. First, in some jurisdictions the effective decision on sentencing is made not by the judge but by the prosecutor during negotiations with the defense. Second, variations in sentencing are widespread. For example, sentences for the same type of defendant in the same type of case often differ from judge to judge in the same jurisdiction.[16] Further, sentences appear to vary by jurisdiction: the South is more harsh than the North, rural justice more stern than urban. The National Advisory Commission finds sentencing disparities a major problem and proposes sentencing agencies to provide more uniformity, as well as appellate court review of sentences (normally appellate courts scrutinize the conduct of the trial, not the propriety of the sentence).

A major policy question involves creating additional sentencing choices. At present the judge has basically two options: placing a person on probation or sending him to prison. Both alternatives fall short of satisfaction: probation officers burdened with large caseloads can supervise only minimally; prisons have few treatment facilities and there are no proved theories of rehabilitation (see Chapter 14 of this volume). One suggested additional option is work release, which operates between probation and prison. The guilty person is detained at night, but during the day works at a job in the community. Attention is also given to greater coordination between the criminal courts and helping agencies (mental health units, for example), in an attempt to provide treatment rather than to incarcerate.

Conclusion

Within a few short years the criminal justice system has gone from being almost totally neglected to being one of the principal claimants for resources. Concern over rising crime has forced a fundamental reexamination of the system. Further, it appears that the changes instituted now will structure the process for a long time. But the focus on reducing crime also produces a major tension within the criminal justice system. More and better facilities efficiently run, with greater options for sentencing and increased fairness, may not reduce crime. This ambivalence is reflected in the National Advisory Commission. Although its major volume, *A National Strategy to Reduce Crime,* speaks of reforming and upgrading the courts to reduce crime, the theme is not sounded in the volume on courts. Moreover, many people question whether the criminal courts do have a significant effect in reducing crime. It can be argued that the main role of the courts is to process those accused of crime, and that courts have at best a limited role in suppressing crime itself. Thus the reforms suggested may only be some things that should be done so that we can more closely approximate the ideals of the system.

Notes

1. Roscoe Pound, "The Causes of Popular Dissatisfaction with the Administration of Justice," *American Bar Association Report* 29 (1906): 395.

2. President's Commission on Law Enforcement and Administration

of Justice, *The Challenge of Crime in a Free Society* (Washington, D.C.: U.S. Government Printing Office, 1967), p. 128.

3. Herbert L. Packer, "Two Models of the Criminal Process," *University of Pennsylvania Law Review* 113 (November 1964): 1-60; Also found in Herbert L. Packer, *The Limits of the Criminal Sanction* (Stanford, Calif.: Stanford University Press, 1968). These two models are placed in an organizational context in Malcolm M. Feeley, "Two Models of the Criminal Justice System: An Organizational Perspective," *Law and Society Review* 7 (Spring 1973): 407.

4. David Neubauer, *Criminal Justice in Middle America* (Morristown, N.J.: General Learning Press, 1974); George Cole, *Politics and the Administration of Justice* (Beverly Hills, Calif.: Sage Publications, 1973).

5. See Herbert Jacob, *Urban Justice* (Boston: Little, Brown, 1973), Ch. 5; Maureen Mileski, "Courtroom Encounters: An Observation Study of a Lower Criminal Court," *Law and Society Review* 5 (May 1971): 473-538. For a journalist's description of a criminal court, see Richard Harris, "Annals of Law," *New Yorker,* April 14, 1973, p. 21.

6. Abraham Blumberg, *Criminal Justice* (Chicago: Quadrangle, 1967); Jonathan Casper, *American Criminal Justice* (Englewood Cliffs, N.J.: Prentice-Hall, 1972); and David Sudnow, "Normal Crimes: Sociological Features of the Penal Code in a Public Defender Office," *Social Problems* 12 (1965): 254-276.

7. James Klonoski and Robert Mendelsohn, eds., *The Politics of Local Justice* (Boston: Little, Brown, 1970).

8. National Advisory Commission on Criminal Justice Standards and Goals, *Report of the Task Force on Courts* (Washington, D.C.: U.S. Government Printing Office, 1973).

9. Robert Reich, "Operations Research and Criminal Justice," *Journal of Public Law* 22 (1973): 362.

10. National Advisory Commission on Criminal Justice Standards and Goals, *A National Strategy to Reduce Crime* (Washington, D.C.: U.S. Government Printing Office, 1973), p. 142.

11. Martin A. Levin, "Delay and Related Policy Topics in Five Criminal Courts," paper delivered at the 1973 Annual Meeting of the American Political Science Association, New Orleans, La. See also Laura Banfield and C. David Anderson, "Continuances in the Cook County Criminal Courts," *University of Chicago Law Review* 35 (1968): 259-316; and Dallin H. Oaks and Warren Lehman, *A Criminal Justice System and the Indigent* (Chicago: University of Chicago Press, 1968).

12. Warren E. Burger, "State of the Federal Judiciary," in George F. Cole, ed., *Criminal Justice: Law and Politics* (North Scituate, Mass.: Duxbury Press, 1972), p. 371.

13. Paul B. Wice and Peter Suwak, "Current Realities of Public De-

fender Programs: A National Survey and Analysis," *Criminal Law Bulletin* 10 (March 1974): 161.

14. Lee Silverstein, *Defense of the Poor* (Chicago: American Bar Foundation, 1965).

15. Charles Reasons and Jack Kuykendall, eds., *Race, Crime and Justice* (Pacific Palisades, Calif.: Goodyear, 1972).

16. Marvin E. Frankel, *Criminal Sentences* (New York: Hill and Wang, 1972). See also Martin A. Levin, "Urban Politics and Policy Outcomes: The Criminal Courts," in Cole, *Criminal Justice,* p. 330.

13

"For the Salvation of Children": The Search for Juvenile Justice in the United States
Jameson W. Doig

New public policies and programs are frequently created to benefit our "less fortunate" citizens. Laws are enacted, institutions created, and new classes of professional expertise are required. Additional structures of power are woven about the client, but whether these operate more to help than hinder the supposed beneficiary is a matter for careful empirical study, not deductive legal reasoning.

This essay is concerned with one of these clusters of laws and institutions, those created "for the salvation of children" who are deemed uncontrollable or who commit criminal acts.[1] Commonly designated as the field of juvenile justice, this area includes governmental action directed toward young people (usually under 18 years of age), when such action is legitimated by a juvenile's alleged violation of a legal code. Thus a number of interesting areas involving control over (and power of) juveniles are excluded, for example, most direct interactions between parents and their children and between children and school authorities, as well as state actions involving "abused" and "neglected" children.[2]

What is included is a vast array of agencies and ideologies, idealistic hopes, recurring fears, and unhappy results (for the client and his "benefactors")—interesting social processes in themselves, and illustrative too of general themes regarding the causes, character, and impact of extensive government intervention in the lives of citizens. The underlying themes of the American experience with juvenile justice are similar to those in the fields of mental illness, drug abuse, and welfare, and in other governmental efforts to reshape individual values and cultures in this country and abroad.[3]

The main purpose of this essay is to identify the primary participants and values in the juvenile justice system today, and to indicate major current policy issues and areas of possible research interest. The comments on research needs are directed mainly toward those interested in political

Thanks are extended to Robert A. Scott and Greg A. Caldeira for their helpful comments, and to The Daniel and Florence Guggenheim Foundation for a grant (to the Woodrow Wilson School, Princeton University) which supported preparation of this paper.

139

science and sociological perspectives, whether as professional researcher, student, or concerned citizen.

In this field as in others, however, an understanding of how policies and agencies were created and evolved is of real assistance in appreciating where we are and where we might go from here. Thus we begin historically and then turn to the contemporary scene.

Divergent Views of History

During the nineteenth and early twentieth centuries, a system of special courts, probation officers, juvenile-aid units in police departments, and juvenile "homes" was created to identify and treat delinquent youths. The reach of these institutions extended well beyond the range of governmental power over adults accused of crime, involving the adoption of laws that applied only to juveniles (for example, truancy and incorrigibility statutes) and judicial acceptance of a lower standard of proof to justify coercive control over errant youths. The motivations for creating and expanding this juvenile justice system have been interpreted in two different ways: first, as shaped by reformers who sought to help young people develop into emotionally and intellectually competent, productive adults; or, second, as generated by the demands of business and political leaders and others, whose concerns were varied, but with little attention to providing a positive outcome for young people themselves.

Those who adopt the first perspective interpret the evolution of the system as follows. First, a system of free public education was created in the early and mid-nineteenth century to ensure education for the lower classes. Attendance was made compulsory (with laws against truancy) in order to safeguard the child's future interests (in being an educated adult) against the immediate pressures of his or her parents (to have the child work instead) and against any shortsighted tendency of the child to remain idle.

Young people who violated truancy laws and other statutes were not to be treated in the harsh, punishment-oriented criminal system. Instead, the reformers succeeded in persuading counties and states to create specialized institutions, whose staff members would be trained to respond to the special problems of juveniles, and whose goal would be rehabilitation, not punishment. Thus, in the early nineteenth century, some states ended the practice of placing juveniles in jails with adult criminals and created special Boys' Homes and Houses of Refuge for errant youths.

The greatest success of the reformers was the creation of the juvenile courts, the first being established in 1899 in Cook County, Illinois. Initially, jurisdiction of the judicial system was limited to violations of specific laws, most of which applied to adults as well as children. But some argued that the juvenile court, and other agencies of social improvement, needed broader scope. If police, schools, and parents could identify juveniles who were "in trouble"—or headed for trouble—then the juvenile justice system must be able to reach out and help them. Persuaded by this argument, most states then added laws which permitted juveniles to be apprehended and treated for a wide variety of activities, including incorrigibility, immorality, knowingly associating with vicious or immoral persons, and deportment endangering the morals, health, or general welfare of the child. Of necessity, wide discretion was given to police, judges, and other officials in deciding who should be identified and treated under these statutes. Thus the reformers hoped to rehabilitate juveniles before their misbehavior reached a serious level, and, more important, to provide the assistance needed by children so that they would grow up to be healthy, productive adults.[4,a]

The second perspective emphasizes the "control and resocialize" face of the juvenile justice system. Recent research suggests that five motives were especially important in the creation and evolving powers of the juvenile courts, boys' and girls' homes, and juvenile probation officers, and in the passage of laws to expand their domain:

1. An interest (on the part of police and other community officials) in removing idle youths from the street, where they might cause trouble or commit crimes.
2. A desire (especially among upper-class leaders) for ways to remove the child from the home (particularly immigrant homes), in order to educate and socialize the young to accept "American" values.[b]

[a] The Supreme Court of Idaho caught this spirit in an early comment on the state's juvenile court: "Its object is to confer a benefit both upon the child and the community in the way of surrounding the child with better and more elevating influences, and of educating and training him in the direction of good citizenship and thereby saving him to society and adding a good and useful citizen to the community." (Ex-parte Sharpe, 15 Idaho 120, 1908). Some reform leaders emphasized that high standards of selection would be required if the new system were to function effectively. For example, Julian Mack argued that an individual chosen as juvenile judge must be not only a trained lawyer but a "student of and deeply interested in the problems of philanthropy and child life, as well as a lover of children . . . [and] patient enough to search out the underlying causes of the trouble and to formulate the plan by which . . . the cure may be effected." See Julian W. Mack, "The Juvenile Court," Harvard Law Review 23 (1909): 104; reprinted in Frederic L. Faust and Paul J. Brantingham, eds., Juvenile Justice Philosophy (St. Paul, Minn.: West, 1974), p. 165. The Idaho court opinion is quoted by Mack on p. 157 of Juvenile Justice Philosophy. This book of readings includes a number of important essays as well as the major court cases through 1971.

[b] Note the comment of Justice Isaac Redfield of Illinois, an early critic of the juvenile statutes: "We do not indeed suppose that the persons mainly instrumental in setting up these things in the country really intend them for their children, or indeed

3. A demand (by businessmen) that young people be taught the discipline and minimal skills necessary to permit the expanding factory system to absorb them and operate efficiently.
4. A need (on the part of some women in the "child-saving" movement) to find acceptable social and professional roles in an industrializing, urbanizing society.
5. Perhaps least important, a concern that young people be given the tools and education needed to earn a living within the existing economic and social structure.[5]

Undoubtedly the creation and evolution of the system of juvenile justice were shaped by both groups: by reformers who were concerned primarily with "helping the young" and by those who saw a need to "control and resocialize" deviant juveniles. In time, a third factor, the natural inclination of agencies to expand their power and their staff, was added to the more external pressures. Throughout these years, however, the clients of the system, unorganized and unenfranchised, contributed little to shaping the goals of government power, except as their misbehavior or docility led the agencies of government marginally to expand or contract resources devoted to monitoring and control of juvenile activities.

The Legacy

As to the outcome of the efforts to create and perfect a system of justice for juveniles, some results can be stated definitively, others only tentatively. It is clear, first, that a very large, specialized structure of governmental institutions has been established during the past century of "reform": there are now about 3000 juvenile courts, more than 15,000 juvenile probation officers, and several hundred residential institutions for delinquent children in the United States. These agencies, together with police departments (many of which have juvenile-aid units), process about two million juveniles each year, sending about 60,000 young people to male correctional centers, "homes for girls," and other residential (total) institutions.[6]

A second firm conclusion is that the standard of procedural fairness applied in juvenile courts is less than that required by the U.S. Constitu-

---

. . . for the children of Protestant parents, to any large extent. We cannot disguise to ourselves that these things do have an ominous squint toward the children of Roman Catholic parents, and of the multitudes of poor emigrants yearly coming to our shores, most of whom are of that faith." *American Law Register* 19 (1871): 372, 373-375, as quoted in D. R. Rendleman, "Parens Patriae: From Chancery to the Juvenile Court," *South Carolina Law Review* 23 (1971): 205; reprinted in Faust and Brantingham.

tion in adult courts. A series of legal challenges (*In re Gault,* 1967, being the leading case) has forced juvenile courts to give greater attention to the right to confront one's accusers, the right to counsel, and other traditional "adult" rights.[7] However, the right to trial by jury is not available to juveniles.[8] Also, implementation of due-process rights for juveniles has proceeded unevenly, because (1) juvenile court actions are generally of very low public visibility (attendance at juvenile hearings is highly restricted, in part to avoid public identification of youthful offenders); (2) the primary potential initiators of public criticism are the parents, who tend to be legally unsophisticated or who have brought the complaint, and the juvenile's lawyer, who is frequently more oriented toward efficient processing at minimal time-cost than toward procedural rights; (3) statutes relating to "incorrigibility" and other juvenile-status offenses grant wide discretion to judges; and (4) the movement toward due-process rights and an adversary procedure violates deeply held views of many juvenile court judges and other members of the judiciary. Thus, two years after *Gault,* a state appeals court rejected the view that the standard of proof in juvenile cases should be "beyond a reasonable doubt," and argued:

> If the emphasis is on constitutional rights something of the essential freedom of method and choice which the sound juvenile court judge ought to have is lost; . . . the danger is that we may lose the child and his potential for good while giving him his constitutional rights.[9]

Under conditions of low visibility, low levels of in-court opposition, and judicial views of this orientation, procedural standards in most juvenile courts appear to be distinctly below those required in adult courts—although admittedly those standards are not adhered to in practice in adult courts either.[10]

Several areas of possible research are suggested by this review of the juvenile court process. For example, studies are needed of the evolving patterns of judicial perceptions and judicial actions since *Gault.*[11] Equally important would be an analysis of the impact of the judicial process on the juvenile defendant's perception of the fairness and legitimacy of the judicial and broader governmental system.[12]

Finally, it appears that this complex and expensive system has had very little success in achieving its primary public goals—the prevention of delinquency, and the rehabilitation of juveniles in trouble with the law.[c]

---

[c] Even those who defend the system acknowledge great defects. Thus Justice Stewart, dissenting in *Gault* (see note 7), commented that "the performance of these agencies has fallen disappointingly short of the hopes and dreams" of the founders; and Justice Blackmun spoke of "disappointments of grave dimensions" while defending the "juvenile concept" in *McKeiver* (see note 8).

144

Nationally, arrests of juveniles since 1960 have increased at several times the increase in the juvenile population, and recidivism in many jurisdictions runs 60 percent and higher. It is, of course, very difficult to know how these rates might have increased or decreased had the juvenile justice system been constructed differently, but intensive studies suggest that some policies and institutions have had destructive effects. In particular, some residential institutions are characterized by staff neglect and brutality, and some juveniles incarcerated for minor offenses (runaway, loitering) learn from their peers in "boys' homes" how to engage in more remunerative or violent crimes.[13] Consequently, some observers argue that juveniles who are apprehended and processed through the system are more likely to become skilled and/or bitter repeaters, labeled and then self-identified as "criminals," than those who are not apprehended after their first delinquent acts.[14]

Lack of effective treatment in such institutions, as well as staff neglect and abuse, has been the subject of a number of court suits and judicial decrees mandating change.[d] Preliminary information indicates, however, that very little effective change is actually produced by such judicial intervention. Staff opposition within the correctional institutions, lack of adequate judicial instruments to monitor change, and other factors appear to have largely nullified court decrees. One important area of research would be an examination of the process through which judicial decrees are modified within the juvenile correctional system and an exploration of ways to implement mandated changes more effectively.[e] Research in this area, as in other areas of criminal justice, will confront substantial obstacles, however, for officials in this field—burdened by poor working conditions, low salaries, and ungrateful clients—often protect "their fragile domain" from outside inquiry with skill and vigor.[15]

---

[d] For example, a federal judge ordered extensive changes at a Texas state "school for boys" after finding that correctional officers administer "various forms of physical abuse, including slapping, punching, and kicking. One form . . . , referred to as 'racking,' consists of requiring the inmate to stand against the wall with his hands in his pockets while he is struck a number of times by blows from the fists of correctional officers"; inmates have been forbidden to speak "for the duration of their confinement except to answer when spoken to"; and the speaking of Spanish "has been the subject of disciplinary action" although some inmates are Mexican-American and speak little English. See *Morales v. Turman,* 364 F. Supp. 166 (E. D. Tex 1973). See also *Nelson v. Heyne,* 355 F. Supp. 451 (N. D. Ind. 1972), affirmed, 491 F. 2d 352 (7th Cir. 1974); Note, "Constitutional Right to Treatment for Juveniles Adjudicated to Be Delinquent," *American Criminal Law Review* 12 (1974): 209.

[e] A study of the problem of implementing judicial orders, primarily focused on adult prisons, was initiated in early 1975 by the Resource Center on Correctional Law and Legal Services of the American Bar Association.

Current Issues and Prospects

The disappointing results of the massive effort to identify and rehabilitate errant youths have generated a number of important questions beyond those noted above and some explorations of alternative policies. Several of these questions and policy options are set forth below.

1. To what extent is the wide discretion given to juvenile justice agencies likely to lead to systematic bias and abuse? More specifically, to what extent does such discretion lead to racial, class, or sex discrimination in the processing of juveniles? Available research suggests that (if the offense is held constant) police in older cities are more likely to refer juveniles to court than are police in suburbs, juveniles from broken homes are more likely to be sent to residential institutions than are those from "intact" families, and both of these patterns result in disproportionate numbers of blacks, chicanos, Puerto Ricans, and low-income children being labeled by the system as delinquent (again, with the offense held constant). In one national sample survey, for example, more than one-half of juveniles in treatment programs were members of minority groups.[16] However, much more empirical research is needed on the patterns and causes of bias, and on the relative impact of various discretionary actions at police and court levels on future careers in delinquency and crime.[f]

Similarly, the few data we have indicate that police and courts tend to treat female juveniles more severely than males (severity being measured by removal of the juvenile from the home to a total institution, with offense level held constant). This disparity appears to be caused mainly by two factors: (1) the judge's self-image as protector of women: "boys will be boys," but girls who run away or engage in morals offenses need to be protected; and (2) the fact that a high proportion of females are brought into court on the initiative of parents (as a result of sex-related charges) and, when the parents refuse custody, institutionalization is often the only readily available alternative.[17] More research is needed into patterns of judicial action and into the impact on the future behavior of young women who become enmeshed in the system.

2. Another area of major concern, partially overlapping that noted

---

[f] This may be an especially appropriate area for evaluation research through controlled and natural experimentation. See Donald T. Campbell and Julian C. Stanley, *Experimental and Quasi-Experimental Designs for Research* (Chicago: Rand McNally, 1963). As causes of bias, the relative impact of organizational pressures, racial discrimination, economic class, and other structural factors needs to be explored. See Schur (cited in note 12), pp. 131ff.; Quinney (cited in note 5); and John M. Martin, J. P. Fitzpatrick, and R. E. Gould, *The Analysis of Delinquent Behavior: A Structural Approach* (New York: Random House, 1970).

above, is the problem of juvenile-status offenders. Nearly half of all young people processed through the courts are charged with truancy, runaway, and other offenses which apply only to juveniles; this total includes perhaps 40 percent of males who come before the court and about two-thirds of all females in the system. In order to avoid mingling these juveniles with those who have committed more serious offenses, 35 states have established a separate category known as persons or juveniles "in need of supervision" (PINS or JINS).[g] Experience with such designations has been mixed: in some states, judges and legislatures have permitted PINS and other delinquents to be placed in the same institutions, because funds for other facilities have not been provided; and some judges have used the commission of a second or third juvenile-status offense as justification for transferring a juvenile out of the PINS category (violation of a court order being the legal rationale).[18] In 1974, New Jersey enacted a JINS law, and state officials are now attempting to construct a system which will avoid the problems found in other states. Reeducation of judges, revitalization of a lethargic youth-services bureaucracy (which places juveniles in foster homes and other facilities), and construction of an effective monitoring and feedback system are all required.

Research into the dynamics of policy innovation (and the "decay" of innovation during implementation) in this area should be of interest to social scientists concerned with the field of juvenile justice, and to those interested in policy innovation and the diffusion of innovation more generally.[19] Policy-makers would also benefit from careful studies of the unanticipated consequences of efforts in New York, Illinois, New Jersey, and other states to restructure traditional patterns of judicial and administrative behavior toward juvenile-status offenders, and from systematic analysis to determine the lessons of such efforts for more effective action in the future.[h]

3. We noted earlier that weaknesses in procedural fairness continue to characterize the juvenile justice system. These problems are especially evident when detention is involved—that is, when officials decide to hold a child in secure custody prior to a court hearing on the alleged offense, rather than permit him or her to remain at home. About 500,000 juveniles

---

[g] With regard to juveniles who commit more serious offenses, the limitations of our knowledge in the areas of deterrence and rehabilitation, and available policy options, are discussed in two chapters, by James Q. Wilson (Chapter 2) and Robert Martinson (Chapter 14), in this volume.

[h] As Robert Scott and Arnold Shore suggest, the social scientist can aid policy-makers "by disclosing complexity where others may see only simplicity; by uncovering irony where others may see only direct cause; by pointing out the latent functions and unanticipated consequences" of current practices ("Sociology and Policy Analysis," 1975, mimeo).

each year are held for days, or in some cases weeks, in detention centers or local jails, and the number appears to have increased significantly during the past decade. In many cities and counties the decision to hold a juvenile is made without clear standards. Moreover, the operation of most detention centers is primarily oriented toward security, with little attention to recreation, education, and other needs of the child. The entire process is carried out at a low level of public visibility and with considerable opportunities for abuse of juvenile rights. When the large number of juveniles consigned to detention, vague standards under which judges detain, and the severe conditions under which the juveniles are held are taken together, detention may be the least satisfactory area of the entire juvenile justice system.[20]

In order to overcome these weaknesses, recent studies urge new legislation and administrative rules which would, among other things, (1) prohibit detention except in certain narrowly defined situations; (2) require that detention decisions be made only by judges and designated court officials, thus precluding police discretion to detain; (3) mandate a prompt hearing for any detained child; and (4) create state agencies to replace local control over detention facilities and programs and to upgrade conditions in those facilities.[21]

Efforts to implement such changes will encounter resistance in most states from police agencies, some court officials, and some detention-facility personnel. Issues of "local control," political patronage in administering and staffing detention centers, and "the need to protect the community from offenders" are likely to shape the public debate and the less visible process through which such proposals are assessed.

At present, we have very little systematic knowledge regarding how detention decisions are actually made, how detention facilities are operated, and what the impact of detention is on the adjudicatory hearing and on the juvenile's future behavior. Studies of the detention process in various localities and of its impact would be valuable, as would analysis of the advantages and limitations of proposed changes.[22] The process through which changes in detention practices are proposed, modified, accepted (or rejected), and implemented in various states is also likely to be a useful area for study by those interested in legislative and bureaucratic decision-making.

4. A concern with the negative impact on juveniles of placing them in total institutions has led to some recent efforts toward "deinstitutionalization" of juveniles—both PINS and those who have committed more serious offenses. The most widely publicized effort has been that of Massachusetts, which closed most of its youth institutions in the early 1970's and has attempted to limit placement to foster homes and small facilities without bars, preferably in the community where the juvenile lives. The processes

and results of the Massachusetts effort have been under close study by the Center for Criminal Justice at the Harvard Law School.[23]

In several states, notably Minnesota and Wisconsin, community-based programs have for some years kept the number of juveniles in total institutions very low. Available evidence indicates that these efforts have been reasonably successful, in terms of recidivism rates and other measures of juvenile behavior, but that high levels of staff leadership and close cooperation with juvenile judges are essential if this approach is to be extended widely, that is, used with "hard-to-reach" juveniles as well as one-time offenders with docile personalities. Otherwise, decarceration at the state level may simply lead to more juveniles being placed in "little prisons" at the local level—a tendency already perceptible in some cities and counties.[24] In those states which are moving toward decarceration of juveniles, analysis of the attitudes and behavior of judges, police, and other officials toward various categories of juvenile offenders is needed. Strategies for creating—and maintaining—effective community programs also warrant close study.[25]

5. Regardless of the success of the decarceration movement, some juveniles will still be committed to residential institutions, and the nature and impact of that confinement should continue to be an important area for study. The courts have recently abandoned their traditional "hands-off" policy toward correctional institutions and have uncovered a wide range of abuses.[26] As noted earlier in this chapter, various forms of harsh treatment, brutality, and insensitivity have been found in juvenile institutions, and efforts are being made to fashion effective remedies. In addition, the courts and administrative officials have begun to recognize inmate rights in a number of areas, such as religious practices, medical care, mail and visitation, and access to the media. In some states, correctional officials have recently encouraged the creation of elected inmate councils and have established grievance mechanisms, in order to provide structured ways for inmates to present individual complaints and their views on broad policy issues to top-level officials.[27]

In the light of these evolving patterns of inmate roles and rights, a number of important questions for study can be suggested: (a) What are the differences between the *formal* changes and the *actual* changes in inmate rights and in the redistribution of power within the institution? For example, a study of grievance mechanisms in 16 juvenile facilities indicates that in some institutions such procedures, though they exist on paper, are largely unknown to the juveniles and unused, while in others the grievance system appears to have led to some identifiable inmate-initiated changes in policy.[28] (b) To what extent do those elected to inmate councils adequately represent the inmate population? [29] (c) What is the impact of these organized mechanisms and other changes on the level of inmate-staff tension and potential inmate violence within the institution? By providing legitimate channels for protest and for resolving problems, do such changes make riots and other kinds of violence less likely? (d) Do such changes have an impact on the inmate's behavior when he or she returns to open society? For example, do they enhance the inmate's feeling of self-worth and "control over his own destiny" and thereby make it more likely that he will be able to function effectively outside the walls?

Viewed more broadly, these changes within correctional institutions can be compared with evolving client rights and roles in other service-delivery systems, such as those of students in schools and universities, patients in hospitals, and clients of welfare and public-housing bureaucracies. The nature of bureaucratic authority and the concept of citizenship in modern society may also be clarified or redefined through comparative studies of this kind.[30]

Conclusion

There is little doubt that the field of juvenile justice will be the object of continued public debate and policy experimentation during the coming decade. As we attempt to make the system fairer and more effective, there are two rather different directions in which policy-makers can proceed.

One direction, already evident in programs established in some states in recent years, is to allocate more funds to community-based facilities, and to reduce the role of the court (in deciding both questions of "guilt" and appropriate treatment) in favor of decisions by youth-services agencies as to *who* receives treatment and *what* treatment is required.[31] Such changes in responsibility—often called "diversion" of juveniles from the full juvenile justice process—offer many advantages, compared with the sombre and often negative impact of judicial action and total institutions. But the new approach, especially if combined with the reformist fervor which marked the efforts of the early 1900's, has potential dangers too: what rights the juveniles have to decline treatment are likely to be a matter of less concern to the service agencies than to courts; increases in the range and depth of bureaucratic intervention in the lives of young people become more likely; and as the amount of money and size of youth agencies' staffs increase, the average quality of staff and program effectiveness will probably decline.

An alternative direction would be to reduce the extent of coercive intervention in the lives of young people. For example, some juvenile-status offenses could be removed from the statute books, thus reducing the range of discretionary powers available to police and the courts. Also, in judging juveniles accused of more serious crimes, juvenile courts might accept more fully the due-process constraints endorsed in *Gault,* rejecting the traditional view that the court should be more concerned with the underlying problems of the juvenile than with the specific offense. Government policy would then focus on providing services which young people could make use of voluntarily (job-training programs, havens for runaways), rather than on compulsory programs for those juveniles who must first be processed through a system which labels them as delinquent or "in need of supervision." The argument for reducing the ease and scope of involuntary government intervention is reinforced by recent evidence that all kinds of intervention to aid offenders seem to be equally unsuccessful.[32]

It appears certain that during the next several years some states will move more strongly in the first of these two directions, and some states and localities will probably move toward the second, while others will try combinations of both.[i] It would not be surprising, perhaps, to see some states experimenting with reform policies along one of these lines and then, failing to reduce recidivism or achieve other measures of success quickly, returning to more restrictive policies and institutions—thus confirming the pessimistic conjecture that children, lacking effective organization and powerful allies, are likely to be the nation's "last oppressed minority."[33] Social scientists may find it useful to monitor and evaluate these evolving patterns, both in order to increase our understanding of the general processes of policy change and the diffusion of innovations, and in order to assist policy-makers in understanding the positive and dysfunctional consequences of various kinds of government intervention in the lives of juveniles.[34]

Notes

1. In the leading case of *Commonwealth v. Fisher,* 213 Pa. 48 (1905), the Supreme Court of Pennsylvania upheld the state's juvenile court act of 1903, concluding that the act was established "not for the punishment of offenders but for the salvation of children."

2. For discussion of child abuse and other areas, see the articles by Brian G. Fraser and J. James McKenna in *American Criminal Law Review* 12 (1974), and several articles in the *Harvard Educational Review*'s special issues on "The Rights of Children" (November 1973, February 1974).

3. See, for example, Nicholas N. Kittrie, *The Right to Be Different*

---

[i] The new federal juvenile justice statute will provide some pressure toward the deinstitutionalization alternative. See note 23.

(Baltimore: Johns Hopkins Press, 1971); David J. Rothman, *Discovery of the Asylum* (Boston: Little, Brown, 1971); and recent studies of the American Indian experience and U.S. policy in Southeast Asia.

4. On the reformist perspective, see Ola Nyquist, *Juvenile Justice* (New York: Macmillan, 1960); Robert Pickett, *House of Refuge* (Syracuse: Syracuse University Press, 1969); and critical discussions in Michael Katz, *The Irony of Early School Reform* (Cambridge, Mass.: Harvard University Press, 1968); Anthony Platt, *The Child Savers* (Chicago: University of Chicago Press, 1969); and Kittrie, Ch. 3.

5. See Platt; Katz; and D. R. Rendleman, "Parens Patriae: From Chancery to the Juvenile Court," *South Carolina Law Review* 23 (1971): 205; reprinted in Frederic L. Faust and Paul J. Brantingham, eds., *Juvenile Justice Philosophy* (St. Paul, Minn.: West, 1974). The development of the juvenile justice system was also closely related to the broad reform efforts of the Progressive Era; see Richard Hofstadter, *The Age of Reform* (New York: Vintage, 1955); and, for a different assessment, Anthony Platt, "The Triumph of Benevolence," in Richard Quinney, ed., *Criminal Justice in America* (Little, Brown, 1974), pp. 364ff.

6. Rosemary Sarri, Robert Vinter, and Rhea Kish, "Juvenile Justice: Failure of a Nation" (National Assessment of Juvenile Corrections, University of Michigan, 1974), p. 15; and see other NAJC reports.

7. See *Kent v. United States,* 383 U.S. 541 (1966); *In re Gault,* 387 U.S. 1 (1967); *In re Winship,* 397 U.S. 358 (1970).

8. *McKeiver v. Pennsylvania,* 403 U.S. 528 (1971).

9. *Samuel W. v. Family Court,* 24 N.Y. 2d 196 (1969); reversed by the U.S. Supreme Court, *In re Winship,* 397 U.S. 358 (1970).

10. See Norman Lefstein, Vaughan Stapleton, and Lee Teitelbaum, "In Search of Juvenile Justice: *Gault* and its Implementation," *Law and Society Review* 3 (1969): 491; also reprinted in Faust and Brantingham. See also Kittrie, Ch. 3. For adult courts, see George F. Cole, ed., *Criminal Justice: Law and Politics* (North Scituate, Mass.: Duxbury Press, 1972); and chapters 11 and 12 of this volume.

11. The roles of other court participants also deserve close study. For two examples, see Richard J. Maiman, "Private Attorneys in Juvenile Court: The Impact of *In re Gault*" (Washington, D.C.: American Political Science Association, 1974); and Elizabeth Laporte, "The Youth Law Center and Reform of the California Juvenile Justice System" (Woodrow Wilson School, Princeton University, 1975).

12. See the discussion by Edwin Schur, *Radical Nonintervention* (Englewood Cliffs, N.J.: Prentice-Hall, 1973), pp. 160ff.

13. See, for example, Birch Bayh, "Juveniles and the Law," *American Criminal Law Review* 12 (1974): 1, and sources cited there; President's

Commission on Law Enforcement and Administration of Justice, *Task Force Report: Corrections* (Washington, D.C.: U.S. Government Printing Office, 1967).

14. National Advisory Commission on Criminal Justice Standards and Goals, *Corrections* (Washington, D.C.: U.S. Government Printing Office, 1973), p. 248; Marvin E. Wolfgang, *Youth and Violence* (Washington, D.C.: U.S. Government Printing Office, 1970), pp. 27ff.

15. Platt, in Quinney, p. 362.

16. Sarri, p. 15.

17. See Carole Upshur, "Delinquency in Girls," in Yitzhak Bakal, ed., *Closing Correctional Institutions* (Lexington, Mass.: Lexington Books D. C. Heath and Company, 1973), pp. 19-30; Gisela Konopka, *The Adolescent Girl in Conflict* (Englewood Cliffs, N.J.: Prentice-Hall, 1966); Suzanne Martin, "Juvenile-Only Offenses" (Woodrow Wilson School, Princeton University, 1974); and Linda Riback, "Juvenile Delinquency Laws: Juvenile Women and the Double Standard of Morality," *UCLA Law Review* 19 (1971): 313.

18. On juvenile-status offenses, see Stuart Stiller and Carol Elder, "PINS—A Concept in Need of Supervision," *American Criminal Law Review* 12 (1974): 33; and "Statement of the Juvenile Rights Division of the Legal Aid Society Concerning Persons in Need of Supervision" (New York City, n.d., ca. 1972), a critique of New York State experience.

19. On the processes and problems of innovation, see, for example, Gerald Zaltman, Robert Duncan, and Jonny Holbek, *Innovation and Organizations* (New York: Wiley, 1973).

20. Daniel J. Freed, Timothy P. Terrell, and J. Lawrence Schultz, "Standards Relating to Reducing Detention," document prepared for the Juvenile Justice Standards Commission (December 1974, draft), p. i, and National Advisory Commission, *Corrections,* pp. 257ff.

21. See National Advisory Commission, *Corrections,* pp. 257-272, 573-575; National Advisory Commission, *Courts,* pp. 296-299; and Freed, Terrell, and Schultz.

22. For a useful study of detention practices, based on field research in one county, see David Beale and Andy Schneider, *Juvenile Justice in New Jersey* (Princeton, N.J.: Center for Analysis of Public Issues, 1973), pp. 27ff.

23. See Bakal; Lloyd Ohlin et al., "Radical Correctional Reform" (Cambridge, Mass.: Center for Criminal Justice, Harvard Law School, 1973); and other Center reports, 1972-1975. Other states which have seen a marked decline during the past five years in the number of institutionalized delinquents include Florida (50 percent reduction), Kentucky (75 percent), and Texas (80 percent). However, the trend in California

and other states has been the reverse: an increase in the number of juveniles in institutions and in the average length of stay. See W. Thomas Jennings, "The California Youth Authority Board" (Youth Law Center, San Francisco, 1974) for comparative data. Florida and California programs are described in *Corrections Magazine* (September 1974). The Juvenile Justice and Delinquency Prevention Act of 1974 includes among its major aims the development of more effective alternatives to institutionalization and a reduction in the use of secure facilities for juveniles. See Senate Report 93-1103 (August 1974).

24. Sarri, p. 4.

25. See Bakal; also Douglas E. Phillips, "The New Crusade: Closing Correctional Institutions for Juvenile Delinquents" (Woodrow Wilson School, Princeton University, 1975), a critique of the decarceration movement.

26. See, for example, *Johnson v. Avery,* 393 U.S. 483 (1969); Sheldon Krantz, *The Law of Corrections and Prisoners' Rights* (St. Paul, Minn.: West, 1973), Chs. 12-20; *Morales v. Turman,* 364 F. Supp. 166 (E. D. Tex 1973); *Nelson v. Heyne,* 355 F. Suppl. 451 (N. D. Ind. 1972), affirmed, 491 F. 2d 352 (7th Cir. 1974); and Note, "Constitutional Right to Treatment for Juveniles Adjudicated to Be Delinquent," *American Criminal Law Review* 12 (1974): 209.

27. See Chapter 15 of this volume; and National Advisory Commission, *Corrections,* Ch. 2 and pp. 362-367. See also Andrew F. Rutherford, "Formal Bargaining in the Prison," *Yale Review of Law and Social Action* 2 (1971): 5; Robert B. Reich, "Bargaining in Correctional Institutions," *Yale Law Journal* 81 (1972): 726; and C. Ronald Huff, "Unionization Behind the Walls," *Criminology* 12 (1974): 175.

28. J. Michael Keating, Jr., et al., *Seen but Not Heard* (Washington, D.C.: Center for Correctional Justice and Institute of Judicial Administration, 1975).

29. See J. E. Baker, "Inmate Self-Government," *Journal of Criminal Law, Criminology and Police Science* 55 (1964): 39; and current study by the Research Program in Criminal Justice, Princeton University.

30. See Rutherford, "Formal Bargaining in the Prison"; J. W. Doig, "Citizens and Serfs: Evolving Patterns of Power in Schools and Prisons" (Woodrow Wilson School, Princeton University, 1975); C. Michael Otten, *University Authority and the Student* (Berkeley: University of California Press, 1970); Robert Rubenstein and Harold D. Lasswell, *The Sharing of Power in a Psychiatric Hospital* (New Haven, Conn.: Yale University Press, 1966); and Philip Selznick, *Law, Society, and Industrial Justice* (New York: Russell Sage Foundation, 1969).

31. For analysis of a system which has substituted lay panels for the

courts in processing a wide range of juvenile offenders, see Sanford J. Fox, "Juvenile Justice Reforms: Innovations in Scotland," *American Criminal Law Review* 12 (1974): 61.

32. See Chapter 14 of this volume; and Schur.

33. Sarri, p. 3.

34. See, for example, the proposed study, "Assessment of Diversion Programs, and Community-Based Alternatives to Incarceration" (Department of Criminal Justice Studies, University of Minnesota, January 1975), to be directed by Andrew Rutherford. A major source of funding for studies of juvenile justice problems and reforms will be the National Institute of Juvenile Justice and Delinquency Prevention, established within the U.S. Department of Justice by the 1974 federal juvenile justice act.

14

What Works? Questions and Answers about Prison Reform
Robert Martinson

In the past several years, American prisons have gone through one of their recurrent periods of strikes, riots, and other disturbances. Simultaneously, and in consequence, the articulate public has entered another one of its sporadic fits of attentiveness to the condition of our prisons and to the perennial questions they pose about the nature of crime and the uses of punishment. The result has been a widespread call for "prison reform," i.e., for "reformed" prisons which will produce "reformed" convicts. Such calls are a familiar feature of American prison history. American prisons, perhaps more than those of any other country, have stood or fallen in public esteem according to their ability to fulfill their promise of rehabilitation.

One of the problems in the constant debate over "prison reform" is that we have been able to draw very little on any systematic empirical knowledge about the success or failure that we have met when we *have* tried to rehabilitate offenders, with various treatments and in various institutional and non-institutional settings. The field of penology has produced a voluminous research literature on this subject, but until recently there has been no comprehensive review of this literature and no attempt to bring its findings to bear, in a useful way, on the general question of "What works?". My purpose in this essay is to sketch an answer to that question.

The Travails of a Study

In 1966, the New York State Governor's Special Committee on Criminal Offenders recognized their need for such an answer. The Committee was organized on the premise that prisons could rehabilitate, that the prisons of New York were not in fact making a serious effort at rehabilitation, and that New York's prisons should be converted from their existing custodial basis to a new rehabilitative one. The problem for the Committee was that there was no available guidance on the question of what had been shown to be the most effective means of rehabilitation. My colleagues and I were hired by the committee to remedy this defect in our knowledge; our job was to undertake a comprehensive survey of what was known about rehabilitation.

In 1968, in order to qualify for federal funds under the Omnibus Crime Control and Safe Streets Act, the state established a planning organization, which acquired from the Governor's Committee the responsibility for our report. But by 1970, when the project was formally completed, the state had changed its mind about the worth and proper use of the information we had gathered. The Governor's Committee had begun by thinking that such information was a necessary basis for any reforms that might be undertaken; the state planning agency ended by viewing the study as a document whose disturbing conclusions posed a serious threat to the programs which, in the meantime, they had determined to carry forward. By the spring of 1972—fully a year after I had re-edited the study for final publication—the state had not only failed to publish it, but had also refused to give me permission to publish it on my own. The document itself would still not be available to me or to the public today had not Joseph Alan Kaplon, an attorney, subpoenaed it from the state for use as evidence in a case before the Bronx Supreme Court.[a]

During the time of my efforts to get the study released, reports of it began to be widely circulated, and it acquired something of an underground reputation. But this article is the first published account, albeit a brief one, of the findings contained in that 1,400-page manuscript.

What we set out to do in this study was fairly simple, though it turned into a massive task. First we undertook a six-month search of the literature for any available reports published in the English language on attempts at rehabilitation that had been made in our corrections systems and those of other countries from 1945 through 1967. We then picked from that literature all those studies whose findings were interpretable— that is, whose design and execution met the conventional standards of social science research. Our criteria were rigorous but hardly esoteric: A study had to be an evaluation of a treatment method, it had to employ an independent measure of the improvement secured by that method, and it had to use some control group, some untreated individuals with whom the treated ones could be compared. We excluded studies only for methodological reasons: They presented insufficient data, they were only preliminary, they presented only a summary of findings and did not allow a reader to evaluate those findings, their results were confounded by extraneous factors, they used unreliable measures, one could not understand their descriptions of the treatment in question, they drew spurious conclusions from their data, their samples were undescribed or too small or provided no true comparability between treated and untreated groups, or they had used inappropriate statistical tests and did not provide enough information

---

[a] Following this case, the state finally did give its permission to have the work published; it will appear in its complete form in a forthcoming book by Praeger.

for the reader to recompute the data. Using these standards, we drew from the total number of studies 231 acceptable ones, which we not only analyzed ourselves but summarized in detail so that a reader of our analysis would be able to compare it with his independent conclusions.

These treatment studies use various measures of offender improvement: recidivism rates (that is, the rates at which offenders return to crime), adjustment to prison life, vocational success, educational achievement, personality and attitude change, and general adjustment to the outside community. We included all of these in our study; but in these pages I will deal only with the effects of rehabilitative treatment on recidivism, the phenomenon which reflects most directly how well our present treatment programs are performing the task of rehabilitation. The use of even this one measure brings with it enough methodological complications to make a clear reporting of the findings most difficult. The groups that are studied, for instance, are exceedingly disparate, so that it is hard to tell whether what "works" for one kind of offender also works for others. In addition, there has been little attempt to replicate studies; therefore one cannot be certain how stable and reliable the various findings are. Just as important, when the various studies use the term "recidivism rate," they may in fact be talking about somewhat different measures of offender behavior—i.e., "failure" measures such as arrest rates or parole violation rates, or "success" measures such as favorable discharge from parole or probation. And not all of these measures correlate very highly with one another. These difficulties will become apparent again and again in the course of this discussion.

With these caveats, it is possible to give a rather bald summary of our findings: *With few and isolated exceptions, the rehabilitative efforts that have been reported so far have had no appreciable effect on recidivism.* Studies that have been done since our survey was completed do not present any major grounds for altering that original conclusion. What follows is an attempt to answer the questions and challenges that might be posed to such an unqualified statement.

Education and Vocational Training

1. *Isn't it true that a correctional facility running a truly rehabilitative program—one that prepares inmates for life on the outside through education and vocational training—will turn out more successful individuals than will a prison which merely leaves its inmates to rot?*

If this *is* true, the fact remains that there is very little empirical evidence to support it. Skill development and education programs are in fact quite common in correctional facilities, and one might begin by examining their effects on young males, those who might be thought most amenable to such efforts. A study by New York State (1964) found that for young males as a whole, the degree of success achieved in the regular prison academic education program, as measured by changes in grade achievement levels, made no significant difference in recidivism rates. The only exception was the relative improvement, compared with the sample as a whole, that greater progress made in the top seven percent of the participating population—those who had high I.Q.'s, had made good records in previous schooling, and who also made good records of academic progress in the institution. And a study by Glaser (1964) found that while it was true that, when one controlled for sentence length, more attendance in regular prison academic programs slightly decreased the subsequent chances of parole violation, this improvement was not large enough to outweigh the associated disadvantage for the "long-attenders": Those who attended prison school the longest also turned out to be those who were in prison the longest. Presumably, those getting the most education were also the worst parole risks in the first place.[b]

Studies of special education programs aimed at vocational or social skill development, as opposed to conventional academic education programs, report similarly discouraging results and reveal additional problems in the field of correctional research. Jacobson (1965) studied a program of "skill re-education" for institutionalized young males, consisting of 10 weeks of daily discussions aimed at developing problem-solving skills. The discussions were led by an adult who was thought capable of serving as a role model for the boys, and they were encouraged to follow the example that he set. Jacobson found that over all, the program produced no improvement in recidivism rates. There was only one special subgroup which provided an exception to this pessimistic finding: If boys in the experimental program decided afterwards to go on to take three or more regular prison courses, they did better upon release than "control" boys who had done the same. (Of course, it also seems likely that experimental boys who did *not* take these extra courses did *worse* than their controls.)

Zivan (1966) also reported negative results from a much more ambitious vocational training program at the Children's Village in Dobbs Ferry, New York. Boys in his special program were prepared for their return to the community in a wide variety of ways. First of all, they were given, in sequence, three types of vocational guidance: "assessment counseling," "development counseling," and preplacement counseling." In addition, they participated in an "occupational orientation," consisting of role-

[b] The net result was that those who received less prison education—because their sentences were shorter or because they were probably better risks—ended up having better parole chances than those who received more prison education.

playing, presentations via audio-visual aids, field trips, and talks by practitioners in various fields of work. Furthermore, the boys were prepared for work by participating in the Auxiliary Maintenance Corps, which performed various chores in the institution; a boy might be promoted from the Corps to the Work Activity Program, which "hired" him, for a small fee, to perform various artisans' tasks. And finally, after release from Children's Village, a boy in the special program received supportive after-care and job placement aid.

None of this made any difference in recidivism rates. Nevertheless, one must add that it is impossible to tell whether this failure lay in the program itself or in the conditions under which it was administered. For one thing, the education department of the institution itself was hostile to the program; they believed instead in the efficacy of academic education. This staff therefore tended to place in the pool from which experimental subjects were randomly selected mainly "multi-problem" boys. This by itself would not have invalidated the experiment as a test of vocational training for this particular type of youth, but staff hostility did not end there; it exerted subtle pressures of disapproval throughout the life of the program. Moreover, the program's "after-care" phase also ran into difficulties; boys who were sent back to school before getting a job often received advice that conflicted with the program's counseling, and boys actually looking for jobs met with the frustrating fact that the program's personnel, despite concerted efforts, simply could not get businesses to hire the boys.

We do not know whether these constraints, so often found in penal institutions, were responsible for the program's failure; it might have failed anyway. All one can say is that this research failed to show the effectiveness of special vocational training for young males.

The only clearly positive report in this area comes from a study by Sullivan (1967) of a program that combined academic education with special training in the use of IBM equipment. Recidivism rates after one year were only 48 percent for experimentals, as compared with 66 percent for controls. But when one examines the data, it appears that this difference emerged only between the controls and those who had successfully *completed* the training. When one compares the control group with all those who had been *enrolled* in the program, the difference disappears. Moreover, during this study the random assignment procedure between experimental and control groups seems to have broken down, so that towards the end, better risks had a greater chance of being assigned to the special program.

In sum, many of these studies of young males are extremely hard to interpret because of flaws in research design. But it can safely be said that they provide us with no clear evidence that education or skill development programs have been successful.

Training Adult Inmates

When one turns to adult male inmates, as opposed to young ones, the results are even more discouraging. There have been six studies of this type; three of them report that their programs, which ranged from academic to prison work experience, produced no significant differences in recidivism rates, and one—by Glaser (1964)—is almost impossible to interpret because of the risk differentials of the prisoners participating in the various programs.

Two studies—by Schnur (1948) and by Saden (1962)—*do* report a positive difference from skill development programs. In one of them, the Saden study, it is questionable whether the experimental and control groups were truly comparable. But what is more interesting is that both these "positive" studies dealt with inmates incarcerated prior to or during World War II. Perhaps the rise in our educational standards as a whole since then has lessened the differences that prison education or training can make. The only other interesting possibility emerges from a study by Gearhart (1967). His study was one of those that reported vocational education to be non-significant in affecting recidivism rates. He did note, however, that when a trainee succeeded in finding a job related to his area of training, he had a slightly higher chance of becoming a successful parolee. It is possible, then, that skill development programs fail because what they teach bears so little relationship to an offender's subsequent life outside the prison.

One other study of adults, this one with fairly clear implications, has been performed with women rather than men. An experimental group of institutionalized women in Milwaukee was given an extremely comprehensive special education program, accompanied by group counseling. Their training was both academic and practical; it included reading, writing, spelling, business filing, child care, and grooming. Kettering (1965) found that the program made no difference in the women's rates of recidivism.

Two things should be noted about these studies. One is the difficulty of interpreting them as a whole. The disparity in the programs that were tried, in the populations that were affected, and in the institutional settings that surrounded these projects make it hard to be sure that one is observing the same category of treatment in each case. But the second point is that despite this difficulty, one can be reasonably sure that, so far, educational and vocational programs have not worked. We don't know why they have failed. We don't know whether the programs themselves are flawed, or whether they are incapable of overcoming the effects of prison life in general. The difficulty may be that they lack applicability to the world the inmate will face outside of prison. Or perhaps the type of educational and skill improvement they produce simply doesn't have very much to do with an individual's propensity to commit a crime. What we do know is that, to date, education and skill development have not reduced recidivism by rehabilitating criminals.

The Effects of Individual Counseling

2. *But when we speak of a rehabilitative prison, aren't we referring to more than education and skill development alone? Isn't what's needed some way of counseling inmates, or helping them with the deeper problems that have caused their maladjustment?*

This, too, is a reasonable hypothesis; but when one examines the programs of this type that have been tried, it's hard to find any more grounds for enthusiasm than we found with skill development and education. One method that's been tried—though so far, there have been acceptable reports only of its application to young offenders—has been individual psychotherapy. For young males, we found seven such reported studies. One study, by Guttman (1963) at the Nelles School, found such treatment to be ineffective in reducing recidivism rates; another, by Rudoff (1960), found it unrelated to *institutional* violation rates, which were themselves related to parole success. It must be pointed out that Rudoff used only this indirect measure of association, and the study therefore cannot rule out the possibility of a treatment effect. A third, also by Guttman (1963) but at another institution, found that such treatment was actually related to a slightly *higher* parole violation rate; and a study by Adams (1959b and 1961b) also found a lack of improvement in parole revocation and first suspension rates.

There were two studies at variance with this pattern. One by Persons (1967) said that if a boy was judged to be "successfully" treated—as opposed to simply being subjected to the treatment experience—he did tend to do better. And there was one finding both hopeful and cautionary: At the Deuel School (Adams, 1961a), the experimental boys were first divided into two groups, those rated as "amenable" to treatment and those rated "non-amenable." Amenable boys who got the treatment did better than non-treated boys. On the other hand, "non-amenable" boys who were treated actually did *worse* than they would have done if they had received no treatment at all. It must be pointed out that Guttman (1963), dealing with younger boys in his Nelles School study, did not find such an "amenability" effect, either to the detriment of the non-amenables who were treated *or* to the benefit of the amenables who were treated. But the Deuel School study (Adams, 1961a) suggests both that there is something to be hoped for in treating properly selected amenable subjects and that if these subjects are *not* properly selected, one may not only wind up doing no good but may actually produce harm.

There have been two studies of the effects of individual psychotherapy on young incarcerated *female* offenders, and both of them (Adams 1959a, Adams 1961b) report no significant effects from the therapy. But one of the Adams studies (1959a) does contain a suggestive, although not clearly interpretable, finding: If this individual therapy was administered by a psychiatrist or a psychologist, the resulting parole suspension rate was almost two-and-a-half times *higher* than if it was administered by a social worker without this specialized training.

There has also been a much smaller number of studies of two other types of individual therapy: counseling, which is directed towards a prisoner's gaining new insight into his own problems, and casework, which aims at helping a prisoner cope with his more pragmatic immediate needs. These types of therapy both rely heavily on the empathetic relationship that is to be developed between the professional and the client. It was noted above that the Adams study (1961b) of therapy administered to girls, referred to in the discussion of individual psychotherapy, found that social workers seemed better at the job than psychologists or psychiatrists. This difference seems to suggest a favorable outlook for these alternative forms of individual therapy. But other studies of such therapy have produced ambiguous results. Bernsten (1961) reported a Danish experiment that showed that socio-psychological counseling combined with comprehensive welfare measures—job and residence placement, clothing, union and health insurance membership, and financial aid—produced an improvement among some short-term male offenders, though not those in either the highest-risk or the lowest-risk categories. On the other hand, Hood, in Britain (1966), reported generally non-significant results with a program of counseling for young males. (Interestingly enough, this experiment *did* point to a mechanism capable of changing recidivism rates. When boys were released from institutional care and entered the army directly, "poor risk" boys among both experimentals *and* controls did better than expected. "Good risks" did worse.)

So these foreign data are sparse and not in agreement; the American data are just as sparse. The only American study which provides a direct measure of the effects of individual counseling—a study of California's Intensive Treatment Program (California, 1958a), which was "psychodynamically" oriented—found no improvement in recidivism rates.

It was this finding of the failure of the Intensive Treatment Program which contributed to the decision in California to de-emphasize individual counseling in its penal system in favor of group methods. And indeed one might suspect that the preceding reports reveal not the inadequacy of counseling as a whole but only the failure of one *type* of counseling, the individual type. *Group* counseling methods, in which offenders are permitted to aid and compare experiences with one another, might be thought to have a better chance of success. So it is important to ask what results these alternative methods have actually produced.

Group Counseling

Group counseling has indeed been tried in correctional institutions, both with and without a specifically psychotherapeutic orientation. There has been one study of "pragmatic," problem-oriented counseling on *young* institutionalized males, by Seckel (1965). This type of counseling had no significant effect. For adult males, there have been three such studies of the "pragmatic" and "insight" methods. Two (Kassebaum, 1971; Harrison, 1964) report no long-lasting significant effects. (One of these two did report a real but short-term effect that wore off as the program became institutionalized and as offenders were at liberty longer.) The third study of adults, by Shelley (1961), dealt with a "pragmatic" casework program, directed towards the educational and vocational needs of institutionalized young adult males in a Michigan prison camp. The treatment lasted for six months and at the end of that time Shelley found an improvement in attitudes; the possession of "good" attitudes was independently found by Shelley to correlate with parole success. Unfortunately, though, Shelley was not able to measure the *direct* impact of the counseling on recidivism rates. His two separate correlations are suggestive, but they fall short of being able to tell us that it really is the counseling that has a direct effect on recidivism.

With regard to more professional group *psychotherapy*, the reports are also conflicting. We have two studies of group psychotherapy on young males. One, by Persons (1966), says that this treatment did in fact reduce recidivism. The improved recidivism rate stems from the improved performance only of those who were clinically judged to have been "successfully" treated; still, the overall result of the treatment was to improve recidivism rates for the experimental group as a whole. On the other hand, a study by Craft (1964) of young males designated "psychopaths," comparing "self-government" group psychotherapy with "authoritarian" individual counseling, found that the "group therapy" boys afterwards committed *twice* as many new offenses as the individually treated ones. Perhaps some forms of group psychotherapy work for some types of offenders but not others; a reader must draw his own conclusions, on the basis of sparse evidence.

With regard to young females, the results are just as equivocal. Adams, in his study of females (1959a), found that there was no improvement to be gained from treating girls by group rather than individual methods. A study by Taylor of borstal (reformatory) girls in New Zealand (1967) found a similar lack of any great improvement for group therapy as opposed to individual therapy or even to no therapy at all. But the Taylor study does offer one real, positive finding: When the "group therapy" girls *did* commit new offenses, these offenses were less serious than the ones for which they had originally been incarcerated.

There is a third study that does report on overall positive finding as opposed to a partial one. Truax (1966) found that girls subjected to group psychotherapy and then released were likely to spend less time reincarcerated in the future. But what is most interesting about this improvement is the very special and important circumstance under which it occurred. The therapists chosen for this program did not merely have to have the proper analytic training; they were specially chosen for their "empathy" and "non-possessive warmth." In other words, it may well have been the therapists' special personal gifts rather than the fact of treatment itself which produced the favorable result. This possibility will emerge again when we examine the effects of other types of rehabilitative treatment later in this article.

As with the question of skill development, it is hard to summarize these results. The programs administered were various; the groups to which they were administered varied not only by sex but by age as well; there were also variations in the length of time for which the programs were carried on, the frequency of contact during that time, and the period for which the subjects were followed up. Still, one must say that the burden of the evidence is not encouraging. These programs seem to work best when they are new, when their subjects are amenable to treatment in the first place, and when the counselors are not only trained people but "good" people as well. Such findings, which would not be much of a surprise to a student of organization or personality, are hardly encouraging for a policy planner, who must adopt measures that are generally applicable, that are capable of being successfully institutionalized, and that must rely for personnel on something other than the exceptional individual.

Transforming the Institutional Environment

3. *But maybe the reason these counseling programs don't seem to work is not that they are ineffective* per se, *but that the institutional environment* outside *the program is unwholesome enough to undo any good work that the counseling does. Isn't a truly successful rehabilitative institution the one where the inmate's whole environment is directed towards true correction rather than towards custody or punishment?*

This argument has not only been made, it has been embodied in several institutional programs that go by the name of "milieu therapy." They are designed to make every element of the inmate's environment a part of his treatment, to reduce the distinctions between the custodial staff and the treatment staff, to create a supportive, non-authoritarian, and non-regimented atmosphere, and to enlist peer influence in the formation of constructive values. These programs are especially hard to summarize because of their variety; they differ, for example, in how "supportive" or "permissive" they are designed to be, in the extent to which they are combined with other treatment methods such as individual therapy, group counseling, or skill development, and in how completely the program is able to control all the relevant aspects of the institutional environment.

One might well begin with two studies that have been done of institutionalized adults, in regular prisons, who have been subjected to such treatment; this is the category whose results are the most clearly discouraging. One study of such a program, by Robison (1967), found that the therapy did seem to reduce recidivism after one year. After two years, however, this effect disappeared, and the treated convicts did no better than the untreated. Another study by Kassebaum, Ward, and Wilner (1971), dealt with a program which had been able to effect an exceptionally extensive and experimentally rigorous transformation of the institutional environment. This sophisticated study had a follow-up period of 36 months, and it found that the program had no significant effect on parole failure or success rates.

The results of the studies of youth are more equivocal. As for young females, one study by Adams (1966) of such a program found that it had no significant effect on recidivism; another study, by Goldberg and Adams (1964), found that such a program *did* have a positive effect. This effect declined when the program began to deal with girls who were judged beforehand to be worse risks.

As for young males, the studies may conveniently be divided into those dealing with juveniles (under 16) and those dealing with youths. There have been five studies of milieu therapy administered to juveniles. Two of them—by Laulicht (1962) and by Jesness (1965)—report clearly that the program in question either had no significant effect or had a short-term effect that wore off with passing time. Jesness does report that when his experimental juveniles did commit new offenses, the offenses were less serious than those committed by controls. A third study of juveniles, by McCord (1953) at the Wiltwyck School, reports mixed results. Using two measures of performance, a "success" rate and a "failure" rate, McCord found that his experimental group achieved both less failure *and* less success than the controls did. There have been two positive reports on milieu therapy programs for male juveniles; both of them have come out of the Highfields program, the milieu therapy experiment which has become the most famous and widely quoted example of "success" via this method. A group of boys was confined for a relatively short time to the unrestrictive, supportive environment of Highfields; and at a follow-up of six months, Freeman (1956) found that the group did indeed show a lower recidivism rate (as measured by parole revocation) than a similar group spending a longer time in the regular reformatory. McCorkle (1958) also reported positive findings from Highfields. But in fact, the McCorkle data show, this improvement was not so clear: The Highfields boys had lower recidivism rates at 12 and 36 months in the follow-up period, but not at 24 and 60 months. The length of follow-up, these data remind us, may have large implications for a study's conclusions. But more important were other flaws in the Highfields experiment: The populations were not fully comparable (they differed according to risk level and time of admission); different organizations—the probation agency for the Highfield boys, the parole agency for the others—were making the revocation decisions for each group; more of the Highfields boys were discharged early from supervision, and thus removed from any risk of revocation. In short, not even from the celebrated Highfields case may we take clear assurance that milieu therapy works.

In the case of male youths, as opposed to male juveniles, the findings are just as equivocal, and hardly more encouraging. One such study by Empey (1966) in a residential context did not produce significant results. A study by Seckel (1967) described California's Fremont Program, in which institutionalized youths participated in a combination of therapy, work projects, field trips, and community meetings. Seckel found that the youths subjected to this treatment committed *more* violations of law than did their non-treated counterparts. This difference could have occurred by chance; still, there was certainly no evidence of relative improvement. Another study, by Levinson (1962-1964), also found a lack of improvement in recidivism rates—but Levinson noted the encouraging fact that the treated group spent somewhat more time in the community before recidivating, and committed less serious offenses. And a study by the State of California (1967) also shows a partially positive finding. This was a study of the Marshall Program, similar to California's Fremont Program but different in several ways. The Marshall Program was shorter and more tightly organized than its Fremont counterpart. In the Marshall Program, as opposed to the Fremont Program, a youth could be ejected from the group and sent back to regular institutions before the completion of the program. Also, the Marshall Program offered some additional benefits: the teaching of "social survival skills" (i.e., getting and holding a job), group counseling of parents, and an occasional opportunity for boys to visit home. When youthful offenders were released to the Marshall Program, either directly or after spending some time in a regular institution, they did no better than a comparable regularly institutionalized population, though both Marshall youth and youth in regular institutions did better than those who were directly released by the court and given no special treatment.

So the youth in these milieu therapy programs at least do no worse than their counterparts in regular institutions and the special programs may cost less. One may therefore be encouraged—not on grounds of rehabilitation but on grounds of cost-effectiveness.

What about Medical Treatment?

4. *Isn't there anything you can do in an institutional setting that will reduce recidivism, for instance, through strictly medical treatment?*

A number of studies deal with the results of efforts to change the behavior of offenders through drugs and surgery. As for surgery, the one experimental study of a plastic surgery program—by Mandell (1967)—had negative results. For non-addicts who received plastic surgery, Mandell purported to find improvement in performance on parole; but when one reanalyzes his data, it appears that surgery alone did not in fact make a significant difference.

One type of surgery does seem to be highly successful in reducing recidivism. A twenty-year Danish study of sex offenders, by Stuerup (1960), found that while those who had been treated with hormones and therapy continued to commit both sex crimes (29.6 percent of them did so) and non-sex crimes (21.0 percent), those who had been castrated had rates of only 3.5 percent (not, interestingly enough, a rate of zero; where there's a will, apparently there's a way) and 9.2 percent. One hopes that the policy implications of this study will be found to be distinctly limited.

As for drugs, the major report on such a program—involving tranquilization—was made by Adams (1961b). The tranquilizers were administered to male and female institutionalized youths. With boys, there was only a slight improvement in their subsequent behavior; this improvement disappeared within a year. With girls, the tranquilization produced worse results than when the girls were given no treatment at all.

The Effects of Sentencing

5. *Well, at least it may be possible to manipulate certain gross features of the existing, conventional prison system—such as length of sentence and degree of security—in order to affect these recidivism rates. Isn't this the case?*

At this point, it's still impossible to say that this is the case. As for the degree of security in an institution, Glaser's (1964) work reported that, for both youth and adults, a less restrictive "custody grading" in American federal prisons was related to success on parole; but this is hardly surprising, since those assigned to more restrictive custody are likely to be worse risks in the first place. More to the point, an American study by Fox (1950) discovered that for "older youths" who were deemed to be good risks for the future, a minimum security institution produced better results than a maximum security one. On the other hand, the data we have on youths under 16—from a study by McClintock (1961), done in Great Britain—indicate that so-called Borstals, in which boys are totally confined, are more effective than a less restrictive regime of partial physical custody. In short, we know very little about the recidivism effects of various degrees of security in existing institutions; and our problems in finding out will be compounded by the probability that these effects will vary widely according to the particular *type* of offender that we're dealing with.

The same problems of mixed results and lack of comparable populations have plagued attempts to study the effects of sentence length. A number of studies—by Narloch (1959), by Bernsten (1965), and by the State of California (1956)—suggest that those who are released earlier from institutions than their scheduled date, or those who serve short sentences of under three months rather than longer sentences of eight months or more, either do better on parole or at least do no worse.[c] The implication here is quite clear and important: Even if early releases and short sentences produce no improvement in recidivism rates, one could at least maintain the same rates while lowering the cost of maintaining the offender and lessening his own burden of imprisonment. Of course, this implication carries with it its concomitant danger: the danger that though shorter sentences cause no worsening of the recidivism rate, they may increase the total amount of crime in the community by increasing the absolute number of potential recidivists at large.

On the other hand, Glaser's (1964) data show not a consistent linear relationship between the shortness of the sentence and the rate of parole success, but a curvilinear one. Of his subjects, those who served less than a year had a 73 percent success rate, those who served up to two years were only 65 percent successful, and those who served up to three years fell to a rate of 56 percent. But among those who served sentences of *more* than three years, the success rate rose again—to 60 percent. These

---

[c] A similar phenomenon has been measured indirectly by studies that have dealt with the effect of various parole policies on recidivism rates. Where parole decisions have been liberalized so that an offender could be released with only the "reasonable assurance" of a job rather than with a definite job already developed by a parole officer (Stanton, 1963), this liberal release policy has produced no worsening of recidivism rates.

findings should be viewed with some caution since Glaser did not control for the pre-existing degree of risk associated with each of his categories of offenders. But the data do suggest that the relationship between sentence length and recidivism may not be a simple linear one.

More important, the effect of sentence length seems to vary widely according to type of offender. In a British study (1963), for instance, Hammond found that for a group of "hard-core recidivists," shortening the sentence caused no improvement in the recidivism rate. In Denmark, Bernsten (1965) discovered a similar phenomenon: That the beneficial effect of three-month sentences as against eight-month ones disappeared in the case of these "hard-core recidivists." Garrity found another such distinction in his 1956 study. He divided his offenders into three categories: "pro-social," "anti-social," and "manipulative." "Pro-social" offenders he found to have low recidivism rates regardless of the length of their sentence; "anti-social" offenders did better with short sentences; the "manipulative" did better with long ones. Two studies from Britain made yet another division of the offender population, and found yet other variations. One (Great Britain, 1964) found that previous offenders—but not first offenders—did better with *longer* sentences, while the other (Cambridge, 1952) found the *reverse* to be true with juveniles.

To add to the problem of interpretation, these studies deal not only with different types and categorizations of offenders but with different types of institutions as well. No more than in the case of institution type can we say that length of sentence has a clear relationship to recidivism.

Decarcerating the Convict

6. *All of this seems to suggest that there's not much we know how to do to rehabilitate an offender when he's in an institution. Doesn't this lead to the clear possibility that the way to rehabilitate offenders is to deal with them* outside *an institutional setting?*

This is indeed an important possibility, and it is suggested by other pieces of information as well. For instance, Miner (1967) reported on a milieu therapy program in Massachusetts called Outward Bound. It took youths 15½ and over; it was oriented toward the development of skills in the out-of-doors and conducted in a wilderness atmosphere very different from that of most existing institutions. The culmination of the 26-day program was a final 24 hours in which each youth had to survive alone in the wilderness. And Miner found that the program did indeed work in reducing recidivism rates.

But by and large, when one takes the programs that have been administered in institutions and applies them in a non-institutional setting, the results do not grow to encouraging proportions. With casework and individual counseling in the community, for instance, there have been three studies; they dealt with counseling methods from psycho-social and vocational counseling to "operant conditioning," in which an offender was rewarded first simply for coming to counseling sessions and then, gradually, for performing other types of approved acts. Two of them report that the community-counseled offenders did no better than their institutional controls, while the third notes that although community counseling produced fewer arrests per person, it did not ultimately reduce the offender's chance of returning to a reformatory.

The one study of a non-institutional skill development program, by Kovacs (1967), described the New Start Program in Denver, in which offenders participated in vocational training, role playing, programmed instruction, group counseling, college class attendance, and trips to art galleries and museums. After all this, Kovacs found no significant improvement over incarceration.

There have also been studies of milieu therapy programs conducted with youthful male probationers not in actual physical custody. One of them found no significant improvement at all. One, by Empey (1966), did say that after a follow-up of six months, a boy who was judged to have "successfully" completed the milieu program was less likely to recidivate afterwards than was a "successful" regular probationer. Empey's "successes" came out of an extraordinary program in Provo, Utah, which aimed to rehabilitate by subjecting offenders to a non-supportive milieu. The staff of this program operated on the principle that they were *not* to go out of their way to interact and be empathetic with the boys. Indeed, a boy who misbehaved was to be met with "role dispossession": He was to be excluded from meetings of his peer group, and he was not to be given answers to his questions as to why he had been excluded or what his ultimate fate might be. This peer group and its meetings were designed to be the major force for reform at Provo; they were intended to develop, and indeed did develop, strong and controlling norms for the behavior of individual members. For one thing, group members were not to associate with delinquent boys outside the program; for another, individuals were to submit to a group review of all their actions and problems; and they were to be completely honest and open with the group about their attitudes, their states of mind, their personal failings. The group was granted quite a few sanctions with which to enforce these norms: They could practice derision or temporary ostracism, or they could lock up an aberrant member for a weekend, refuse to release him from the program, or send him away to the regular reformatory.

One might be tempted to forgive these methods because of the success that Empey reports, except for one thing. If one judges the program not only by its "successful" boys but by all the boys who were subjected to it —those who succeeded and those who, not surprisingly, failed—the totals show *no* significant improvement in recidivism rates compared with boys on regular probation. Empey did find that both the Provo boys and those on regular probation did better than those in regular reformatories—in contradiction, it may be recalled, to the finding from the residential Marshall Program, in which the direct releases given no special treatment did *worse* than boys in regular institutions.

The third such study of non-residential milieu therapy, by McCravey (1967), found not only that there was no significant improvement, but that the longer a boy participated in the treatment, the *worse* he was likely to do afterwards.

Psychotherapy in Community Settings

There is some indication that individual psychotherapy may "work" in a community setting. Massimo (1963) reported on one such program, using what might be termed a "pragmatic" psychotherapeutic approach, including "insight" therapy and a focus on vocational problems. The program was marked by its small size and by its use of therapists who were personally enthusiastic about the project; Massimo found that there was indeed a decline in recidivism rates. Adamson (1956), on the other hand, found no significant difference produced by another program of individual therapy (though he did note that arrest rates among the experimental boys declined with what he called "intensity of treatment"). And Schwitzgebel (1963, 1964), studying other, different kinds of therapy programs, found that the programs *did* produce improvements in the attitudes of his boys—but, unfortunately, not in their rates of recidivism.

And with *group* therapy administered in the community, we find yet another set of equivocal results. The results from studies of pragmatic group counseling are only mildly optimistic. Adams (1965) did report that a form of group therapy, "guided group interaction," when administered to juvenile gangs, did somewhat reduce the percentage that were to be found in custody six years later. On the other hand, in a study of juveniles, Adams (1964) found that while such a program did reduce the number of contacts that an experimental youth had with police, it made no ultimate difference in the detention rate. And the attitudes of the counseled youth showed no improvement. Finally, when O'Brien (1961) examined a community-based program of group psychotherapy, he found not only that the program produced no improvement in the recidivism rate, but that the experimental boys actually did worse than their controls on a series of psychological tests.

Probation or Parole Versus Prison

But by far the most extensive and important work that has been done on the effect of community-based treatments has been done in the areas of probation and parole. This work sets out to answer the question of whether it makes any difference how you supervise and treat an offender once he has been released from prison or has come under state surveillance in lieu of prison. This is the work that has provided the main basis to date for the claim that we do indeed have the means at our disposal for rehabilitating the offender or at least decarcerating him safely.

One group of these studies has compared the use of probation with other dispositions for offenders; these provide some slight evidence that, at least under some circumstances, probation may make an offender's future chances better than if he had been sent to prison. Or, at least, probation may not worsen those chances.[d] A British study, by Wilkins (1958), reported that when probation was granted more frequently, recidivism rates among probationers did not increase significantly. And another such study by the state of Michigan in 1963 reported that an expansion in the use of probation actually improved recidivism rates—though there are serious problems of comparability in the groups and systems that were studied.

One experiment—by Babst (1965)—compared a group of parolees, drawn from adult male felony offenders in Wisconsin, and excluding murderers and sex criminals, with a similar group that had been put on probation; it found that the probationers committed fewer violations if they had been first offenders, and did no worse if they were recidivists. The problem in interpreting this experiment, though, is that the behavior of those groups was being measured by separate organizations, by probation officers for the probationers, and by parole officers for the parolees; it is not clear that the definition of "violation" was the same in each case, or that other types of uniform standards were being applied. Also, it is not clear what the results would have been if subjects had been released directly to the parole organization without having experienced prison first. Another such study, done in Israel by Shoham (1964), must be interpreted cautiously because his experimental and control groups had slightly different characteristics. But Shoham found that when one compared a suspended sentence plus probation for first offenders with a one-year prison sentence, only first offenders under 20 years of age did better on probation; those from 21 to 45 actually did *worse*. And Shoham's findings also differ from Babst's in another way. Babst had found that parole rather

---

[d] It will be recalled that Empey's report on the Provo program made such a finding.

than prison brought no improvement for recidivists, but Shoham reported that for recidivists with four or more prior offenses, a suspended sentence was actually *better*—though the improvement was much less when the recidivist had committed a crime of violence.

But both the Babst and the Shoham studies, even while they suggest the possible value of suspended sentences, probation, or parole for some offenders (though they contradict each other in telling us *which* offenders), also indicate a pessimistic general conclusion concerning the limits of the effectiveness of treatment programs. For they found that the personal characteristics of offenders—first-offender status, or age, or type of offense—were more important than the form of treatment in determining future recidivism. An offender with a "favorable" prognosis will do better than one without, it seems, no matter how you distribute "good" or "bad," "enlightened" or "regressive" treatments among them.

Quite a large group of studies deals not with probation as compared to other dispositions, but instead with the type of treatment that an offender receives once he is *on* probation or parole. These are the studies that have provided the most encouraging reports on rehabilitative treatment and that have also raised the most serious questions about the nature of the research that has been going on in the corrections field.

Five of these studies have dealt with youthful probationers from 13 to 18 who were assigned to probation officers with small caseloads or provided with other ways of receiving more intensive supervision (Adams, 1966—two reports; Feistman, 1966; Kawaguchi, 1967; Pilnick, 1967). These studies report that, by and large, intensive supervision does work— that the specially treated youngsters do better according to some measure of recidivism. Yet these studies left some important questions unanswered. For instance, was this improved performance a function merely of the number of contacts a youngster had with his probation officer? Did it also depend on the length of time in treatment? Or was it the quality of supervision that was making the difference, rather than the quantity?

Intensive Supervision: The Warren Studies

The widely-reported Warren studies (1966a, 1966b, 1967) in California constitute an extremely ambitious attempt to answer these questions. In this project, a control group of youths, drawn from a pool of candidates ready for first admission to a California Youth Authority institution, was assigned to regular detention, usually for eight to nine months, and then released to regular supervision. The experimental group received considerably more elaborate treatment. They were released directly to probation status and assigned to 12-man caseloads. To decide what special treatment was appropriate within these caseloads, the youths were divided according to their "interpersonal maturity level classification," by use of a scale developed by Grant and Grant. And each level dictated its own special type of therapy. For instance, a youth might be judged to occupy the lowest maturity level; this would be a youth, according to the scale, primarily concerned with "demands that the world take care of him. . . . He behaves impulsively, unaware of anything except the grossest effects of his behavior on others." A youth like this would be placed in a supportive environment such as a foster home; the goals of his therapy would be to meet his dependency needs and help him gain more accurate perceptions about his relationship to others. At the other end of the three-tier classification, a youth might exhibit high maturity. This would be a youth who had internalized "a set of standards by which he judges his and others' behavior. . . . He shows some ability to understand reasons for behavior, some ability to relate to people emotionally and on a long-term basis." These high-maturity youths could come in several varieties—a "neurotic acting out," for instance, a "neurotic anxious," a "situational emotional reactor," or a "cultural identifier." But the appropriate treatment for these youths was individual psychotherapy, or family or group therapy for the purpose of reducing internal conflicts and increasing the youths' awareness of personal and family dynamics.

"Success" in this experiment was defined as favorable discharge by the Youth Authority; "failure" was unfavorable discharge, revocation, or recommitment by a court. Warren reported an encouraging finding: Among all but one of the "subtypes," the experimentals had a significantly lower failure rate than the controls. The experiment did have certain problems: The experimentals might have been performing better because of the enthusiasm of the staff and the attention lavished on them; none of the controls had been *directly* released to their regular supervision programs instead of being detained first; and it was impossible to separate the effects of the experimentals' small caseloads from their specially designed treatments, since no experimental youths had been assigned to a small caseload with "inappropriate" treatment, or with no treatment at all. Still, none of these problems were serious enough to vitiate the encouraging prospect that this finding presented for successful treatment of probationers.

This encouraging finding was, however, accompanied by a rather more disturbing clue. As has been mentioned before, the experimental subjects, when measured, had a lower *failure* rate than the controls. But the experimentals also had a lower *success* rate. That is, fewer of the experimentals as compared with the controls had been judged to have successfully completed their program of supervision and to be suitable for favorable release. When my colleagues and I undertook a rather laborious reanalysis of the Warren data, it became clear why this discrepancy had appeared. It turned out that fewer experimentals were "successful" because the experimentals were actually committing more offenses than their controls. The reason that the experimentals' relatively large number of offenses was not being reflected in their failure rates was simply that the experimentals' probation officers were using a more lenient revocation policy. In other words, the controls had a higher failure rate because the controls were being revoked for less serious offenses.

So it seems that what Warren was reporting in her "failure" rates was not merely the treatment effect of her small caseloads and special programs. Instead, what Warren was finding was not so much a change in the behavior of the experimental youths as a change in the behavior of the experimental *probation officers,* who knew the "special" status of their charges and who had evidently decided to revoke probation status at a lower than normal rate. The experimentals continued to commit offenses; what was different was that when they committed these offenses, they were permitted to remain on probation.

The experimenters claimed that this low revocation policy, and the greater number of offenses committed by the special treatment youth, were *not* an indication that these youth were behaving specially badly and that policy makers were simply letting them get away with it. Instead, it was claimed, the higher reported offense rate was primarily an artifact of the more intense surveillance that the experimental youth received. But the data show that this is not a sufficient explanation of the low failure rate among experimental youth; the difference in "tolerance" of offenses between experimental officials and control officials was much greater than the difference in the rates at which these two systems detected youths committing new offenses. Needless to say, this reinterpretation of the data presents a much bleaker picture of the possibilities of intensive supervision with special treatment.

"Treatment Effects" vs. "Policy Effects"

This same problem of experimenter bias may also be present in the predecessors of the Warren study, the ones which had also found positive results from intensive supervision on probation; indeed, this disturbing question can be raised about many of the previously discussed reports of positive "treatment effects."

This possibility of a "policy effect" rather than a "treatment effect" applies, for instance, to the previously discussed studies of the effects of intensive supervision on juvenile and youthful probationers. These were the studies, it will be recalled, which found lower recidivism rates for the intensively supervised.[e]

One opportunity to make a further check on the effects of this problem is provided, in a slightly different context, by Johnson (1962a). Johnson was measuring the effects of intensive supervision on youthful *parolees* (as distinct from probationers). There have been several such studies of the effects on youths of intensive parole supervision plus special counseling, and their findings are on the whole less encouraging than the probation studies; they are difficult to interpret because of experimental problems, but studies by Boston University in 1966, and by Van Couvering in 1966, report no significant effects and possibly some bad effects from such special programs. But Johnson's studies were unique for the chance they provide to measure both treatment effects and the effect of agency policy.

Johnson, like Warren, assigned experimental subjects to small caseloads and his experiment had the virtue of being performed with two separate populations and at two different times. But in contrast with the Warren case, the Johnson experiment did not engage in a large continuing attempt to choose the experimental counselors specially, to train them specially, and to keep them informed about the progress and importance of the experiment. The first time the experiment was performed, the experimental youths had a slightly lower revocation rate than the controls at six months. But the second time, the experimentals did *not* do better than their controls; indeed, they did slightly worse. And with the experimentals from the first group—those who *had* shown an improvement after six months—this effect wore off at 18 months. In the Johnson study, my colleagues and I found, "intensive" supervision did *not* increase the experimental youths' risk of detection. Instead, what was happening in the Johnson experiment was that the first time it had been performed—just as in the Warren study—the experimentals were simply revoked less often per number of offenses committed, and they were revoked for offenses more serious than those which prompted revocation among the controls. The second time around, this "policy" discrepancy disappeared; and when it did, the "improved" performance of the experimentals disappeared as well. The enthusiasm guiding the project had simply worn off in the absence of reinforcement.

One must conclude that the "benefits" of intensive supervision for youthful offenders may stem not so much from a "treatment" effect as from a "policy" effect—that such supervision, so far as we now know, results not in rehabilitation but in a decision to look the other way when an offense is committed. But there is one major modification to be added

---

[e] But one of these reports, by Kawaguchi (1967), also found that an intensively supervised juvenile, by the time he finally "failed," had had more previous detentions while under supervision than a control juvenile had experienced.

to this conclusion. Johnson performed a further measurement (1962b) in his parole experiment: He rated all the supervising agents according to the "adequacy" of the supervision they gave. And he found that an "adequate" agent, whether he was working in a small *or* a large caseload, produced a relative improvement in his charges. The converse was not true: An *in*adequate agent was more likely to produce youthful "failures" when he was given a *small* caseload to supervise. One can't much help a "good" agent, it seems, by reducing his caseload size; such reduction can only do further harm to those youths who fall into the hands of "bad" agents.

So with youthful offenders, Johnson found, intensive supervision does not seem to provide the rehabilitative benefits claimed for it; the only such benefits may flow not from intensive supervision itself but from contact with one of the "good people" who are frequently in such short supply.

Intensive Supervision of Adults

The results are similarly ambiguous when one applies this intensive supervision to adult offenders. There have been several studies of the effects of intensive supervision on adult parolees. Some of these are hard to interpret because of problems of comparability between experimental and control groups (general risk ratings, for instance, or distribution of narcotics offenders, or policy changes that took place between various phases of the experiments), but two of them (California, 1966; Stanton, 1964) do not seem to give evidence of the benefits of intensive supervision. By far the most extensive work, though, on the effects of intensive supervision of adult parolees has been a series of studies of California's Special Intensive Parole Unit (SIPU), a 10-year-long experiment designed to test the treatment possibilities of various special parole programs. Three of the four "phases" of this experiment produced "negative results." The first phase tested the effect of a reduced caseload size; no lasting effect was found. The second phase slightly increased the size of the small caseloads and provided for a longer time in treatment; again there was no evidence of a treatment effect. In the fourth phase, caseload sizes and time in treatment were again varied, and treatments were simultaneously varied in a sophisticated way according to personality characteristics of the parolees; once again, significant results did not appear.

The only phase of this experiment for which positive results were reported was Phase Three. Here, it was indeed found that a smaller caseload improved one's chances of parole success. There is, however, an important caveat that attaches to this finding: When my colleagues and I divided the whole population of subjects into two groups—those receiving supervision in the North of the state and those in the South—we found that the "improvement" of the experimentals' success rates was taking place primarily in the North. The North differed from the South in one important aspect: Its agents practiced a policy of returning both "experimental" and "control" violators to prison at relatively high rates. And it was the North that produced the higher success rate among its experimentals. So this improvement in experimentals' performance was taking place only when accompanied by a "realistic threat" of severe sanctions. It is interesting to compare this situation with that of the Warren studies. In the Warren studies, experimental subjects were being revoked at a relatively *low* rate. These experimentals "failed" less, but they also committed more new offenses than their controls. By contrast, in the Northern region of the SIPU experiment, there was a policy of *high* rate of return to prison for experimentals; and here, the special program *did* seem to produce a real improvement in the behavior of offenders. What this suggests is that when intensive supervision *does* produce an improvement in offenders' behavior, it does so not through the mechanism of "treatment" or "rehabilitation," but instead through a mechanism that our studies have almost totally ignored—the mechanism of *deterrence*. And a similar mechanism is suggested by Lohman's study (1967) of intensive supervision of probationers. In this study intensive supervision led to higher total violation rates. But one also notes that intensive supervision combined the highest rate of technical violations with the lowest rate for *new* offenses.

The Effects of Community Treatment

In sum, even in the case of treatment programs administered outside penal institutions, we simply cannot say that this treatment in itself has an appreciable effect on offender behavior. On the other hand, there is one encouraging set of findings that emerges from these studies. For from many of them there flows the strong suggestion that even if we can't "treat" offenders so as to make them do better, a great many of the programs designed to rehabilitate them at least did not make them do *worse*. And if these programs did not show the advantages of actually rehabilitating, some of them did have the advantage of being less onerous to the offender himself without seeming to pose increased danger to the community. And some of these programs—especially those involving less restrictive custody, minimal supervision, and early release—simply cost fewer dollars to administer. The information on the dollar costs of these programs is just beginning to be developed but the implication is clear: *that if we can't do more for (and to) offenders, at least we can safely do less.*

There is, however, one important caveat even to this note of optimism: In order to calculate the true costs of these programs, one must in each case include not only their administrative cost but also the cost of maintaining in the community an offender population increased in size. This population might well not be committing new offenses at any greater rate; but the offender population might, under some of these plans, be larger in absolute *numbers*. So the total number of offenses committed might rise, and our chances of victimization might therefore rise too. We need to be able to make a judgment about the size and probable duration of this effect; as of now, we simply do not know.

Does Nothing Work?

7. *Do all of these studies lead us irrevocably to the conclusion that nothing works, that we haven't the faintest clue about how to rehabilitate offenders and reduce recidivism? And if so, what shall we do?*

We tried to exclude from our survey those studies which were so poorly done that they simply could not be interpreted. But despite our efforts, a pattern has run through much of this discussion—of studies which "found" effects without making any truly rigorous attempt to exclude competing hypotheses, of extraneous factors permitted to intrude upon the measurements, of recidivism measures which are not all measuring the same thing, of "follow-up" periods which vary enormously and rarely extend beyond the period of legal supervision, of experiments never replicated, of "system effects" not taken into account, of categories drawn up without any theory to guide the enterprise. It is just possible that some of our treatment programs *are* working to some extent, but that our research is so bad that it is incapable of telling.

Having entered this very serious caveat, I am bound to say that these data, involving over two hundred studies and hundreds of thousands of individuals as they do, are the best available and give us very little reason to hope that we have in fact found a sure way of reducing recidivism through rehabilitation. This is not to say that we found no instances of success or partial success; it is only to say that these instances have been isolated, producing no clear pattern to indicate the efficacy of any particular method of treatment. And neither is this to say that factors *outside* the realm of rehabilitation may not be working to reduce recidivism— factors such as the tendency for recidivism to be lower in offenders over the age of 30; it is only to say that such factors seem to have little connection with any of the treatment methods now at our disposal.

From this probability, one may draw any of several conclusions. It may be simply that our programs aren't yet good enough—that the education we provide to inmates is still poor education, that the therapy we administer is not administered skillfully enough, that our intensive supervision and counseling do not yet provide enough personal support for the offenders who are subjected to them. If one wishes to believe this, then what our correctional system needs is simply a more full-hearted commitment to the strategy of treatment.

It may be, on the other hand, that there is a more radical flaw in our present strategies—that education at its best, or that psychotherapy at its best, cannot overcome, or even appreciably reduce, the powerful tendency for offenders to continue in criminal behavior. Our present treatment programs are based on a theory of crime as a "disease"—that is to say, as something foreign and abnormal in the individual which can presumably be cured. This theory may well be flawed, in that it overlooks—indeed, denies—both the normality of crime in society and the personal normality of a very large proportion of offenders, criminals who are merely responding to the facts and conditions of our society.

This opposing theory of "crime as a social phenomenon" directs our attention away from a "rehabilitative" strategy, away from the notion that we may best insure public safety through a series of "treatments" to be imposed forcibly on convicted offenders. These treatments have on occasion become, and have the potential for becoming, so draconian as to offend the moral order of a democratic society; and the theory of crime as a social phenomenon suggests that such treatments may be not only offensive but ineffective as well. This theory points, instead, to decarceration for low-risk offenders—and, presumably, to keeping high-risk offenders in prisons which are nothing more (and aim to be nothing more) than custodial institutions.

But this approach has its own problems. To begin with, there is the moral dimension of crime and punishment. Many low-risk offenders have committed serious crimes (murder, sometimes) and even if one is reasonably sure they will never commit another crime, it violates our sense of justice that they should experience no significant retribution for their actions. A middle-class banker who kills his adulterous wife in a moment of passion is a "low-risk" criminal; a juvenile delinquent in the ghetto who commits armed robbery has, statistically, a much higher probability of committing another crime. Are we going to put the first on probation and sentence the latter to a long term in prison?

Besides, one cannot ignore the fact that the punishment of offenders is the major means we have for *deterring* incipient offenders. We know almost nothing about the "deterrent effect," largely because "treatment" theories have so dominated our research, and "deterrence" theories have been relegated to the status of a historical curiosity. Since we have almost no idea of the deterrent functions that our present system performs or that future strategies might be made to perform, it is possible that there is indeed something that works—that to some extent is working right now in front of our noses, and that might be made to work better—something that deters rather than cures, something that does not so much reform convicted offenders as prevent criminal behavior in the first place. But whether that is the case and, if it is, what strategies will be found to make our deterrence system work better than it does now, are questions we will not be able to answer with data until a new family of studies has been brought into existence. As we begin to learn the facts, we will be in a better position than we are now to judge to what degree the prison has become an anachronism and can be replaced by more effective means of social control.

Bibliography of Studies Referred to by Name

Adams, Stuart. "Effectiveness of the Youth Authority Special Treatment Program: First Interim Report." Research Report No. 5. California Youth Authority, March 6, 1959. (Mimeographed.)

Adams, Stuart. "Assessment of the Psychiatric Treatment Program: Second Interim Report." Research Report No. 15. California Youth Authority, December 13, 1959. (Mimeographed.)

Adams, Stuart. "Effectiveness of Interview Therapy with Older Youth Authority Wards: An Interim Evaluation of the PICO Project." Research Report No. 20. California Youth Authority, January 20, 1961. (Mimeographed.)

Adams, Stuart. "Assessment of the Psychiatric Treatment Program, Phase I: Third Interim Report." Research Report No. 21. California Youth Authority, January 31, 1961. (Mimeographed.)

Adams, Stuart. "An Experimental Assessment of Group Counseling with Juvenile Probationers." Paper presented at the 18th Convention of the California State Psychological Association, Los Angeles, December 12, 1964. (Mimeographed.)

Adams, Stuart, Rice, Rogert E., and Olive, Borden. "A Cost Analysis of the Effectiveness of the Group Guidance Program." Research Memorandum 65-3. Los Angeles County Probation Department, January 1965. (Mimeographed.)

Adams, Stuart. "Development of a Program Research Service in Probation." Research Report No. 27 (Final Report, NIMH Project MH007 18.) Los Angeles County Probation Department, January 1966. (Processed.)

Adamson, LeMay, and Dunham, H. Warren. "Clinical Treatment of Male Delinquents. A Case Study in Effort and Result," *American Sociological Review,* XXI, 3 (1956), 312-320.

Babst, Dean V., and Mannering, John W. "Probation versus Imprisonment for Similar Types of Offenders: A Comparison by Subsequent Violations," *Journal of Research in Crime and Delinquency,* II, 2 (1965), 60-71.

Bernsten, Karen, and Christiansen, Karl O. "A Resocialization Experiment with Short-term Offenders," *Scandinavian Studies in Criminology,* I (1965), 35-54.

California, Adult Authority, Division of Adult Parolees. "Special Intensive Parole Unit, Phase I: Fifteen Man Caseload Study." Prepared by Walter I. Stone. Sacramento, Calif., November 1956. (Mimeographed.)

California, Department of Corrections. "Intensive Treatment Program: Second Annual Report." Prepared by Harold B. Bradley and Jack D. Williams. Sacramento, Calif., December 1, 1958. (Mimeographed.)

California, Department of Corrections. "Special Intensive Parole Unit, Phase II: Thirty Man Caseload Study." Prepared by Ernest Reimer and Martin Warren. Sacramento, Calif., December 1958. (Mimeographed.)

California, Department of Corrections. "Parole Work Unit Program: An Evaluative Report." A memorandum to the California Joint Legislative Budget Committee, December 30, 1966. (Mimeographed.)

California, Department of the Youth Authority. "James Marshall Treatment Program: Progress Report." January 1967. (Processed.)

Cambridge University, Department of Criminal Science. *Detention in Remard Homes.* London: Macmillan, 1952.

Craft, Michael, Stephenson, Geoffrey, and Granger, Clive. "A Controlled Trial of Authoritarian and Self-Governing Regimes with Adolescent Psychopaths," *American Journal of Orthopsychiatry,* XXXIV, 3 (1964), 543-554.

Empey, LeMar T. "The Provo Experiment: A Brief Review." Los Angeles: Youth Studies Center, University of Southern California. 1966. (Processed.)

Feistman, Eugene G. "Comparative Analysis of the Willow-Brook-Harbor Intensive Services Program, March 1, 1965 through February 28, 1966." Research Report No. 28. Los Angeles County Probation Department, June 1966. (Processed.)

Forman, B. "The Effects of Differential Treatment on Attitudes, Personality Traits, and Behavior of Adult Parolees." Unpublished Ph.D. dissertation, University of Southern California, 1960.

Fox, Vernon. "Michigan's Experiment in Minimum Security Penology," *Journal of Criminal Law, Criminology, and Police Science,* XLI, 2 (1950), 150-166.

Freeman, Howard E., and Weeks, H. Ashley. "Analysis of a Program of Treatment of Delinquent Boys," *American Journal of Sociology,* LXII, 1 (1956), 56-61.

Garrity, Donald Lee. "The Effects of Length of Incarceration upon Parole Adjustment and Estimation of Optimum Sentence: Washington State Correctional Institutions." Unpublished Ph.D. dissertation, University of Washington, 1956.

Gearhart, J. Walter, Keith, Harold L., and Clemmons, Gloria. "An Analysis of the Vocational Training Program in the Washington State Adult Correctional Institutions." Research Review No. 23. State of Washington, Department of Institutions, May 1967. (Processed.)

Glaser, Daniel. *The Effectiveness of a Prison and Parole System.* New York: Bobbs-Merrill, 1964.

Goldberg, Lisbeth, and Adams, Stuart. "An Experimental Evaluation of the Lathrop Hall Program." Los Angeles County Probation Department, December 1964. (Summarized in: Adams, Stuart. "Development of a Program Research Service in Probation," pp. 19-22.)

Great Britain. Home Office. *The Sentence of the Court: A Handbook for Courts on the Treatment of Offenders.* London: Her Majesty's Stationery Office, 1964.

Guttman, Evelyn S. "Effects of Short-Term Psychiatric Treatment on Boys in Two California Youth Authority Institutions." Research Report No. 36. California Youth Authority, December 1963. (Processed.)

Hammond, W. H., and Chayen, E. *Persistent Criminals: A Home Office Research Unit Report.* London: Her Majesty's Stationery Office, 1963.

Harrison, Robert M., and Mueller, Paul F. C. "Clue Hunting About Group Counseling and Parole Outcome." Research Report No. 11. California Department of Corrections, May 1964. (Mimeographed.)

Havel, Joan, and Sulka, Elaine. "Special Intensive Parole Unit: Phase Three." Research Report No. 3. California Department of Corrections, March 1962. (Processed.)

Havel, Joan. "A Synopsis of Research Report No. 10, SIPU Phase IV— The High Base Expectancy Study." Administrative Abstract No. 10. California Department of Corrections, June 1963. (Processed.)

Havel, Joan. "Special Intensive Parole Unit—Phase Four: 'The Parole Outcome Study.'" Research Report No. 13. California Department of Corrections, September 1965. (Processed.)

Hood, Roger. Homeless Borstal Boys: *A Study of Their After-Care and After-Conduct.* Occasional Papers on Social Administration No. 18. London: G. Bell & Sons, 1966.

Jacobson, Frank, and McGee, Eugene. "Englewood Project: Re-education: A Radical Correction of Incarcerated Delinquents." Englewood, Colo.: July 1965. (Mimeographed.)

Jesness, Carl F. "The Fricot Ranch Study: Outcomes with Small versus Large Living Groups in the Rehabilitation of Delinquents." Research Report No. 47. California Youth Authority, October 1, 1965. (Processed.)

Johnson, Bertram. "Parole Performance of the First Year's Releases, Parole Research Project: Evaluation of Reduced Caseloads." Research Report No. 27. California Youth Authority, January 31, 1962. (Mimeographed.)

Johnson, Bertram. "An Analysis of Predictions of Parole Performance and of Judgments of Supervision in the Parole Research Project," Research Report No. 32. California Youth Authority, December 31, 1962. (Mimeographed.)

Kassebaum, Gene, Ward, David, and Wilnet, Daniel. *Prison Treatment and Parole Survival: An Empirical Assessment.* New York: Wiley, 1971.

Kawaguchi, Ray M., and Siff, Leon, M. "An Analysis of Intensive Probation Services—Phase II." Research Report No. 29. Los Angeles County Probation Department, April 1967. (Processed.)

Kettering, Marvin E. "Rehabilitation of Women in the Milwaukee County Jail: An Exploration Experiment." Unpublished Master's Thesis, Colorado State College, 1965.

Kovacs, Frank W. "Evaluation and Final Report of the New Start Demonstration Project." Colorado Department of Employment, October 1967. (Processed.)

Lavlicht, Jerome, et al., in *Berkshire Farms Monographs,* I, 1 (1962), 11-48.

Levinson, Robert B., and Kitchenet, Howard L. "Demonstration Counseling Project." 2 vols. Washington, D.C.: National Training School for Boys, 1962-1964. (Mimeographed.)

Lohman, Joseph D., et al., "The Intensive Supervision Caseloads: A Preliminary Evaluation." The San Francisco Project: A Study of Federal Probation and Parole. Research Report No. 11. School of Criminology, University of California, March 1967. (Processed.)

McClintock, F. H., *Attendance Centres.* London. Macmillan, 1961.

McCord, William and Joan. "Two Approaches to the Cure of Delinquents," *Journal of Criminal Law, Criminology, and Police Science,* XLIV, 4 (1953), 442-467.

McCorkle, Lloyd W., Elias, Albert, and Bixby, F. Lovell. The Highfields Story: *An Experimental Treatment Project for Youthful Offenders.* New York: Holt, 1958.

McCravy, Newton, Jr., and Delehanty, Dolores S. "Community Rehabilitation of the Younger Delinquent Boy, Parkland Non-Residential Group

Center." Final Report, Kentucky Child Welfare Research Foundation, Inc., September 1, 1967. (Mimeographed.)

Mandell, Wallace, *et al.* "Surgical and Social Rehabilitation of Adult Offenders." Final Report. Montefiore Hospital and Medical Center, with Staten Island Mental Health Society. New York City Department of Correction, 1967. (Processed.)

Massimo, Joseph L., and Shore, Milton F. "The Effectiveness of a Comprehensive Vocationally Oriented Psychotherapeutic Program for Adolescent Delinquent Boys," *American Journal of Orthopsychiatry,* XXXIII, 4 (1963), 634-642.

Minet, Joshua, III, Kelly, Francis J., and Hatch, M. Charles. "Outward Bound Inc.: Juvenile Delinquency Demonstration Project, Year End Report." Massachusetts Division of Youth Service, May 31, 1967.

Narloch, R. P., Adams, Stuart, and Jenkins, Kendall J. "Characteristics and Parole Performance of California Youth Authority Early Releases." Research Report No. 7. California Youth Authority, June 22, 1959. (Mimeographed.)

New York State, Division of Parole, Department of Correction. "Parole Adjustment and Prior Educational Achievement of Male Adolescent Offenders, June 1957—June 1961." September 1964. (Mimeographed.)

O'Brien, William J. "Personality Assessment as a Measure of Change Resulting from Group Psychotherapy with Male Juvenile Delinquents." The Institute for the Study of Crime and Delinquency, and the California Youth Authority, December 1961. (Processed.)

Persons, Roy W. "Psychological and Behavioral Change in Delinquents Following Psychotherapy," *Journal of Clinical Psychology,* XXII, 3 (1966), 337-340.

Persons, Roy W. "Relationship Between Psychotherapy with Institutionalized Boys and Subsequent Community Adjustment," *Journal of Consulting Psychology,* XXXI, 2 (1967), 137-141.

Pilnick, Saul, *et al.* "Collegefields: From Delinquency to Freedom." A Report . . . on Collegefields Group Educational Center. Laboratory for Applied Behavioral Science, Newark State College, February 1967. (Processed.)

Robison, James, and Kevotkian, Marinette. "Intensive Treatment Project: Phase II. Parole Outcome: Interim Report." Research Report No. 27. California Department of Corrections, Youth and Adult Correctional Agency, January 1967. (Mimeographed.)

Rudoff, Alvin. "The Effect of Treatment on Incarcerated Young Adult Delinquents as Measured by Disciplinary History." Unpublished Master's thesis, University of Southern California, 1960.

Saden, S. J. "Correctional Research at Jackson Prison," *Journal of Correctional Education,* XV (October 1962), 22-26.

Schnur, Alfred C. "The Educational Treatment of Prisoners and Recidivism," *American Journal of Sociology,* LIV, 2 (1948), 142-147.

Schwitzgebel, Robert and Ralph. "Therapeutic Research: A Procedure for the Reduction of Adolescent Crime." Paper presented at meetings of the American Psychological Association, Philadelphia, Pa., August 1963.

Schwitzgebel, Robert and Kolb, D. A. "Inducing Behavior Change in Adolescent Delinquents," *Behavior Research Therapy,* I (1964), 297-304.

Seckel, Joachim P. "Experiments in Group Counseling at Two Youth Authority Institutions." Research Report No. 46. California Youth Authority, September 1965. (Processed.)

Seckel, Joachim P. "The Fremont Experiment, Assessment of Residential Treatment at a Youth Authority Reception Center." Research Report No. 50. California Youth Authority, January 1967. (Mimeographed.)

Shelley, Ernest L. V., and Johnson, Walter F., Jr. "Evaluating an Organized Counseling Service for Youthful Offenders," *Journal of Counseling Psychology,* VIII, 4 (1961), 351-354.

Shoham, Shlomo, and Sandberg, Moshe. "Suspended Sentences in Israel: An Evaluation of the Preventive Efficacy of Prospective Imprisonment," *Crime and Delinquency,* X, 1 (1964), 74-83.

Stanton, John M. "Delinquencies and Types of Parole Programs to Which Inmates are Released." New York State Division of Parole, May 15, 1963. (Mimeographed.)

Stanton, John M. "Board Directed Extensive Supervision." New York State Division of Parole, August 3, 1964. (Mimeographed.)

Stuerup, Georg K. "The Treatment of Sexual Offenders," *Bulletin de la societe internationale de criminologie* (1960), pp. 320-329.

Sullivan, Clyde E., Mandell, Wallace. "Restoration of Youth Through Training: A Final Report." Staten Island, New York: Wakoff Research Center, April 1967. (Processed.)

Taylor, A. J. W. "An Evaluation of Group Psychotherapy in a Girls' Borstal," *International Journal of Group Psychotherapy,* XVII, 2 (1967), 168-177.

Truax, Charles B., Wargo, Donald G., and Silber, Leon D. "Effects of Group Psychotherapy with High Adequate Empathy and Nonpossessive Warmth upon Female Institutionalized Delinquents," *Journal of Abnormal Psychology,* LXXI, 4 (1966), 267-274.

Warren, Marguerite. "The Community Treatment Project after Five Years." California Youth Authority, 1966. (Processed.)

Warren, Marguerite, *et al.* "Community Treatment Project, an Evaluation of Community Treatment for Delinquents: a Fifth Progress Report." C.T.P. Research Report No. 7. California Youth Authority, August 1966. (Processed.)

Warren, Marguerite, *et al.* "Community Treatment Project, an Evaluation of Community Treatment for Delinquents: Sixth Progress Report." C.T.P. Research Report No. 8. California Youth Authority, September 1967. (Processed.)

Wilkins, Leslie T. "A Small Comparative Study of the Results of Probation," *British Journal of Criminology,* VIII, 3 (1958), 201-209.

Zivan, Morton. "Youth in Trouble: A Vocational Approach." Final Report of a Research and Demonstration Project, May 31, 1961—August 31, 1966. Dobbs Ferry, N.Y., Children's Village, 1966. (Processed.)

15 New Perspectives on Corrections Policy
Erika S. Fairchild

Failure has been endemic to the corrections system in this country. Whether one perceives its function to be deterrence, rehabilitation, or simple punishment, its failure is attested to by high recidivism, increasing crime rates, and the remoteness of the criminal act itself from the offender's preoccupation with the intricacies and injustices of his passage through the criminal justice system. In addition to the failure of the system in terms of operational results, the inhumaneness of much of the corrections apparatus makes it all the more unacceptable.

Although the failure of the corrections system to "correct" has been long recognized by its students, typically that very aspect of the criminal justice system has been most neglected by legislators, pressure groups, and the general public, all of whom have been interested chiefly in keeping down costs and in not allowing the prison apparatus to intrude upon their consciousness. The apathy and ignorance surrounding corrections is reinforced by the judicial system, which has generally adopted a "hands-off" policy by refusing to consider cases involving prison conditions and prisoners' rights. The underlying assumption of this hands-off policy is that a judge cannot evaluate the peculiar needs and conditions existing in a prison community and therefore should not interfere with prison administrators.

Forces for Change

In contrast to the inertia which has historically prevailed in the area of corrections, recent years have seen the development of a sense of urgency, ferment, change, and public awareness which has made corrections an important issue of national and state policy. This development is in part a spin-off from the fact that crime itself and crime control have become major political issues, especially in large urban areas and on the national level. In addition, several other interrelated developments have contributed to ferment and change in the field of corrections:

1. Certain elements of the general public have become active in prison reform. Under the impetus of the civil-rights movement of the 1960's,

lawyers, civil-rights advocates, minority pressure groups, and other noncriminologists have become involved in representing prisoners and in advocating change in the corrections system.

2. Prisoners themselves have pressured for change. Prisoner unrest resulting in riots and disturbances has brought prison policy into prominent public notice. Furthermore, politicization of prisoners is a new and growing phenomenon, and organization of prisoners into identity groups and unions is spreading.

3. The realization has become widespread that advanced programs of flexibility and rehabilitation undertaken in some prison systems, notably in California, during the 1950's and early 1960's were not successful in achieving rehabilitation, humane incarceration, or even stability in the prisons. This realization has caused a search for new ways to handle the problem of social control and, more specifically, the problem of sanctions for convicted offenders.

4. Federal and state governments increasingly have become involved in correctional reform, with the federal government planning to take the lead in creating a model correctional system. In addition, increasing amounts of public money have become available for corrections. Law Enforcement Assistance Administration seed money has become available for evaluation of, and experimentation in, rehabilitation programs. State legislatures have also begun to place higher priority than ever before on funding for corrections.

The most noteworthy aspect of the above developments is the shifting and balancing of the power distribution which is taking place with regard to correctional policy. Larger numbers of political actors—litigants, judges, interest groups, federal government personnel, legislators, and inmates themselves—have become involved in bringing about change. Corrections administrators are being forced to play a more intense game of bargaining, compromise, shift in policy focus, etc., than was customary in the past. In short, the corrections system has become more politicized, reflecting the heightened politicization of American society in general. Especially among black prisoners, the feeling is strong that in many cases they are political prisoners incarcerated because of the faults of a society which has treated them unequally.

Despite the above developments, it is important not to overstate the extent and significance of actual reforms which have taken place in corrections. Much of the change that has occurred has been a change in expectations and the climate of opinion, rather than reform in the operations of particular prison systems. The picture in the latter case is decidedly mixed, partially as a result of disagreement about what actually constitutes progress. For example, at a time when many authorities, including the

National Advisory Commission on Criminal Justice Standards and Goals, are calling for a moratorium on construction of prisons, several states, including New York, California, and North Carolina, are proceeding with plans to build large new maximum-security institutions. On the other hand, some of the more notorious prison systems, such as those of Mississippi and Arkansas, are planning important reforms in their operations.

Trends in Corrections Policy

Three major trends can be discerned in corrections policy today: (a) the strengthening of (and change in) the custody-treatment, or "medical," model which has dominated enlightened thinking in the field for many years; (b) more widespread and innovative uses of decentralized, or community-based, correctional facilities and programs; and (c) the development of client-input movements and programs in which the prisoner himself is directly involved in influencing policy. While these are the major trends in corrections that will be discussed here, it must be remembered that, in addition, sentencing and parole practices are important aspects of corrections policy and that the injustice, chaos, and confusion surrounding these practices are major sources of frustration for offenders and indicate serious need of comprehensive reform.

Change in the "Custody-Treatment," or "Medical,"
Model of Corrections

The medical model presumes that, for various psychological and social reasons, the offender has been unable to cope with modern society; that his crime is a sign of pathology; and that the obligation of the corrections system is to treat, rehabilitate, or resocialize him through counseling, education, psychotherapy, vocational training, work experience, etc. This approach to corrections is the most prevalent one among students of criminology and enlightened penal administrators, despite the fact that little evidence exists to suggest that this nonpunitive approach is any more effective in reducing recidivism than is simple retribution or punishment. Proponents of the medical model assume that its lack of success has been the result of insufficient resources to implement it and of the fact that an ideal program of implementation has not yet been discovered. Those who criticize the medical model qua model, i.e., are critical of the underlying assumptions of the model, point out that there is a basic inconsistency between the security goals of custody and the individual-responsibility goals of treatment. In addition, many offenders have come to object to the image of themselves as sick, unfree, or deviant, an image which they may find more threatening than that of simply being law-breakers by choice.

In recent years, some adherents to the medical model have undertaken a series of new programs of rehabilitation and treatment. These programs are generally called "behavior modification," and include such more or less radical practices as psychosurgery, sensory deprivation (removal of environmental stimuli), aversive conditioning (association of a disagree-able response with an antisocial stimulus), operant conditioning (intensive reward-punishment responses), and drug therapy. Such practices have occasioned great protest from civil-rights and prisoner groups, and might be considered a radical fringe in corrections.

Much of the new money which has become available to correctional systems through the federal and state governments has not gone to be-havior-modification programs, but has been devoted to expansion of the more conventional custody-treatment programs, as well as to greater efforts to evaluate their effectiveness. Despite these renewed efforts, a sense of failure is apparent in much of the writing about custody-treatment as a solution to the problems posed by the need for more effective corrections policy.

Community-Based Correctional Facilities and Programs

The great expectations which at one time were entertained for the custody-treatment model have been transferred today to plans for a variety of programs referred to as "community-based" programs. The purpose of community-based programs is to avoid the warehousing of prisoners in large maximum-security institutions with few or no contacts with the out-side world. These programs are not new in conception, nor do they nec-essarily preclude the concept of treatment for pathology. They include such well-known devices as probation, parole, halfway houses, furloughs, work release, and community volunteer programs. The difference today is one of emphasis, with the hope that a large proportion of the 85 percent of offenders not considered dangerous will be able to participate in community-based programs. Proponents of community-based corrections also hope that large maximum-security facilities will become obsolete, and that those which continue to exist will be broken down into smaller units with a less dehumanizing atmosphere. The philosophy behind the push for community-based facilities has been well expressed by the National Advisory Commission on Criminal Justice Standards and Goals:

Perhaps the major contribution of the community-based programs is that they keep the offender in the community where he must ultimately live, rather than in an isolated institution where all decisions are made for him and he becomes less and less able to cope with life on the outside.[1]

More cynical individuals adopt the position that, since nothing seems to reduce recidivism or otherwise change the offender for the good, we might as well pursue the cheapest program which is consistent with a humane penology. Community-based corrections, with its emphasis on probation and work release, seems to be, at least in the long run, the most inexpensive correctional option.

The greatest stumbling block to the increased use of community-based programs is the public's fear of the convicted offender. A viable community-based program is dependent upon willingness to risk losing track of larger numbers of offenders, and also upon the willingness of the public to interact with offenders. If the hesitation of the public can be overcome, community-based corrections is the policy option which will no doubt undergo the greatest development in the coming decade.

Development of Client-Input Programs and Movements

Client-input programs and activities are those in which the offender himself is involved in decision-making about his future and about prison administration, especially the latter. The cluster of trends and activities included under this heading might properly be called a *political* approach to corrections, in that the offender has become aware of, and tries to manipulate for his own good, the power structure which dispenses the goods and values of the prison system.

Some client-input activities are undertaken without the cooperation and, indeed, despite the hostility of prison administrators. The politicization of prisoners, partially through contact with outside political, racial, and ethnic groups, and partially through organization within the prison walls, threatens to have an increasingly important influence in shaping prison policy. Organization of prisoners for collective self-help has even taken the form of traditional unionism with its goals of collective bargaining for better wages and better working conditions. The best-known of these unions is the California-based Prisoner's Union, which claims a membership of 15,000 (out of a total prison population of somewhat more than 200,000 in this country). The increased involvement of lawyers and prisoners in litigation dealing with prison conditions and prisoners' rights might also be regarded as client-input activities which are undertaken without the cooperation of prison officials.

More conventional client-input activities are those which have been adopted as policy by the correctional authorities themselves. Examples are the "mutual-agreement" or "prescription" programs that are being tried in several states, and the experiments in greatly expanded prisoner self-government. In the prescription programs, the offender draws up a contract with officials under the terms of which his release time for parole is dependent upon his meeting certain measurable behavioral objectives. While the inmate in this program does not act in a political manner to influence his future, the program does give him a greater opportunity for self-determination of his future, and is an important device in helping him to combat the frustrations and confusions that indeterminate or semideterminate sentences so often cause.

Expanded inmate self-government also has been tried recently, most notably in the state of Washington. It consists of a network of communications, committees, councils, etc., which are designed to allow maximum formal inmate participation (as opposed to the informal power arrangements which have always characterized inmate input into institutional management) in decision-making regarding the operations and policy of the prison community.

True self-government is, to be sure, incompatible with maximum-security custody arrangements, as well as with continued veto power by wardens. Nevertheless, inmate self-government is an interesting experiment, and it probably helps to overcome some of the feelings of powerlessness, alienation, and hostility felt by many prisoners. As an attempt to find a better way to run large maximum-security prisons, which no doubt will continue to exist into the foreseeable future, it deserves more widespread use.

Client-input programs clearly show that the corrections system is reflecting the increased politicization of the larger society. On a less dramatic level, however, these programs can also be seen as a reflection of the emergent management philosophy which stresses participation in decision-making by the rank and file in large organizations, and which attempts to develop a client-centered orientation among bureaucrats in general.

Further Prescriptions for Basic Change

Despite the difficulties inherent in implementing the above trends in corrections policy, each of the trends is tied to a program of action and progress within the constraints of the currently operating corrections system. Increasingly, however, a sense of futility about the efficacy of these programs for change is becoming apparent in the literature on criminal justice and corrections. This sense of futility is related at least in part to the apparent lack of success of any known corrections policy in reducing recidivism among offenders. It is perhaps also related to the general confusion of goals and implementation strategy in the American criminal justice system, and a conviction that matters are getting worse and we really have no effective way of dealing with them. The difficulty, for example, of trying to balance an act-oriented legal system with an offender-oriented penal system has resulted in problems and disillusionment among both administrators and offenders.

This emergent sense of futility can be discerned in at least two philosophies about corrections and society, both of which abandon rehabilitation as a goal for corrections. The first of these philosophies might be described as a counsel of despair: it suggests that the only purpose which can be served by a corrections system is, on the one hand, to segregate dangerous individuals from the population at large and, on the other hand, to serve as a deterrent for those offenders or potential offenders who are indeed likely to be deterred by the possibility of a prison sentence. This apparently simple approach, to be sure, masks a host of problems which have so far eluded solution. It is notoriously difficult to determine whether or not an individual with a history of violent behavior continues to be dangerous after a period of incarceration. In addition, segregation of individuals from society on the basis of their potential danger to others seems more appropriately the function of a mental health program than of a criminal justice program, whose function, according to law, is punishment for crime rather than treatment for individuals. The nature and extent of a deterrent function which might be served by the corrections system are also matters about which, despite much speculation and research, little agreement exists. It is apparent, however, that those who are most likely to be deterred—i.e., middle-class white-collar criminals—are also least likely to be found in prison. One is left with the impression that this first philosophy really only calls for maximum-security housing for offenders with the sole purpose of postponing the crimes which they are inevitably going to commit upon release.

The second philosophy relates crime and criminality to a basic dysfunction in American society which cannot be ameliorated by patchwork or incremental reforms. It sees the offender as suffering from a lack of commitment to the social order precisely because this social order has little to offer him but conformity to a lower-class life style which he finds undignified and unrewarding. The conventional rehabilitation programs suggest that the individual wants to be rehabilitated, that all he is lacking are the educational and psychological tools which will help him to cope with and conform to the conventional society. While it has long been claimed that poor social conditions breed crime, the system-dysfunction theory presumes a more basic problem than poor social conditions. It suggests that, since almost all imprisoned offenders are low-status individuals who are not active participants in creating the social order, and whose status as criminals has been defined by others, the loss or lack of commitment to the social order cannot be ameliorated by conventional efforts at rehabilitation, and that a more fundamental change is needed in the class structure or the social conformation of American society.

Such a basic reevaluation of all of American society, however, goes much beyond considerations of corrections policy, which is essentially a small part of the major social change that is called for. In terms of grappling with present problems in administration of policy, this second philosophy offers little of substance. Nevertheless, both this philosophy of major social change and the philosophy of segregation and deterrence, while they do not immediately present guidelines to action, reflect an emergent intellectual stance which may well affect future attempts to deal with corrections policy at an operational level.

Research Needs

With few exceptions, corrections officials in the United States have not been receptive to research by outsiders and have not chosen to invest in programs of ongoing research and evaluation as part of their own operations. Thus there are many research needs in the field of corrections, three of which are particularly pressing.

The first need is for expanded evaluation of various strategies for handling offenders. The fact is that we do not have a valid, empirical basis for making rational choices among alternatives—it is simply not known how effective correctional programs are relative to one another. This lack of knowledge has been compounded by overreliance upon a single indicator of effectiveness, namely recidivism. The bases for development of recidivism statistics have fluctuated markedly from one jurisdiction to another, making comparison difficult. In addition, the assumptions upon which these statistics are based are not generally well known or understood, and the statistics themselves are therefore misleading. Furthermore, recidivism is a rather crude yardstick that measures efficiency in terms of reducing corrections costs, but indicates little about the desirability in terms of human development of alternative correctional programs. Other, more refined standards of evaluation are needed on a program-by-program basis.

Closely related to the need for more useful standards of evaluation is the need for valid, uniform data on correctional programs and offender populations on a national basis. These data, which are currently very fragmentary, are important for effective prison administration and rational policy choice, and are also essential for meaningful work by researchers and policy analysts. The development of such a uniform data base has been stressed as a priority by the National Advisory Commission on Criminal Justice Standards and Goals.

The third need, which is especially relevant for political scientists, is for intensive research into changes in prisoner outlook and changes in the power relationships which determine correctional policy. The prison community studies conducted by sociologists over the years are in need of reconsideration and updating. Furthermore, political scientists should undertake such research on-site in prisons and other correctional situations instead of depending solely upon the writings of militants such as George Jackson and Angela Davis for information. The need, despite difficulties of access and methodology, is for a more in-depth analyses of the conventional prison inmate and prison society as important keys to understanding the legal culture of our society.

Notes on the Literature

Corrections literature reflects both current policy trends and the scholarly background of researchers. The field has been dominated by psychologists and sociologists, who have traditionally studied prisons as communities, bureaucracies, social systems, and rehabilitation experiments.[2] More recently the sociologists Richard Quinney, John Irwin, and Edwin Schur have emphasized an approach to an understanding of crime and corrections policy which is more closely related to considerations of public policy and power structure.[3] A summary of old and somewhat newer trends in thinking among sociologists can be found in the selections in *Prisoners in America*.[4]

The interest of legally trained scholars in the matter of prisoners' rights has resulted in the important volume *After Conviction*[5] and in the ACLU handbook *The Rights of Prisoners*.[6] The law journals frequently carry articles relating to prisoners' rights, and the best way to find these articles is through the *Index to Legal Periodicals*.

Political scientists, as mentioned before, have done little research in corrections, and therefore have contributed little to the literature. A few volumes which have stressed a political-system approach to corrections have appeared within the past year, but these have been in large part compilations of writings by prisoners, lawyers, and others with experience in prison systems.[7] In general, systematic research from the perspective of the political scientist remains to be done.

The various national-level commission and task-force reports are the most comprehensive efforts to assess the state of corrections and to offer proposals for change. Two of them are particularly important. The recent report *Corrections,* issued by the National Advisory Commission on Criminal Justice Standards and Goals, attempts to set performance goals for change and no doubt will become the standard reference in the field of corrections for the next few years.[8] The 1967 *Task Force Report: Corrections* of the President's Commission on Law Enforcement and Administration of Justice analyzed many of the same problems and made many of the same proposals for change.[9] The NACCJSG report, however, puts great emphasis on the matter of prisoners' rights, a topic whose parameters were less well defined in the earlier PCLEAJ report.

In addition to the national commission reports, a thoughtful and influential product of committee effort is the American Friends Service Committee report *Struggle for Justice.*[10] This is a small volume which is concerned with the inadequacies and discretionary latitude of the treatment philosophy in corrections.

A number of periodicals appear in this field. Scholarly journals which often report on corrections research include the *Journal of Research in Crime and Delinquency; Criminology, An Interdisciplinary Journal;* and the *Journal of Criminal Law and Criminology. Crime and Delinquency,* the "professional forum" of the National Council on Crime and Delinquency, should also be of interest to policy researchers. Information about new programs, professional meetings, personnel changes, and even equipment may be found in the *American Journal of Corrections,* which is the official publication of the American Correctional Association. News of programs and problems as seen from the prisoners' or "consumers'" point of view can be found in various prison newsletters and, on a national scale, in *The Outlaw,* the bimonthly publication of the Prisoner's Union in San Francisco.

Notes

1. National Advisory Commission on Criminal Justice Standards and Goals, *A National Strategy to Reduce Crime* (Washington, D.C.: U.S. Government Printing Office, 1973), p. 123.
2. See, for example, Donald Clemmer, *The Prison Community* (New York: Holt, Rinehart, 1958); Donald Cressey, ed., *The Prison: Studies in Institutional Organization and Change* (New York: Social Science Research Council, 1960); Erving Goffman, *Asylums* (Chicago: Aldine, 1961); Gresham Sykes, *Society of Captives* (Princeton, N.J.: Princeton University Press, 1958); H. Ashley Weeks, *Youthful Offenders at Highfields* (Ann Arbor, Mich.: University of Michigan Press, 1958).
3. Richard Quinney, *The Social Reality of Crime* (Boston: Little,

Brown, 1970), and *Critique of Legal Order* (Boston: Little, Brown, 1973); John Irwin, *The Felon* (Englewood Cliffs, N.J.: Prentice-Hall, 1970); and Edwin Schur, *Our Criminal Society* (Englewood Cliffs, N.J.: Prentice-Hall, 1969).

4. Lloyd E. Ohlin, *Prisoners in America* (Englewood Cliffs, N.J.: Prentice-Hall, 1973).

5. Ronald Goldfarb and Linda Singer, *After Conviction* (New York: Simon and Schuster, 1973).

6. David Rudovsky, *The Rights of Prisoners* (New York: Avon, 1973).

7. Burton Atkins and Henry Glick, *Prisons, Protest, and Politics* (Englewood Cliffs, N.J.: Prentice-Hall, 1972); Erik Olin Wright, *The Politics of Punishment* (New York: Harper and Row, 1973).

8. National Advisory Commission on Criminal Justice Standards and Goals, *Corrections* (Washington, D.C.: U.S. Government Printing Office, 1973).

9. President's Commission on Law Enforcement and Administration of Justice, *Task Force Report: Corrections* (Washington, D.C.: U.S. Government Printing Office, 1967).

10. American Friends Service Committee, *Struggle for Justice* (New York: Hill and Wang, 1973).

Index of Names

Index of Subjects

About the Editors and Contributors

John A. Gardiner is head of the Department of Political Science at the University of Illinois at Chicago Circle. He previously taught at the University of Wisconsin–Madison and the State University of New York at Stony Brook, and served as Assistant Director of the National Institute of Law Enforcement and Criminal Justice. He is the author of *Traffic and the Police* (Harvard University Press, 1969) and *The Politics of Corruption* (Russell Sage Foundation, 1970), and coeditor of *Theft of the City: Readings on Corruption in Urban America* (Indiana University Press, 1974).

Michael A. Mulkey is a political scientist with the National Institute of Law Enforcement and Criminal Justice of the Law Enforcement Assistance Administration; he is involved in efforts to evaluate the effectiveness of various law enforcement and criminal justice programs.

Carl Akins is a senior program officer with the Drug Abuse Council in Washington, D.C., an independent research, information, and policy evaluation organization established in 1972. He is the coeditor and an author of the Public Policy Forum, "Minority Perspectives on Bureaucracy," in the Summer 1973 issue of *The Bureaucrat,* and the coauthor of *Governmental Response to Drugs: Fiscal and Organizational* (Drug Abuse Council, 1974). Prior to joining the council staff, Dr. Akins was affiliated with American University, the Brookings Institution, and the University of Houston.

Lief H. Carter is an assistant professor of political science at the University of Georgia at Athens; he previously taught at the University of Tennessee at Chattanooga. He received the J.D. from Harvard University and the Ph.D. in political science from the University of California at Berkeley. He is the author of *The Limits of Order* (Lexington Books, 1974).

George F. Cole, an associate professor of political science at the University of Connecticut, is the author of *Politics and the Administration of Justice* (Sage Publications, 1973) and *The American System of Criminal Justice* (Duxbury, 1976), and is editor of *Criminal Justice: Law and Politics* (Duxbury, 1972).

Thomas J. Cook is an associate professor of political science at the University of Illinois at Chicago Circle. He received the Ph.D. from Florida

State University in 1969, and taught at Pennsylvania State University before joining the faculty at Chicago Circle. He was Principal Investigator on an NSF grant evaluating volunteer programs, and has served as a consultant on program evaluation to federal, state, and local governments. He serves on the editorial boards of *The Experimental Study of Politics* and *Policy Studies Journal*.

Jameson W. Doig is professor of politics and public affairs in the Woodrow Wilson School and the Department of Politics, Princeton University. He is also director of the School's Research Program in Criminal Justice. He has written articles concerning the police and the criminal justice system in the *Public Administration Review* and in the book, *Agenda for a City* (Sage Publications, 1970), and he is the author or coauthor of books on transportation politics and administrative behavior. Dr. Doig has been a member of the Governor's Council Against Crime, State of New Jersey, and has served as a consultant to the American Bar Association's Center for Administrative Justice, New Jersey's Office of Juvenile Justice, and other organizations.

Erika S. Fairchild is an instructor in political science at Meredith College in Raleigh, North Carolina. She recently received the Ph.D. at the University of Washington; her dissertation concerned the politicization of prisoners in the Washington prison system. Dr. Fairchild has been a Fulbright Scholar at the University of Aix-Marseilles and a management analyst for the U.S. Department of Health, Education, and Welfare.

Michael D. Maltz is a visiting associate professor in the Departments of Criminal Justice and Systems Engineering at the University of Illinois at Chicago Circle. He received the Ph.D. in electrical engineering from Stanford University and conducted post-doctoral research at the Technical University of Denmark. He has served as an operations research analyst with Arthur D. Little, Inc., and with the National Institute of Law Enforcement and Criminal Justice. Dr. Maltz is the author of *Evaluation of Crime Control Programs* (Law Enforcement Assistance Administration, 1972).

Robert Martinson is an associate professor and former chairman of the Department of Sociology at the City College of the City University of New York. He received the Ph.D. in 1968 from the University of California at Berkeley, and is coprincipal investigator of the Crime Deterrence and Offender Career project in New York City. Dr. Martinson is coauthor of *The Effectiveness of Correctional Treatment* (Praeger, forthcoming).

David W. Neubauer, an assistant professor of political science at the University of New Orleans, is the author of *Criminal Justice in Middle America* (General Learning Press, 1974). He is involved in research on variations in justice among American communities.

Roger B. Parks is a research associate in the Workshop in Political Theory and Policy Analysis at Indiana University. He has also been a systems analyst for McDonnell-Douglas and the Radio Corporation of America. He is the author of several studies of police services in metropolitan areas published in *Public Administration Review* and *Publius*.

Robert P. Rhodes received the Ph.D. from the Maxwell School of Syracuse University in 1971, and is a professor of political science at Edinboro State College in Pennsylvania. As a consultant on research and evaluation to the Pennsylvania Governor's Justice Commission, he is the author of the Commission's reports *Delay and the Quality of Justice* (1973), *A Comparison of Effectiveness for Privately Retained Counsel and Public Defender* (1974), and of *The Insoluble Problems of Crime* (John Wiley, forthcoming in 1976).

Leonard Ruchelman is an associate professor of political science and Director of the Urban Studies Program at Lehigh University. He received the Ph.D. from Columbia University, and is the author of *Big City Mayors* (Indiana University Press, 1969), *Political Careers: Recruitment through the Legislature* (Fairleigh Dickinson Press, 1970), *Who Rules the Police?* (New York University Press, 1973), and *Police Politics: A Comparative Study of Three Cities* (Ballinger, 1974).

Frank P. Scioli, Jr., is an associate professor of political science at the University of Illinois at Chicago Circle and Director of the Ph.D. program in Public Policy Analysis. He received the Ph.D. from Florida State University in 1970. He is a coprincipal investigator of a National Science Foundation (RANN Division) project evaluating volunteer programs and also research associate on a project studying tall buildings. Dr. Scioli is coeditor of the *Journal for Experimental Study of Politics* and the *Policy Studies Journal*. He has served as a consultant to federal, state, and local agencies.

Wesley G. Skogan is an assistant professor of political science and urban affairs at Northwestern University. His research interests include the police, courts, crime policy, measurement theory, and computer applications in social science.

James Q. Wilson is Henry Lee Shattuck Professor of Urban Government at Harvard University. He has served as Chairman of the Advisory Committee of the Special Action Office for Drug Abuse Prevention, as Vice-Chairman of the Police Foundation, and as a consultant to the President's Commission on Law Enforcement and Administration of Justice. Among his major publications are *Political Organizations* (Basic Books, 1973), *Varieties of Police Behavior* (Harvard University Press, 1968), *The Amateur Democrat* (University of Chicago Press, 1962), *Negro Politics* (Free Press, 1960), and *City Politics* (Harvard University Press, 1963).